WILD AIR

ALSO BY JAMES MACDONALD LOCKHART

Raptor

WILD AIR

IN SEARCH OF BIRDSONG

JAMES MACDONALD
LOCKHART

4th ESTATE • *London*

4th Estate
An imprint of HarperCollins*Publishers*
1 London Bridge Street
London SE1 9GF

www.4thestate.co.uk

HarperCollins*Publishers*
Macken House, 39/40 Mayor Street Upper
Dublin 1, D01 C9W8, Ireland

First published in Great Britain in 2023 by 4th Estate

1

A catalogue record for this book is available from the British Library

ISBN 978-0-00-839953-5

Extract on p. 281 is from *Through the Woods* by H. E. Bates (1936). Reproduced with permission of Curtis Brown Group Ltd, London on behalf of The Estate of H. E. Bates. Copyright © H. E. Bates.

Quote on p. 17 is taken from *The Peregrine* by J. A. Baker, HarperCollins*Publishers*, 1970.

Quotes on p. 121 are taken from *Voices of the Wild* by Eric Simms, Putnum, 1957.

Quotes on p. 154, p. 164–6 and p. 178 are taken from *Mind of the Raven: Investigations and Adventures with Wolf-Birds* by Bernd Heinrich, Cliff Street Books, 2000.

Quote on p. 277 is taken from *Nightingale* by Bethan Roberts, Reaktion Books, 2021.

Quote on p. 278 is taken from *Whistling in the Dark: In Pursuit of the Nightingale* by Richard Mabey, Sinclair-Stevenson Ltd, 1993.

Quote on p. 278 is taken from *The Nightingale: Notes on a Songbird* by Sam Lee, Century, 2021.

Set in Emona
Printed and bound in the UK using 100% renewable electricity at CPI Group (UK) Ltd

This book is produced from independently certified FSC™ paper to ensure responsible forest management.

For more information visit: www.harpercollins.co.uk/green

For Davina
1981–2020

Norman Arlott

1947–2022

Norman Arlott sadly passed away just after supplying the wonderful illustrations in this book and on the cover. One of Britain's leading bird illustrators, his encyclopaedic knowledge of birds and his talent as an artist were a rare mix. He will be greatly missed.

Contents

Introduction

Shortly before she died, my granny told me a story about how she used to help her father – my great-grandfather – with his bird studies. My great-grandfather's name was Seton Gordon and during a long life he published many books on the wildlife of the Scottish Highlands. As a naturalist, his interests were wide-ranging: snowfields, alpine flora, history and folklore are all components of his work. But birds were his abiding love and interest. In particular, the birds of the high mountains: dotterel, ptarmigan, golden eagle and snow bunting, species that he studied, photographed and wrote about throughout his career, from his teenage years, cycling around Deeside in the first decade of the twentieth century with his half-plate Thornton-Pickard Ruby camera, to an old man in his eighties, still climbing the Cairngorms, still wearing his tatty kilt, searching for his beloved birds. Granny lent me her father's books, showed me his photographs. She also lent me books by contemporary naturalists who had followed in Gordon's pioneering wake. I devoured the books, and fell under the spell of the birds and the landscapes my great-grandfather wrote about.

It's hard to get a sense of what Gordon was like from his writing. He doesn't dwell much on himself. Instead, his focus is always on the birds, the plants, the weather in the mountains (his moustache was often frozen and cycle tyres frequently froze to his bike's mudguards). But that self-effacement made me curious about him. What was he like? His books did offer the occasional insight. He could be dryly humorous: 'I would strongly advise any ornithologist who decides on studying the habits of the hill birds to procure a good strong tent ... and a plentiful supply of rugs.' The rugs were needed not just to keep warm at night but also, reminding us of the huge technological advances that have occurred in photography, to change photographic plates under during the summer months in the Highlands, when there is little darkness. So, beneath that frozen Edwardian moustache, there was a twinkling humour, though I sometimes find it hard to disentangle humour from eccentricity in his work. In one of his books, he describes a snowstorm in the mountains that is so severe his friend loses his way trying to find his way back from a well only 25 metres from the bothy they are staying in. What to do in such a crisis? Gordon's answer is, naturally, to consider tuning up his bagpipes to guide his friend back to the shelter. Often with Gordon, his eccentricities were simply his modus operandi. I expect he carried his bagpipes into the mountains as you would a mobile phone today; to him, the pipes were a useful safety precaution, which you could hear wailing through the fiercest storm.

But eccentricity can lean towards loneliness. And Gordon often seems to me to cut a lonely figure in the landscape, with his camera and telescope, when most other people in the corries and glens of the Cairngorms at that time would have carried a gun. In an era when egg collecting and the persecution of birds were rife, Gordon's despair, his pleas for better understanding and protection of the birds, surface throughout his work. He was the only full-time naturalist working in Scotland in the first decades of the twentieth century; at times, it must have felt like the loneliest job in the world. Here is his account of coming across a dead peregrine in 1906:

> It was plain that the keeper had crept up the rock from the west side and shot the bird while she was unsuspectingly brooding. On receiving the shot she had, in her agony, fluttered along the ledge for about two feet, carrying two of the eggs with her, and I could see the marks made by her claws as she writhed in her death agony. Numbers of her feathers were lying around, some of the under-feathers being of extraordinary beauty – tinged with greenish yellow.

This is a moving description, written by someone who was deeply affected by this horrible scene. The detail is harrowing: the dying bird's claw marks, the pathos in the beauty of the peregrine's under-feathers. It's writing like this that pulled me in to Gordon's work and that, in turn, made me curious to find out more about him. So, I pestered Granny for titbits: 'What was my great-grandfather like?' She got to the point with characteristic bluntness: 'Well, the thing about dad was that he was very deaf, his deafness was something which came on in his twenties.' There followed a story about how he used to judge piping competitions (he was as obsessed with bagpipes as he was with birds) by removing his shoes so that he could better feel the vibrations from the bagpipes through the ground. 'He listened with his feet!' Then came the story of how she used to assist him with his bird studies. 'You see, Dad could no longer hear the birds he loved.' So Granny was recruited to serve as his pair of ears. 'My role was to scurry ahead of him like a dog!' She would describe the birdsongs she heard, painting a sound-picture for her father. 'I'd report back – sing back – what I was hearing: greenshank, oystercatcher, golden plover … skylark, meadow pipit, willow warbler.' Back home, in the evening, Gordon would sometimes take out his practice bagpipe chanter and play back the bird songs his daughter had described to him, as though he was checking his memory, holding on to the soundscape he knew before his deafness took hold.

In the following chapters I've set out to write about a series of birds as though I had my Granny's role, listening to the birds' songs and calls, relaying what I heard: from a nightjar's strange churring song on a heath in the south of England, to a lapwing displaying over the machair in the Outer Hebrides. I write about eight different birds and, while I encountered many different species along the way, these eight are the birds I spent most time with, returned to most often. If this book has a guiding principle, it was simply that: to spend as much time as I could, observing and listening to each of these fascinating birds.

The eight species I chose to concentrate on were all representative of, or at least located in, a different habitat. Nightjars on a lowland heath; shearwaters on a mountain overlooking the sea; dippers on a river; skylarks in farmland; ravens in woodland; divers on a loch; lapwings on the coast; and nightingales in dense scrub. While each chapter focuses on an individual species, other birds, inevitably, make their appearance as part of the wider soundscape of each habitat. So, there are 'cameo' roles from birds including woodcock, stone-curlew, song thrush, snipe, oystercatcher and many others.

Each of the eight birds I focus on drew me to them, primarily, because I was interested in listening to the sounds they made. Not all of the birds are songbirds in the traditional sense, though each possesses its own distinctive music. That music can vary from the strange, as in the weird gurgling sound a shearwater makes inside its burrow, to the joyous exuberance of the skylark's song. Sometimes, I heard a lot, and saw little (shearwaters in the pitch dark); sometimes I saw a lot, but heard little (black-throated divers on their loch). The sounds the birds made were, for me, a way in to writing about each bird more generally, their behaviour, their movements, their conservation status. I also found myself as drawn to the ornithological literature for each species as I was to observing the birds in the field. So, what follows is a blend of my experiences and the observations of others, including my great-grandfather, whose work I draw on periodically through the book, particularly with respect to those birds Gordon also had an interest in and which were a part of the Highland fauna he studied.

One of the birds he studied and photographed was a rare, beautiful wading bird called the greenshank, whose song, he wrote, though 'rarely heard', is 'in certain respects ... the most beautiful and certainly the wildest of all the bird songs of Britain'. He acknowledged, however, that he struggled to describe the greenshank's song in writing. 'It is impossible to set down the greenshank's song in words,' he concluded. 'It is usually uttered in groups of two notes, the first two notes in a low key, the second two in a higher. They are somewhat as follows: *teuchi, teuchi, clever, clever*.' He found instead that it was easier for him to transcribe the greenshank's song as music: 'On returning home after having listened for half an hour to a greenshank's song I found that the notes could be reproduced closely on the chanter of the Highland bagpipe.'

Is it impossible, as Gordon found with the greenshank, to set down birdsong in words? I think it probably is, for the majority of birds; our ears cannot register the speed, range and complexity of most birdsong. For one thing, birds can sing with 'two voices'; their syrinx, the equivalent of our voice box, is divided into two separate parts, or chambers, located at the bottom of the bird's trachea. Imagine the bag on Gordon's bagpipes repurposed so that it is divided into two separate bags, representing the syrinx, with the chanter, extending out from the bag, representing the trachea, or windpipe. Each of these chambers in the syrinx can produce sounds; either by one side acting alone, both parts acting together, or by alternating from one chamber to the other. When both sides of the syrinx produce a sound simultaneously, it may be the same sound, or it may be two entirely different sounds, with a different pitch and frequency. The syrinx is the organ that enables birds such as song thrushes and nightingales, for example, to sing such intricate, varied songs; to sing, as it were, with two voices.

Daines Barrington, the eighteenth-century naturalist with whom Gilbert White corresponded, described the song of a nightingale he kept as something that 'eludes all verbal description'. It may well indeed be impossible to transcribe a bird's song in words. But you can, at least, attempt to put into words the experience of listening to birdsong. That is what I have tried to do in this book.

Seton Gordon died two years after I was born. There is a photo of us together at a family gathering in the 1970s. I am the chubby toddler beside his thin old age. In his frayed kilt and Highland bonnet, my great-grandfather looks like he has walked out of a different era to join us that day. I sometimes wonder, if he were still alive, what he would make of the changes in our avifauna since he died four decades ago. He would be delighted, I'm sure, by the re-establishment of birds such as the osprey and sea eagle, both of which became extinct as breeding species when he was a young man. However, I'm certain he would also be distraught at the catastrophic declines that have occurred among many of our birds. Some of those declines were evident while Gordon was still alive, as he observed in 1970, writing that the corn bunting was 'everywhere in Scotland ... much scarcer than it used to be', and that 'we are in danger of losing the corncrake as a nesting species.' But he would, I'm also sure, be utterly dismayed and shocked by the acceleration in losses of so many other species, including ones he loved like the lapwing and curlew.

I would like to have been able to share some of the experiences I had with birds, while researching this book, with my great-grandfather. I would like to have been able to ask him questions about the birds, about some of the things that puzzled me. And I would have liked to relay, as my granny did, the music I heard back to him. I think he would have enjoyed hearing about some of the birds I listened to.

I

The Bird that Hides its Shadow

Nightjar

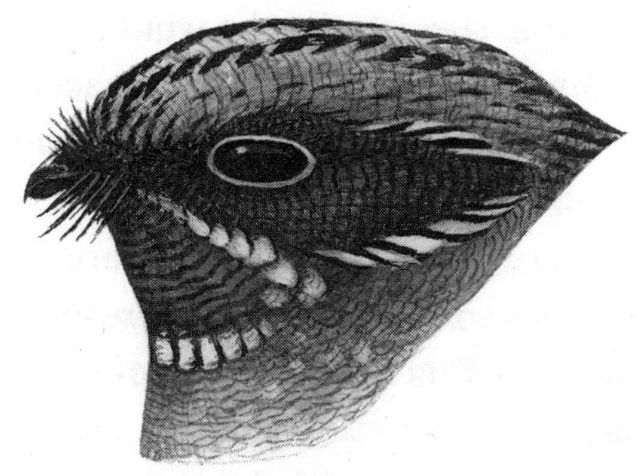

Midsummer on the outskirts of London. I'm standing in the middle of a heath, waiting for it to get dark. Heather, pine and birch; a sharp smell of bracken; stonechats clicking from their perch. Nine p.m. and it's still so light, I'm worried it will never grow dark. A low-pitched hum; traffic on the distant motorway sounds like heavy rain. Aeroplanes bank slowly over Heathrow to the north.

I'd spent the last few hours following sandy paths around the heath. I loved the place instantly. It felt like an act of resistance, a small pocket of wilderness encircled by noise and roads. Half a mile to the south was the motorway, to the east, the rattle and screech of trains. Roads, houses, building sites ... And the heath like a pause in the middle of it all, quiet after the day's heat. The heather was dry and dusty, and there was a strange mirage effect where hundreds of ants moving up and down a tree made it look as if the trunk were twitching. I stopped to watch a pair of stonechats fuss and skitter through a gorse bush. The male's chest glowed inside the gorse; as he moved through the bush, I caught glimpses of brightness as though a bulb were flickering in there. For an hour I saw nobody. Then a mountain bike zipped past me, its tyres making a loud crunching noise on the dried mud. In a gap between the pine trees, I watched a rotary sprinkler twitching over a golf course; the mist coming off its spray looked like smoke rising above the trees.

I'd come to the heath to listen to a bird called the nightjar. I didn't expect to see one, as nightjars are among the most perfectly camouflaged birds. Their plumage is all vermiculated browns, greys and blacks, flecked with gold and white. The colour and texture of the bird's patterning is close to mimicry; it resembles flakes of bark or a lichen-encrusted boulder. If you were to hold a nightjar in your hand it would look like you had scooped up a trembling clump of woodland floor. Stitch together a bird-shaped cloak, about the length of a brick, using dead leaves, lichen, moss and bark, and you have a nightjar.

There is some climatic variation across the species; in Britain, European nightjars are darker in appearance than those that breed in the arid regions of Central Asia. The dark and light shading across the nightjar's plumage deceives the eye to focus on the contours of the patterning, rather than the outline of the bird. It is only when you notice the nightjar's huge dark brown eyes, set laterally in the middle of its head, that its camouflage morphs into something like a bird. Perched on a branch or on the ground beside leaves and sticks, nightjars look like an appendage of their perch. Lying up to roost on the low bough of a tree during the day, the birds fold themselves into the tree. They habitually roost lengthways so that their long tail aligns with the branch, head held low, body pressed flat, their enormous eyes closed except for a thin slit through which the bird keeps watch. If, when they alight on a branch, they land so they are perched across it, nightjars will usually adjust their position, turning around so they are lying lengthways, or 'closing up' as this movement is beautifully termed. The naturalist John Walpole-Bond, writing in the 1930s, even came across one nightjar lying lengthways along 'the narrowest of railings'.

There is a sense with the nightjar of a bird constantly tuning its camouflage. They have an astonishing awareness of how to make themselves disappear and are more likely to roost during the day on the ground than on a branch. If the sun is bright, nightjars will track the sun's course, periodically shifting their position so they are always facing the sun in order to minimise their shadow. This is a bird that has so perfected its camouflage, that is so reliant on camouflage for survival, it even hides its shadow.

I spent those hours before dusk on the heath scanning every low branch, every pile of brash for nightjars, hoping that through my binoculars I might detect some anomaly in the structure of the bark. It was like trying to conjure a ghost; every dark gnarl in the wood was an eye.

If the nightjar does have a weak spot in its camouflage, it lies with the colour of its eggs rather than with the bird. Its eggs are a pale moon white, dabbed with faint grey and brown blotches. The white predominates, making the eggs stand out, albeit faintly, on the ground. Nightjar eggs have not evolved the level of protective colouration found in most ground-nesting birds. One explanation for this could be that the colour of the eggs serves to help these crepuscular and nocturnal birds locate them in the dark. It's almost as though the faint grey and brown blotching on the shells is a gesture towards a compromise between camouflage and visibility, with the latter taking precedence.

Nightjars appear, however, to have evolved two notable habits that compensate for their eggs' exposure. First, the birds are exceptionally close sitters; they tend not to rise from the nest until an intruder is almost on top of them. When they do rise, the movement is so sudden their eggs will sometimes roll away from under them. So long as the parent nightjar is incubating, the eggs are protected by the bird's camouflage. Second, nightjars start incubating their first egg as soon as it is laid, rather than deferring incubation until the full clutch is produced, as is the case with most other birds. Unusually, one habit nightjars have not adopted to compensate for the colour of their eggs is the removal of the eggshells from the nest area after the young hatch. Though the shells are eventually trodden on and broken up, their presence around the nest site still risks attracting predators.

One of the reasons nightjar breeding success correlates so closely with the amount of human disturbance to the nest site is that if the birds are disturbed when incubating, the visibility of their eggs makes them especially vulnerable to predation. Some adult nightjars, disturbed from the nest, have been observed taking up to 15 minutes to return to the clutch, ample time for a predator such as a crow to locate the eggs. A study of nightjars in Dorset in 2002 found that the probability of nest survival was only 12 per cent, with the incubation stage being by far the most vulnerable period. Sixty per cent of the nests in the study failed; 93 per cent of those failures were due to predation, with the majority of nests predated by corvids.

At 9.40 p.m. I hear the first nightjar – a short burst of churring that only lasts a few seconds, then the heath is quiet again. I think of cold mornings when my car won't start. The ignition clicks, coughs, then an engine-ticking pause, a prayer to the engine gods, before I try the key once more. Male nightjars often start their dusk song tentatively. The first churr is like a sound-check, a throat-clearing before they really get going. And when they do, it's not unusual for a male to sing uninterrupted for as long as 9 minutes. Some birds have been observed singing, with only very short pauses, for up to 19.5 minutes.

It's the speed of the song that is so remarkable. The churring (I've also heard it described as 'skirling') comprises 28 to 42 notes, or pulses, per second, with an interval of no more than 40 milliseconds between notes. The song is unlike any other produced by a bird. It's more reminiscent of (and more easily confused with) the pulsing sound made by a cricket – in particular, the mole-cricket – as the insect rubs, or stridulates, its wings together. The nightjar's churring is so unusual it doesn't easily fit into what we perceive as birdsong. But song is what it is, the male nightjar's display song, advertising his presence, asserting his territory, singing his night music.

Several nightjars were calling now. I hopped about, balancing on a bench, straining my ears, trying to work out where the calls were coming from. It was difficult to pinpoint where the birds were. I gazed hopefully in one direction, only for the churring to circle round behind me. I felt like I'd stumbled upon a ventriloquists' convention. The ability of nightjars to throw their voices like this adds to the weirdness of the sound. They are among the most ventriloquial of birds, the males turning their head as they churr so that their song swings back and forth, chasing itself.

Ventriloquism in birdsong serves as a defence mechanism. The purpose is to deceive or confuse predators as to the location of the singer, who is exposed, perched in the open, preoccupied with his song. Where a bird's song, or alarm call, has a restricted high-frequency range, as is the case with the nightjar's churr, the effect is particularly ventriloquial to the ears of a larger predator. It works differently on avian and mammalian ears, but the disorientating effect is the same. With an avian predator, the single-frequency call from a smaller bird exploits the air passage that connects a bird's two inner ear cavities, with the sound waves produced by the call hitting both sides of the larger bird's eardrum at the same time. In some instances, this might result in these high-frequency calls sounding louder in the ear that is furthest away from the source of the call, causing the predator to misconstrue the location of the source. For a mammal with large external ears, the high-frequency sound waves bounce off the ear in a number of places, making it seem like the call itself has come from several locations. It is much easier to locate a call made up of multiple frequencies – such as a blackbird's song – as each frequency reflects differently on the ear, producing a series of clues, or reference points, to the sound's origin.

Just as the nightjar hides its shadow, it also hides its song, not only through ventriloquism, but also imitation.

The similarity between the nightjar's churr and the sound produced by a stridulating mole-cricket is unlikely to be coincidence. While the mole-cricket is rare across the nightjar's breeding range in Britain, it is a common insect across the bird's range in continental Europe. The mole-cricket and nightjar also overlap with the timing of their song, at dusk and after dark, throughout the spring and summer months. Writing in the eighteenth century, the English naturalist Gilbert White observed this similarity between insect and bird when he wrote of the mole-cricket:

> In fine weather, about the middle of April, and just at the close of day, they begin to solace themselves with a low, dull, jarring note, continued for a long time without interruption, and not unlike the chattering of the fern-owl, or goat-sucker, but more inward.

'Fern-owl' and 'goat-sucker' are both names for the nightjar. 'More inward' is a wonderful, accurate distinction; the mole-cricket's song has been described as more 'chirr' than 'churr'. But the similarity between the two sounds can sometimes confuse even seasoned ornithologists, particularly when wind or distance blurs the quality of the sound. The nightjar's churr has also been likened to a chorus of wood-crickets, even the nocturnal rattling calls of natterjack toads.

Mimicry of insect sounds by birds is a type of acoustic camouflage. It is most pronounced in the insect-like songs of some warbler species, such as the grasshopper warbler and river warbler, in the way their songs mimic the pulsing sound made by stridulating crickets. Where a few birds are singing amid thousands of similar-sounding insects, the birds are camouflaged by the acoustic backdrop.

As it got darker on the heath, the nightjar calls sounded louder and their churring lasted longer. I had this sense of the birds hurrying the dark along, as well as of the birds testing and adapting to the acoustics of the heath, moving from perch to perch, trying out a different space in which to throw their song. Just before 10 p.m., one nightjar started up close to me, followed by another on the other side of the path. Their calls spun in and out of each other, so the heath felt like it was vibrating. I thought of earth tremors, wheels spinning on an upturned bike, a distant generator whirring in its shed. But the churring, when you hear it, is not really like a machine. There is a pulsing energy to the sound, like listening to a speeded-up heartbeat. But there is also a sense of hesitancy, of the sound falling and wavering; the writer J. A. Baker described the nightjar's song as 'like the sound of a stream of wine spilling from a height into a deep and booming cask'.

Not like a machine, then, though a machine could confuse someone listening out for nightjars. A small-engined motorbike, heard in the distance, has sometimes stood in for a churring nightjar. If you are waiting in the dark for a bird you cannot see – a superb ventriloquist, who hides its call among insect calls – it's easy to seize on any sound that might conjure up the bird.

The many names for the nightjar – local, archaic, often onomatopoeic – reflect the distinctiveness of the bird's song: 'night churr', 'scissor grinder', 'razor grinder', 'screech hawk', 'churr owl', 'eve churr', 'eve jar', 'jar owl', 'wheel bird', 'spinner', and, in Welsh, *aderyn-y-droell*: the spinning-wheel bird. Other names reflect the nightjar's hunting habits, its flight prowess, its habitat: 'moth hawk', 'gnat hawk', 'night hawk', 'night swallow', 'night crow', 'dor hawk' (the name Wordsworth used for the bird – 'dor' being an old name for beetle – 'The buzzing dor-hawk, round and round, is wheeling'), and Gilbert White's name, 'fern-owl', reflecting the bird's association with heathland where fern, or bracken, is common.

White's other name for the bird, 'goat-sucker', has its origins in the long-held belief that nightjars stole the milk from goats and other livestock at night. Variations on this name include 'goat owl' and 'goat chaffer', while in Spain the nightjar is sometimes called *engana pastor*: 'shepherd's deceiver'. The view that this nocturnal bird hovered around livestock, sucking milk from the animals, persisted from Aristotle and led Linnaeus, in the eighteenth century, to give the European nightjar its current scientific name, *Caprimulgus europaeus*, from the Latin *capra*, a nanny goat, and *mulgere*, to milk; *Caprimulgus* is therefore a 'milker of goats'. Hovering around livestock at dusk is something nightjars do; the birds are drawn to the animals in the same way they are sometimes drawn to streetlights and stagnant water, to predate the insects that gather in these places. The irony is that nightjars, rather than stealing milk, benefited livestock by predating the insects that plagued them.

Another name for the nightjar, 'Puckeridge' (also 'Puck-bird'), derives from a skin infection found in cattle caused by the warble fly laying its eggs under the skin on the animal's back. In Gilbert White's time it was thought this infection was caused by nightjars striking at cattle with their beaks (blindness in animals was another condition attributed to nightjars sucking the milk of livestock). 'Puckeridge', perhaps derived from the malignant spirit Puck, was the name given to the skin infection and, by association, to the birds themselves. White was quick to dismiss this belief; he realised that the nightjar's bill was far too weak to puncture cattle hide, and when he dissected the contents of a nightjar's stomach he found it to comprise entirely of insects.

The nightjar's association with darkness has, like the owls, bestowed on the bird a whole baggage of folklore, superstition and prejudice. 'Lichfowl', meaning a corpse-fowl, is another local name for the nightjar, as is 'gabble ratchet', meaning a corpse hound. In parts of Germany the nightjar was known as *Todtenvogel*, meaning the 'death bird'. The souls of unbaptised children were thought to lodge in nightjars, with the birds seen as vessels for the wanderings of these restless souls. There is even a species of nightjar, *Eurostopodus diabolicus*, found in Sulawesi, whose name, the diabolical or Satanic nightjar, stems from the bird's distinctive plip-plop call, thought to be the sound it makes when pulling out people's eyeballs.

It had become much darker, and I could no longer see the trees on the far side of the heath. Every so often an aeroplane passed low overhead and the roar of its engines shook the place. I wondered how the nightjars coped being so close to an airport. The frequent noise of aircraft made it feel like an impossible place to be a bird, for their song to be heard. Human-generated noise, or anthrophony, as it has collectively been termed, is sometimes described as 'aural litter' or 'audible trash'. It's an appropriate description for how anthrophony pollutes and impacts the biophony, the sounds produced by living organisms. I felt that impact acutely with the noise of the aircraft; their intrusion was as much a blight on the heath as if someone had dumped a pile of litter there. It was always such a relief once the planes had passed.

I decided to walk slowly in the direction of where I thought one of the nightjars was calling. Every few metres I stopped to listen. The bird's churr had a rolling rhythm to it, a rising and falling pitch. There are two principal phrases to the nightjar's song (a 'song phrase', or 'motif', comprises an arranged sequence of 'syllables', each syllable being made up of one or more notes grouped together). The song has a long, high-frequency phrase (the major phrase), which runs for roughly 10 seconds, before it jolts into a brief, lower-frequency phrase (the minor phrase), which lasts for around a second. The major phrase has a frequency of about 1.7

kHz and a pulse rate of 24 pulses per second. The minor phrase has a lower frequency of around 1.2 kHz, but a higher pulse rate of 40 pulses per second. Once the minor phrase finishes, there is no pause; instead, the song reverts straight back to the high-frequency major phrase. The effect is a bit like listening to a slowed-down ambulance siren, or of a radio dial being gradually turned through distant static. The nightjar's churring follows this pattern of phrases on continuous loop, until it abruptly stops.

Occasionally, the song ends with a gurgling, bubbling sound, as though its last moments are caught in the swirl of a plughole. This distinctive ending, known as the 'terminal phrase', has also been described as sounding like a 'clockwork toy running down'. Why some male nightjars end their song this way is not clear, though birdsong with a distinctive ending, referred to as 'accented' song, tends to be produced when a female is present, and is thus associated with courtship and pair bonding, while 'unaccented' song, where there is no distinctive finale, is more associated with territorial defence. A 2020 study of nightjars in Nottinghamshire suggested that the terminal phrase in male nightjar song is more prevalent in June, when pairs have bonded and laid their first clutch of eggs, as opposed to earlier in the season, in May, when the males first arrive and have not yet paired, and when the tendency is for the nightjars to end their churring song abruptly.

The switch between major and minor phrase in the song was for a long time thought to be produced by the bird turning its head from side to side. In fact, the rising and falling pattern of the churr is more likely to be a result of the bird's breathing rhythm. I wonder if this helps to explain why I found the noise so captivating; as well as hearing the nightjar's music, I was also listening to the bird breathing.

The puzzle of the nightjar's song is how a bird of this size manages to churr for such an extended period without seeming to pause to take a breath. If the bird is singing non-stop for nearly 10 minutes, producing 40 notes per second with a gap of only 40 milliseconds between notes, how does it draw enough air to vocalise? How does the bird breathe? The answer appears to lie with the pattern of the song. When the nightjar switches to the minor phrase, faster and much shorter in duration than the major phrase, the bird inhales, exhaling when he reverts to the louder and longer major component of the churr. Most bird species sing while exhaling and pause during their song to draw in oxygen and air. The male nightjar seems to have found a way to not stop singing – a slight shift in pitch and amplitude, air is drawn in, and the bird continues singing uninterrupted. Not only does this change in pitch facilitate breathing, it also breaks the monotony of the song. I loved hearing that sudden shift in pitch; it gave the churr its rhythm, made the song more like a song. You can understand why the sound was attributed to the bird moving its head; the shift in pitch creates a sense of movement, as though the bird has suddenly shifted position, jumped to a different perch.

But why does the nightjar not interrupt its song, as most birds do, to pause and breathe? Presumably, the duration of the male's song is key to both sexual selection and territorial claim over other males. The slightest pause in the song could signal a lack of fitness. There's a peculiar male-madness at work here; testosterone eclipses oxygen, breath becomes secondary to song. All that matters is the length and volume of the song. At peak volume, if conditions are right, the male nightjar's churr can carry for 600 metres and is easily heard 200 metres away. As the breeding season progresses, the song becomes quieter. So, by the middle of August, the churr is usually weaker than it is in May and June.

I found it impossible to distinguish between the different males calling on the heath. But it's feasible, with the right recording equipment, to identify individual males from their song and in doing so build up a picture of their habits, of foraging movements and migration patterns, by documenting which individuals return to the same territories year on year. It's as though the song holds the key to unlocking the bird's immaculate crypsis; by analysing the texture, the temporal features of their song, individuals are revealed. Each male nightjar's song has its own signature pattern, so that by recording the length of each phrase, as well as the speed and number of pulses per second in the churr, it's possible to distinguish between individuals. Each nightjar's song carries its own unique and subtle fingerprint.

* * *

Before I heard the first nightjar of the evening, I had been hearing and seeing woodcock displaying over the heath. The inky sky showed their profile beautifully. A stiffness to the way they held themselves in flight, a tautness around the chest, wings flickering rapidly. The woodcock patrolled the heath in low, wide arcs, announcing themselves with a loud popping squeak: *pee-zisp*, *pee-zisp*, the *zisp* like a small, explosive spit. The effect was very different from the nightjar's ventriloquism. As soon as a woodcock made its high-pitched squeak, I looked up and found the bird instantly. Silhouetted against the sky, its long, aerial-like bill was clearly visible. The bill was held at about 45° to the ground, so that it seemed as though the woodcock was looking down its length towards me as it passed overhead. The prominence of the bill and its downward tilt gave the impression of the bird interacting with the ground, of the pulse-like squeaks it emitted being directed at the ground, as though to bounce them back like sonar. One woodcock passed close overhead and I watched as it opened its bill to call. The mandibles parted enough to see a slice of sky between them. But the bill didn't open fully; the section nearest the bird's head stayed joined, as though the bill were hinged there.

The woodcock's 'squeak' call is often followed, or underlaid, with a strange croaking noise that the male makes during his display flight. The 'croak' is a kind of throaty burp, lower and softer (and harder to detect) than the far-carrying *pee-zisp* call. It's a bit like a frog's croak, but deeper and more creaky-sounding. The woodcock usually makes its croak in quick succession, two, sometimes three or four times, the repetition giving the sound a sense of friction. When I heard it, I thought of a stiff, creaky door, its frame swollen with damp, being coaxed open. If, like (some) human burps, you could smell a woodcock's croak, it would smell, I think, of mud and marsh and mulch. Just before it makes the croak, the woodcock pulls up out of its swift flight to pause in the air, hesitates there, wings flickering, head pointed downwards. Briefly, it is held in the air by its song.

There was a regularity to the woodcock fly-pasts. Their roding (the name for the male woodcock's display flight) appeared to follow the same flight path, so the effect was like watching a lighthouse beam, seeing it flash then disappear, waiting for the beam to make another pass. I thought how the woodcock and nightjar shared the evening shift between them. You could devise a light meter around the emergence times of the two species. Woodcock-light is a thin evening light, where there is still enough light to see them in the distance as they circle the heath in their fast roding displays. Nightjar-light is barely light at all; just as you start to worry the birds are not there and that it will soon be dark, the first nightjar begins to churr.

I walked further along the path and the churring became more intense. A duck-like gulping noise sounded to my left, a high-pitched *ker-ick*, *ker-ick*: a nightjar's contact call. I looked up to see a nightjar silhouetted against the sky, hanging in the air, just clearing the top of a birch tree. A slow, hovering flight, the bird looking down at me, with such a distinctive profile, its long, narrow tail tilted downwards. As I had been watching woodcock earlier, the nightjar's tail looked like a counterbalance to the woodcock's downwards-pointed bill. The nightjar's wings also appeared long and narrow, so that the impression was of looking up at a cross hanging in the air. I was surprised how close the bird came to me. It flipped low over my head, silent, moth-like, fluttering past me. I followed the nightjar as it swung over the heath, flickering above the shorter birch trees. That long tail again; it's the angle of the tail that stands out, held downwards, almost at a right angle to the nightjar's head and neck, like a keel beneath the bird. Then the nightjar flew on, and it was too dark to see anything more.

I went back to the heath again. I got better at timing my arrival so that I hadn't too long to wait to hear the nightjars. It was an odd sort of ritual, leaving work in the evening, driving along the M25, turning off the motorway, and, shortly after, finding myself alone in the middle of the heath, waiting for dark. Anxious that the nightjars would still be here, longing to hear them.

Some evenings the light left the heath so slowly it was as though there were a blockage in the air. On other nights, the temperature would suddenly drop, and the light seemed then to rush out of the heath. As the summer went on, the displaying woodcock became fewer until I no longer heard or saw the birds, and the heath was given over to nightjars.

I tried to time my visits to coincide as closely as possible with a full moon. I scanned weather forecasts, tried to work out which nights would have the best visibility. I became apprehensive of cloud density. I worried that some nights might be too cold for insects and so reduce the nightjars' activity.

If conditions are unfavourable for hunting, nightjars (like hummingbirds and swift nestlings) are able to conserve energy by entering a state of torpidity; that is, the birds can lower their body temperature to reduce the rate of metabolism in order to survive periods of fasting. Nightjars are especially vulnerable to starvation because they rely on such narrow periods of the day – after sunset and just before sunrise – for hunting. If conditions are unfavourable during these times, then the birds can initiate torpidity to conserve vital energy. A North American relative of the nightjar, the common poorwill, is the only species of bird known to enter a state of hibernation, though in the poorwill's case there is some debate as to whether the bird enters a state of prolonged torpor, rather than true hibernation. European nightjars, however, are unable to prolong torpidity in the way the poorwill can, and nightjars therefore need to migrate to sub-Saharan Africa in order to survive the winter.

Because nightjars hunt visually, not acoustically as bats do, they require some degree of light in the sky against which they can silhouette their insect prey. Moths comprise the bulk of their prey species, with beetles and true flies also being significant. Nestling nightjars are initially fed with micro-moths and smaller flies, which the adult birds hunt very low over the ground, skimming the heather and bracken tops. As the young birds grow, their diet shifts towards the larger staple insects their parents feed on, which are brought to the young in a bolus, a saliva-bound ball of compacted insects. Nightjars have several notable adaptations that help them detect their insect prey in poor light conditions. Like owls, they have a tapetum at the back of their eyes. The tapetum works like a mirror, reflecting any unabsorbed light back through the retina, where it is detected by photoreceptor cells. The presence of the tapetum in the bird's retina means that nightjars are exceptionally light-sensitive. They can detect the faintest of light, and then enhance it. It's not so much that nightjars can see in the dark (pitch darkness slows their activity substantially), rather that they are adept at retrieving what light there is from within the dark.

Another specialised adaptation nightjars possess is a frog-like ability to open their mouth extremely wide, both vertically and horizontally, enabling them to more easily catch insects in poor visibility. As well as a wide gape, nightjars also possess a number of long rictal bristles around their mouth. It's thought that these specialised feathers enhance tactility, functioning as a sensory backup when visibility is especially poor and assisting the birds in locating their prey through touch.

While nightjars require some degree of light to hunt in, too much light can have an adverse effect on these highly light-sensitive birds. A recent study in Switzerland concluded that a failure to curb light pollution has brought the nightjar to the brink of extinction in that country. High levels of artificial light disrupt the contrast between insect and background so that nightjars find it difficult to silhouette their insect prey. Where bright and permanent artificial light encroaches on nightjar habitat, for example, the birds will be blinded by such light, their hypersensitive retinas overloaded and dazzled by the glare.

One source of light, however, which is beneficial to nightjars, is the moon. In fact, moonlight is so important to nightjars that it plays a significant role in the bird's behaviour. Moonlight not only enhances hunting conditions, it also prolongs the period in which nightjars can hunt, beyond those narrow dusk and pre-dawn windows. Under bright moonlight, nightjars will often utilise the conditions to static hunt, waiting on a perch before swooping down on passing insects. In darker conditions, the birds tend to forage continuously, flying about looking for prey in a much less energy-efficient way than hunting from a perch allows. Nightjars will also synchronise their reproductive cycle with the lunar cycle. Birds that arrive on their breeding territories in May will usually set about nesting as quickly as possible, presumably to maximise the chance of raising a second brood in July. Those birds that arrive a little later in June, however, synchronise laying so that their eggs hatch during a young waxing moon. This way, the period of peak moonlight coincides with the period when the adult birds need to provide the most food for their young. Nightjars are, to a large extent, moon-birds, lunarphilic in their behaviour, dependent upon the light of the moon to hunt effectively, to conserve energy and to raise their young.

When the first nightjar of the evening started to sing, I was always struck by how loud it sounded. It was as though a tap had been turned on to release a rush of whirring noise. The birds dominated the soundscape. The sound of the distant motorway and the traffic on nearby roads was pushed out by the nightjar's churr. Another Spanish name for the nightjar, *papa ventos*, translates as 'father of the wind'. This might refer to the bird's wide gape, as though, when fully open, the nightjar is releasing a gust of wind, but also, perhaps, to the loud wind-like whirring of its song; similarly, the French word for a nightjar is *engoulevent*: 'wind crow'.

I cheered when I heard that first bird of the evening and felt the volume of its song increasing. A six-lane motorway? Europe's busiest airport? The nightjars took them on and made the soundscape their own. Only the low-flying aircraft swamped the birds' song, but they didn't deter them. Once the planes had passed, the nightjars would always resume their churring. Sometimes that first song of the evening would quickly stall. Then there would be a pause of 5, maybe 10, minutes before I heard the next churr. It was as though that first explorative song had found the conditions wanting. I thought of the nightjars then as bird-barometers, testing the acoustics, the temperature, the accumulation of dew, waiting for the optimum conditions for them to sing. The darker it got, the more the heath became a theatre for their song.

Nightjar song is enhanced by night. As it gets dark, a temperature inversion occurs; the ground temperature cools, while the temperature of the air increases, as warmth released by the cooling ground rises. It is the reverse of what occurs during the day, when the ground temperature rises as it absorbs the sun's warmth. This temperature inversion makes sound behave differently at night. During the day, sound waves speed up over the warm ground and are refracted, bent upwards and lost. At night, sound waves are bent away from the warmer air towards the cooler ground. It's not so much that it is quieter at night, rather that sound is louder and carries further because sound waves are not dissipated in the way they are during the day. Instead of bending away from us, the sound waves bend back towards us. For animals that communicate over long distances, night offers the best conditions to vocalise. For instance, the foxes I sometimes hear screech-barking at night in midwinter are often half a mile away. Nightjars appear to utilise these conditions too, waiting for that temperature inversion to occur so that their song can carry further and sound louder. Nightjar song feels like a release, as though the churr has built up during the day and is then let go in a whirligig of sound. Night is the trigger; as warmth departs the ground, the song departs the bird.

* * *

Go deeper into the night and, just as the woodcock gives way to the nightjar, the nightjar gives way to other birds on the heath. Though I kept coming back to that heath by the motorway on the outskirts of London, I explored other heathlands that summer. I travelled to the stony Breckland heaths of East Anglia, past vast American air bases, walking for miles along sandy tracks through the pine woods that dominate the landscape.

On the walk out through the trees, I watched a whitethroat bending bracken tips as it flicked from stem to stem. And on the way back in the dark, a long-eared owl swooped round me, as one of its young, perched in a nearby tree, made a loud, far-carrying begging call, *pee-yip*, *pee-yip*, which followed me most of the way back through the forest. I heard nightjars churring in the clearings among the pines and watched a mistle thrush cast its tall shadow over the ground, its bill so full of leggy insects that it looked like it was gathering twigs. There were lapwings out on the heath there, a large flock of 50 birds, restless and quivering. Stone-curlews were there too, with their long, yellow legs and huge lemony eyes. I watched four of them fly low in front of me, calling, whistling as they flew. The white markings on their wings flashed as they passed. The flock landed on a stony patch of the heath and I immediately lost them as they just seemed to fold into the dusty ground. I marked the spot carefully and walked slowly towards it, but the birds might as well have turned themselves to stone.

Later, when it was much darker and I was starting to wonder if I had imagined the encounter, I jumped when a stone-curlew suddenly called out with its loud, piercing *kuu-lie, kuu-lie*. 'I'm here! I'm here!' it seemed to say. It was too dark to locate the caller, so I sat down beneath a tree and listened to the bird's wailing, which grew louder and closer the darker it became. Its call was not unlike a curlew's, enough to make me hesitate when I heard it. But the stone-curlew's call lacks the curlew's bubbling, watery richness. It's as though both species draw their call from the landscape; the curlew's wetlands and damp moorlands, the stone-curlew's drier, sandy, stony heathlands. As it got darker out on the Brecks, the nightjars became quieter and stone-curlews – one local name for them is 'night curlew', another is 'shriek owl' (though my favourite is 'wailing heath chicken') – took over the night with their strange wailing.

Back on the heath between the railway and the motorway, I began to build up a sense of where the best spots to see the nightjars were. One place I often encountered the birds was where a path split a small group of birch trees. The low evening sun often lit these birches as if from the inside, so that their leaves glowed red. I frequently saw nightjars there, hovering over the trees. One male used the birches as his churring perch and would move between branches to sing from different vantage points.

Some of the encounters I had with nightjars at that spot were among the most exhilarating I've had with any bird. I became so distracted watching the nightjars, I'd forget how dark it had become and how far I had to drive before I'd get home. Not only did the birds transform the soundscape of the place, but they also alleviated the dark, the uneasiness of being alone in it. It took me a few visits to get used to the pitch black; I'd step from the glare of the motorway into this pool of darkness out on the heath. But I soon grew to value that darkness, appreciating how the absence of light pollution was such an essential component of the nightjar's habitat.

Some evenings I would find myself in the centre of a nightjar dance. It would start with a glimpse of a nightjar flickering bat-like between the trees. The way the birds twisted, hovered and spun in the air was dizzying to watch. They had this serpentine agility, as though they could double back and coil through their own trajectory. There was something both erratic and graceful about their flight; I thought of a kite jinking as its flyer tugs at the lines, trying to coax and lift it back into flight. The nightjars dipped over my head, close enough to see the sooty browns of their feathers. Quiet, soft as owls. And on one occasion two birds shot past me at head height, one close behind the other, at such a speed they made a whirring sound as they brushed the air beside my ear ('and often by his head/Wizzes as quick as thought' is how John Clare vividly describes these nightjar flypasts in his poem, 'The Fern Owl's Nest'). Suddenly, another nightjar appeared, as though it had been shaken out of the heather, and I watched as the pair shivered about each other. I could see the white spots – the prominent display markings – on the underside of the male's wings and tail as he shook in the air around the other bird.

Sometimes, when the pair edged away from me and the light was too poor to see them clearly, the male's white wing-spots were all I could make out, like will-o'-the-wisps in the dark.

The birds seemed largely oblivious to me and several times they swirled over and around me as I stood amazed in the middle of the path. Then a *kip*, *kip* noise would start up as the male began wing-clapping. This sound, a feature of nightjar displays, is produced by the bird striking its wings together above its back; occasionally the wings are also slapped together on the down beat. Wing-clapping is the male's percussive accompaniment to his churring song. He wing-claps to advertise to females and in territorial disputes with other males. The clapping I heard was not especially loud, like somebody tapping against a door. But the combination of wing-clapping, churring and the birds' dancing flypasts made it feel like the whole heath had suddenly woken up.

The ornithologist David Lack, who made several studies of nightjars in the twenties and thirties, proposed an interesting theory concerning injury-feigning in nightjars. Rather than the adult bird deliberately trying to draw a predator away from the nest area by simulating a broken wing, as several ground-nesting species do, Lack suggested that this behaviour in nightjars could be induced by shock. An intruder so startles the bird that it becomes partially paralysed, its movements uncoordinated. Lack noted that with nightjars the feigning performance lessens in vigour the more often the nest is visited, suggesting that the effects of the shock on the bird diminished with repetition. He also pointed out that because nightjars are such close sitters, they must rarely need to divert intruders through an injury-feigning display. Lack thought that the shock of startling a crepuscular species during the day might be greater than for a diurnal species. As though, vampirically, daylight is as much a part of the shock to a nightjar as the presence of an intruder.

I was fascinated by this idea of Lack's, which was borne out of his close observations of nightjars and through comparing their actions to injury-feigning in other species. The idea that our presence could so shock and alarm a bird that it induced in them a state of partial paralysis was striking. It felt like a metaphor for our intrusion on so much of the natural world; our presence is so intrusive, so damaging, that we shock the natural world, Gorgon-like, into a state of paralysis. In our wake we leave anxiety, trembling.

Up until 2017, nightjars were on the UK's Birds of Conservation Concern Red List, which highlights those species of most concern and in urgent need of help. The nightjar population had been in marked decline since at least the 1950s. Between 1972 and 1981 their numbers in Britain are thought to have halved, to leave a population of roughly 2,100 calling males. Alongside this numerical decline, range contraction has also been a serious problem for the nightjar. Contraction has been especially accelerated across Scotland, Wales, Northern Ireland (where nightjars are likely now extinct), as well as northern and central England. Since the 1980s there has been a partial recovery of numbers plus range expansion, notably in southern England where 66 per cent of the population is located. In 2004 the population was estimated at 4,024 males, a 30 per cent increase since 1992. It is a rare and welcome conservation success story, with the preservation and restoration of southern heathland being a crucial factor in stabilising the nightjar population in England. However, the increase has largely been confined to the core population areas in the south, which accounted for 88.6 per cent of the national increase. This increase in the south is balanced by declines in the north-west of the UK, and it remains the challenge to restore the species to much of its former breeding range across the country.

What has driven this range contraction in the nightjar? Climate is one factor that affects the breeding success of the species. The range contraction for nightjars across Britain during the second half of the twentieth century closely follows climatic trends, with the population contracting to the drier coastal fringes and warmer southern parts of the country. Poor weather during spring migration can delay arrival times and therefore limit the chances of this often double-brooded species raising a second brood. One of the striking differences between David Lack's studies of nightjars and more recent studies of the bird is that double-brooding in nightjars is far less common now than it was in the 1930s. Wet, cold summers are disastrous for nightjars, severely limiting their ability to catch sufficient insect prey to raise their young. And there is also a close correlation between cold nights, when insect prey is suppressed, and poor growth rates and death rates in young nightjars.

But it is the recent calamitous declines in insect populations, largely driven by agricultural intensification with its widespread use of synthetic pesticides, that have posed the most serious threat to this insectivorous bird. It's estimated that more than 40 per cent of all insect species across large swathes of Western Europe are in rapid decline, with a third of insect species threatened with extinction. Within Europe and North America, the UK currently shows the highest rate of insect declines, with a shocking 60 per cent of species documented as being in decline. At least 337 moth species in England – a crucial prey species for nightjars – have shown declining populations of 12 per cent every 10 years. In the south of England, where nightjars are most concentrated, these moth species are declining at an even faster rate of 17 per cent per decade.

Habitat loss has been another significant factor in driving declines in the nightjar population since the 1950s, and it is an issue that continues to threaten the species across its range. Wherever heathland, downland and marginal land are under threat from development, housing, golf courses or agricultural intensification, the nightjar is threatened.

Fragmentation of these habitats also impacts the species: not only by isolating breeding populations, but where roads dissect these habitats they pose a threat to resident birds, collision with vehicles being one of the principal causes of death among nightjars. The heath where I spent time listening to nightjars, for all its sense of refuge, filled me with concern for the birds because of the proximity of so many busy roads.

Maintenance of heathland (in the 2004 national survey, 46.4 per cent of male nightjars were associated with heathland) is also crucial for nightjars. One of the reasons there was such a thriving population on the heath I visited was because the habitat was being carefully managed, notably through the presence of a small herd of Belted Galloway cattle, whose grazing helped to maintain the structure of the heath by removing coarse grasses, breaking up dense vegetation and keeping the heath open. If heathland becomes overrun with birch or pine, then it soon becomes unsuitable for nightjars.

Beyond the bird's traditional heathland breeding territories, consideration also needs to be given to their wider foraging areas. Nightjars will forage some distance from their nest site, often travelling to adjoining farmland. If that wider foraging zone is denuded of insects, or if there aren't adequate corridors to link breeding territories with the birds' foraging areas, then nightjars will struggle to raise their young. A study in Belgium has recommended that the country's conservation policy for nightjars needs to be adjusted to take the importance of these wider foraging areas into account. If access to, and provision for, adequate wider foraging zones for nightjars are limited, then the birds can become trapped within the confines of their breeding habitat. This is one of the main issues facing nightjars in Britain today; the bird's difficulty in expanding beyond its current heartlands in the south means that it has essentially become isolated in a few select breeding areas, which are a fraction of its former range.

One thing I learnt spending time listening to nightjars that summer was that the birds made a variety of sounds. The churring dominated their soundtrack but I also frequently heard wing-clapping and their soft *co-ic* contact calls, as well as the occasional bubbling sound made at the end of a sequence of churring. Occasionally, I also heard the birds make a short chuckling sound a bit like a blackbird's alarm call. In addition to these, I'd read that when the male relieves the female from incubation for short spells at dawn and dusk he makes a bubbling call to her. The female will then reply by making trembling movements with her tail and body, while the male raises his wings above his back before carefully lowering and folding them. This encounter between the pair sounded like the most balletic, intimate changeover at the nest. It made me realise that what I had witnessed of the nightjars – what I had heard of them – was just a fraction of their lives, that there was a whole soundscape of intimacy between the birds that I could not hear.

One evening, under a huge red moon, I stayed late on the heath. There was a partial eclipse that night as the earth's shadow slid across the moon. The eclipse reminded me of something my young son once said; standing in the back garden, three or four years old, he pointed up at the quarter moon and said, 'Look, a broken moon!'

I didn't want to leave the nightjars that night. Waves of churring rolled across the heath as though the place were murmuring to itself. I kept seeing silhouettes of nightjars against the sky. One bird sat on a branch above me. I could see the outline of its long tail, the kink of its neck, the helmet-looking head. Very slowly, I walked towards it. The brittle heather branches snapped under my weight, and I thought every step I made would scare the nightjar from its perch. But he kept singing. I was close enough to see the bird's dark eyestripe. The earth's shadow looked like an eyelid closing over the moon. I stood there, just a few feet away, and listened to the nightjar's strange music, felt the air vibrating with its churr.

II

Mountain of the Trolls

Shearwater

It's the end of July and I'm walking up a mountain on the Isle of Rum. The wind is shaking the heather and slamming into my back. I can see a distant waterfall struggling in the gale, spray pouring back over the lip of the hill so that it looks like the waterfall has grown a crest. I turn off the path and begin to climb the boggy lower slopes of the mountain. A snipe bursts from the rushes with a sharp sneezing sound. Then a male hen harrier flies out of the wind, jinking and silvery, and is gone in an instant.

I'd come to Rum to listen to the midnight song of the Manx shearwater. My plan was to camp on the mountain for a few days, spending the nights up at the shearwaters' colony among the burrows where the birds nest. I had seen some shearwaters earlier, from the windy deck of the ferry; sooty-black on their upper parts and white below, as the birds skimmed over the waves they flickered black and white. Their dark back and upper wings blended with the colour of the sea so that the birds always seemed on the verge of disappearing. A flash of white, a roll of the wings, and they vanished, before their white breasts blinked into view again. Several shearwaters gliding together gave off a shimmering effect as their wings tipped between dark and light, as though the birds kept interrupting their own shadows.

I pitched my tent on a plateau that was like a shelf on the side of the mountain. Cliffs below, and steep slopes of rock and scree all the way to the summit. So much spilt rock, it looked, in places, like the mountain was crumbling. Cloud shadows raced over the plateau. The wind slapped my tent, sprayed it with rain, then seconds later blew it dry again. There were large bare patches of earth scraped across the ground where wind and water had scoured the vegetation. Red deer hooves scuffed and patterned these scrapes. I sometimes saw the deer moving along the ridgelines, and in the evening they grazed on the slope above where I camped. The deer were so well camouflaged among the tumble of rocks, their sudden movements looked like boulders coming loose.

There is an unusual relationship between the red deer on Rum and the Manx shearwater colony on the island. The deer graze around the shearwater burrows, attracted to the vegetation that flourishes where the shearwaters' droppings have fertilised the ground. But the deer don't just feed on the vegetation, they also eat the shearwaters themselves. Not the adult birds; the deer only predate the fledgling shearwaters, and specifically during the period late in the breeding season when the young shearwaters start to emerge from their burrows at night to wing-exercise. Away from the safety of their burrows, the young shearwaters are vulnerable to the deer, which graze both at night and during the day, and those fledglings that fail to make it back to their burrows by daybreak are especially susceptible to predation. In what seems to be methodical rather than aberrant behaviour, a deer will seize a shearwater, bite off then swallow its head, before proceeding to chew the bird's wings and legs to extract the bones. It's the calcium in the bird's bones that the deer are after, and it is assumed that the mineral-poor montane vegetation of Rum causes the deer to make up for the mineral deficiencies in their regular diet by eating the bones of the abundant and easily available young shearwaters. Retrieved shearwater carcasses typically show the bones almost completely removed by the deer from both the bird's legs and the carpal areas of the wing, with the shearwater's skin, flesh and feathers left mostly intact. It's as if the deer have sucked the bones out of the shearwater's body; the deer don't so much pick the bones clean, as clean the carcass itself of bones.

This phenomenon, though certainly unusual among herbivores, is not unique to the deer on Rum as it has also been observed in sheep living on another island, Foula in Shetland, where sheep have been observed predating unfledged Arctic tern chicks. On Rum, the deer's behaviour creates an interesting interdependence between the deer and the island's more conventional predators, the ravens and golden eagles, which benefit from the discarded shearwater carcasses the deer leave behind, just as they also benefit from mortality among the deer themselves. Numbers of shearwater chicks killed by the deer on Rum remain small (no more than 4 per cent of all fledglings) and their predation has little impact on the overall shearwater population. Still, I watched the deer with added interest as they moved around the colony, and it was never too far from my mind that I was camped alone on a mountain surrounded by flesh-eating, bone-sucking deer.

That first afternoon on Rum I spent exploring the mountain. There were shearwater burrows all the way up its slopes, some only a few feet from my tent, and I even came across burrows close to the summit cairn. Tier upon tier of burrows, thousands of birds, the whole mountain pockmarked with holes. The burrows were concentrated across the soft grassy areas between the rocks. And the grass around the burrows was flushed a denser green where it had been manured by the shearwaters' guano. Wherever the hillside glowed green, I found burrows. Their entrances were roughly the size of a rabbit hole, the span of my little finger to thumb on my outstretched hand. There was often an overhang of rock that formed a ceiling to the entrance, so the tunnel burrowed down beneath the rock. Several of the burrows had wisps of dead grass beside the opening, like a doormat, where the birds had plucked at the grass around the entrance.

Some openings had small spills of soil down their lip, like gritty brown tongues. The ground in front of the burrows was compressed, smoothed down by the birds standing there. One or two burrows had a white feather caught in the grass or the soil outside them. Some had feathers dropped in the dark of the hole, as though a light had been left on in the burrow. The entrances had a musty smell like the pages of an old book. There was no sound coming from any of the burrows. Apart from the wind and the occasional raven passing overhead, the mountain was quiet.

I never got used to that tension in the place, that beneath me there were thousands of birds, tucked in their burrows, yet during the day there was neither sign nor sound of them. It was only when it became properly dark, around midnight, that the mountain erupted into one of the eeriest and most clamorous displays of birdsong I experienced on these journeys.

* * *

Manx shearwaters belong to the order of ocean-wandering, tube-nosed birds known as the Procellariiformes. These are the 'storm birds', from the Latin *procella*, a storm, and they are pelagic in their habits, at home in the stormiest seas. The order includes the storm petrels, diving petrels, fulmars and albatrosses, often referred to collectively as the 'petrels', and also known as the 'tubenoses'. The prominent tube-shaped nostrils these birds possess, like a tube of penne pasta strapped to the top of their bill, enable them to eject salt in the form of a saline solution that drips from their nasal glands. The petrels are also distinctive in possessing a high concentration of olfactory cells in their brains, equipping them with an exceptional sense of smell with which to both navigate and detect their marine prey.

These are long-lived birds, typically around 15 years for Manx shearwaters, though the oldest Manx shearwater recorded was a bird ringed on 17 May 1957 on Bardsey Island off the Welsh coast and caught by a ringer on the same island on 8 May 2008, making it an astonishing 50 years, 11 months and 21 days old. 'Manxies' are largely monogamous, slow to reach breeding age (around 6 years old), with chicks that spend a lengthy 10 weeks in the nest before they fledge. Bill to tail, they are slightly longer than a rugby ball, and weigh about the same as the ball, between 400 to 450 grams. Their wingspan, at around 80 centimetres, is twice the length of their body, so when they glide on those long, straight wings, there is something runic about their profile – a line with a dash through the middle.

Manx shearwaters arrive at their breeding grounds around the British Isles in late March, having spent the winter in the South Atlantic off the coasts of Brazil and Patagonia. They breed around the British and Irish coasts in large numbers, up to 300,000 pairs (90 per cent of the global population) concentrated in just a handful of locations, with Rum in the Hebrides, the islands of Skomer and Skokholm off the Pembrokeshire coast, Bardsey Island off the Llŷn Peninsula in Gwynedd and Puffin Island in Co. Kerry, Ireland, holding the densest colonies. The Manx shearwater population on Rum is estimated to be 100,000 pairs, around a quarter of the world population.

Shearwaters generally mate for life and, although they separate during the winter, pair bonds are re-established when the birds return to their breeding grounds, where they will nest, if possible, in the same burrow year after year. The burrows, which tend to be between 70 centimetres and 3 metres deep, are given a spring clean by the returning birds. Walls are sanded down with their chisel-like bills and any loose soil is swept back with their wings, then kicked out the entrance with their feet. The previous year's nest material is similarly ejected and fresh bedding (mostly moss on Rum) is gathered to replenish the nest. The birds rake the moss out of the surrounding grass using the curved tip of their bill, then drag the moss into the hole to line the burrow. Shearwaters are diligent gardeners; by raking out the moss from the sward, the birds aerate the ground; by raking out last year's composted nest material, they fertilise the ground in front of the burrows. Birds arriving back to the mountains on Rum in early spring will often find their burrows still buried under snow, and those bills and sharp-clawed feet then serve as shovels to clear the burrow entrances.

A single large white egg is laid in the burrow around the beginning of May. There follows an exceptionally long incubation period (51 days) and subsequent nestling period (71 days), before the chick fledges towards the end of August and beginning of September. During incubation, the adult pair alternate long shifts in the burrow of between 6 to 7 days. One adult remains with the egg, not eating, losing around 10 g in weight per day, while its mate can travel hundreds of miles from the nest site, feeding out at sea, diving to depths of up to 100 ft in pursuit of small fish, cephalopods (particularly squid) and small crustaceans, building up sufficient fat reserves for its turn in the burrow. Male shearwaters tend to spend about a day and a half longer incubating than females; the male's larger size means they lose a smaller proportion of their body reserves each day and can therefore afford to spend longer at the nest.

These marathon incubation shifts by the adult pair are a remarkable feat of endurance, and the overall energetic costs of such a long breeding season – four months from egg laying to fledging – must be substantial. One way that shearwaters alleviate these energy costs is by lowering their body temperature by around 2°C while they are incubating; thus, in a similar way to nightjars, reducing their metabolic rate and saving energy while they are fasting. The birds may even enter a state of mild torpor during their time in the burrow. In addition, shearwater eggs are able to withstand lengthy periods of cooling (up to 7 days) and still remain viable.

Both the adult shearwater's ability to reduce its body temperature, and the egg's ability to survive periods of cooling, are innovative solutions to the shearwater's habit of ranging long distances in search of food. The egg's capacity to withstand periods of cooling presumably insures against the possibility of the incubating bird needing to leave the nest to feed should its mate be delayed – by weather or by sheer distance – in returning to the burrow. The adult bird who is not on incubation duty can forage out at sea for days on end, conserving energy on these long-distance flights by gliding over the waves on its long, narrow, almost rigid wings.

Everything about the shearwater seems designed to equip them with the ability to keep on wandering. Even when they have to spend time on land, the birds do so equipped in such a way that allows their partner to keep wandering far out at sea. I love that about the birds, that the sea is so much a part of them that when shearwaters do have to come ashore, they do so in a way that insures them against the pull the sea has over them.

When the shearwater chick finally hatches it resembles one of those balls of matted dust that spill from the bag of a vacuum cleaner. Over the following days the chick's down turns a slightly darker grey, and thickens, like a cloud filling with rain. For the first week one of the adults guards the chick, then the parents leave the young bird in its burrow, while they forage out at sea, returning most nights to feed the nestling. This troglodyte existence continues for around 60 days, by which time a well-fed chick has reached one and a half times the weight of its parents. It will also fledge a darker, blacker bird on its upper parts than its parents, whose worn plumage is much browner at this stage of the breeding season. Night-time feeds then cease, and the adults desert their chick to commence their migration to the South Atlantic. The young shearwater spends its final eight days on the island fasting, emerging from the burrow at night to exercise its wings before, on one of these nocturnal excursions, finding a breeze to lift it from a rock or tumbling into flight off a cliff.

Light pollution can pose a hazard on these maiden flights, with young shearwaters disorientated by lights on the mainland and even by household lights in the small village on Rum. I chatted to a man on the ferry who told me how he monitored the shoreline below the port on the mainland each September to check for stranded shearwaters – their bearings confused by the town's lights – which he gathered up and released from the ferry when safely out at sea. Autumn gales can prove even more hazardous to young shearwaters, blowing them far inland to incongruous locations miles from the coast. Hazards aside, by October the majority of young shearwaters will have joined their parents in the South Atlantic, their fat reserves fuelling them for the long migration. These birds won't touch land again for another two years.

I settled into a routine over the following days. In the morning I washed in the burn, collected water, then made some breakfast. The rest of the day I spent wandering over the mountain, exploring the shearwater burrows. I'd return to my camp in the late afternoon, make some tea, rest and wait for nightfall. Much of these daytime recces was spent thinking about how the mountain would look and feel in the dark. There were practical reasons for this; I needed to not get lost, to find my way around safely in the dark. So I tried to memorise the mountain, study the routes up and down, which sections to avoid, which prominent boulders to make for when descending. The larger boulders were useful markers, but no matter how much I rehearsed these routes, how much I tried to acclimatise to the dark, the reality of the mountain at night was always disorientating.

One striking aspect of Manx shearwater behaviour is their ability to navigate around their colonies in the dark, and for each bird to locate its burrow among the many thousands of others. As I stumbled around the rocky slopes at night, shearwaters shot past me in the dark, landed and quickly made straight for their burrows. Meanwhile, I could barely work out where my tent was. How did the shearwaters know where their burrows were? How did the birds navigate so effectively in the dark? Several studies have set out to try and answer these questions. Auditory clues – birds calling to one another to locate their burrows – do not appear to be used by Manx shearwaters; for the majority of the breeding season, adult birds are returning to a solitary, silent chick in its burrow. It's also the case that breeding adult Manx shearwaters are largely silent around the colony from May onwards; it's the non-breeding birds that make all the noise. The most obvious navigational sense employed by the birds, aside from vision, would be the use of olfactory clues, particularly in a bird with such a developed sense of smell. However, experiments that tested the shearwater's use of smell in locating their burrows provided no evidence that smell was utilised by the birds. This is backed up by the fact that on Rum, returning shearwaters are able to locate their burrows buried under snow and ice, when presumably there is minimal scent to guide the birds.

Visual cues, therefore, do seem to be the most significant navigational tool used by shearwaters around the colony at night. Their eyesight has some notable adaptations that enhance the birds' ability to see in the dark. For example, they have a high percentage of colourless droplets in the receptor cells in their retinas (a feature common in other nocturnal birds). Manx shearwaters also have a relatively flat cornea (the outer covering of the eye), so it is their lens, rather than their cornea, that refracts, or bends, the most light to produce an image on their retina. Consequently, a shearwater possesses a shorter focal length than, for example, a pigeon, a similar-sized diurnal bird whose cornea is highly curved and refracts most of the light onto their retina. Pigeons have a wider field of vision than the shearwater and a pigeon will see an image, in normal light conditions, in greater detail than a shearwater can. The shearwater's shorter focal length, however, means it sees a smaller but brighter image; its eyesight has a greater image brightness than a pigeon's, so it can see better in poor light.

However, Manx shearwaters' eyes are not perfectly adapted to the dark; their eyes, for example, are not as efficient as those of largely nocturnal species such as owls, mice or rats. Shearwaters seem to hover somewhere on the eyesight spectrum between diurnal and nocturnal species, and it may be that the open habitat of their colonies, on treeless offshore islands, means that the adaptations to their vision are good enough for the habitats they frequent. Anywhere more enclosed by a canopy of vegetation, for example, and the birds would probably struggle to navigate efficiently. On Rum, it's likely that the shearwaters also make use of the prominent boulders, some larger than cars, dotted over the mountain as visual cues, waymarks to steer by, as though the birds carry a map of the mountain's boulder fields inside them.

To watch the shearwaters come in through the dark and the mists and read the mountain so that they know exactly where to land is an extraordinary thing. Even the final scramble, from the point where they touch down to the entrance of their burrow, seems a small navigational miracle. The birds usually land several feet away from the entrance, then pause for a short period before setting off to their burrows. Pitch dark, rocks strewn everywhere.

Do they head up or down the slope? Which burrow entrance, among the numerous others to choose from, is theirs? Do they navigate those last few feet to their burrow entrance through a combination of senses? Vision, perhaps supplemented with, as has been suggested, 'proprioception', the sense that registers the body's position and movement, much as we find our way to the bathroom in the dark in the middle of the night, our limbs having memorised the route?

Manx shearwaters are justly famed for their ability to navigate across thousands of miles of ocean and find their way back to their burrow, even when they have been taken from their nests and released in unfamiliar locations hundreds of miles away. Ronald Lockley's homing experiments with Manx shearwaters from Skokholm in the late 1930s, which documented the swift return of birds to their island burrows from places as far flung as the Isle of May in the Firth of Forth, Venice and, perhaps most notably, in 1952, Boston, Massachusetts, provided the first proof of the shearwater's exceptional homing ability. Not all of the birds in these experiments returned to Skokholm, but many did, often covering the great distances in remarkably short time. There is almost the sense, reading Lockley's accounts, that you could release a Manx shearwater anywhere in the Northern Hemisphere and it would still find its way back to its musty burrow on a small island off the coast of Pembrokeshire. And more recently, research showing how shearwaters navigate the oceans using their sense of smell, how the birds remember what different parts of the ocean smell like, documented by Adam Nicolson in his book *The Seabird's Cry*, are as astonishing as Lockley's findings from the 1930s. But I also find the shearwater's ability to navigate on the local level just as remarkable, finding their way to a small hole on a mountainside among many thousands of other holes, among all those rocks and tussocks, in the pitch dark, somehow steering, sensing their way to their nest.

After I'd finished tea and washed up, there was always a long wait till dusk. I sometimes read or went for a walk around the plateau, exploring the jumble of boulders and volcanic rocks. One evening, I watched a large garden spider spinning its web between the tent's guy ropes and the ground; its web was so large, it looked like the spider was reinforcing the ropes, pulling them taut with its thread. And when the wind suddenly dropped one evening, I was grateful to the spider for the midges it caught. The spider became a sort of caretaker while I was away from the tent, working its way along the ropes, checking their tension. When I returned to the tent in the early hours of the morning, I was always careful to tread cautiously so as not to damage its web in the dark.

At dusk I packed a small bag for the night, zipped up the tent, then began to pick my way up the mountain's rocky slope. This was when I always felt most anxious. I was glad to be heading out to find the shearwaters, but I was uncertain when they would start to arrive, if they would arrive and in what sort of numbers. I was never quite sure how long I would have to wait up on the mountain. My experience of listening to birds over the course of these journeys was as much about searching for the right conditions, the right moment, to hear their song, as it was about searching for the birds. Moonlight, cloud cover, wind speed ... I must have spent as much time looking at weather forecasts as I did planning my itineraries. The mountain epitomised that experience; the birds were here in their thousands, but I needed to find that moment, the precise light conditions, that unlocked the shearwaters' song.

After a climb of 30 minutes or so I reached a mossy boulder field three-quarters of the way up the mountain. I took off my backpack and sat down on the soft grass, with burrows all around me. I could see my tent far below, and behind it the shallow loch. A few pink clouds slid over Canna to the west; to the north lay Skye and the Cuillin's serrated ridge. Then suddenly clouds rushed in across the mountain and shut the place down, engulfing me in a thick, swirling mist. I could make out my boots stretched out in front of me, but not much beyond them. My first panicked thought was, where has my tent gone? But then I started to relax; I knew the tent was down there somewhere, and I hoped that this cloud cover might usher in the shearwaters a little sooner.

Why do Manx shearwaters wait so long into the night before returning to their burrows? What were the birds doing while I sat on the mountain, waiting for them to return? The answer to the first question is because solid ground is a precarious element for shearwaters; they are not suited to moving about on the ground. Shearwaters are supremely adapted to a life in the air and in water, but with their pale, greyish-pink legs set far back on their bodies to assist with propulsion through water, the birds move awkwardly on land, often using their wings and beaks to assist with scrambling up slopes. And this clumsiness makes them vulnerable to predation; a Manx shearwater stumbling to its burrow would make an easy meal for a great black-backed gull, great skua or golden eagle. Shearwaters wait till night to return to the colony because it is much safer for them to do so under the cover of darkness.

It is while they are waiting for darkness to fall that the shearwaters perform something beautiful. This is what the birds were doing as I sat on the mountain, waiting for their return. The shearwaters were gathering just offshore of the island in what are known as 'rafts', large concentrations of birds sitting together on the surface of the sea, marking time until nightfall. Why the shearwaters form these rafts is not entirely clear. The rafts may assemble because shearwaters often forage large distances from the colony, and so the birds cannot reliably time their return to coincide with nightfall. So the rafts might act like a waiting room, a kind of offshore transit lounge, before the birds are ready to fly into the colony itself. These gatherings might also be an arena for communication exchange, social interaction and courtship. Then again, the rafts might simply be somewhere the birds rest and preen, in the safety of numbers.

But it is their movement, the progression of these rafts towards the island, that perhaps offers the best explanation for their purpose. Individual rafts made up of hundreds, sometimes thousands, of birds are often located in a circle around the island colony. As they start to gather, the rafts are around 650 ft from the shore, creating a halo effect around the island's perimeter. I have looked at GPS tracking images of these rafts and the pattern they form is striking; island, sea, then a ring of birds like the dark circle around the iris. As it begins to get darker, the rafts start to drift closer to the shore, and the halo contracts. It is possible that this is a mass gathering to assess the island for predators and weather conditions, before the birds take to the wing and fly into the colony. It's as if they are in a holding pattern around the island, waiting for the instruction that it's safe to land. To start with, while there is still plenty of daylight, the rafts are positioned safely offshore. But they move closer and closer to the island as the light starts to fail, as, presumably, the birds need to be closer in the fading light to see what is happening on the island. Are there peregrines patrolling the colony? Where are the great black-backed gulls stationed? How thick is the cloud cover? It's an exercise in mass information gathering by a nervous flotilla of birds that pulses closer to the colony the nearer it gets to nightfall, a ring of birds turning slowly towards the island, adjusting its focus, as though the halo were the focusing ring on a binoculars' lens.

* * *

As I waited for the shearwaters on the mountain, I visualised them pulling nearer in their rafts, scanning the skyline for gulls, ravens, eagles. The clouds grew thicker, and it started to get cold. There were brief moments of brightness when the clouds swept through, parted, and I could see my tent again, far below. But these windows closed as quickly as they opened. Then, gradually, it began to get darker, as though the clouds were bruising over. I don't think I had anticipated hearing any birds as much as I did with the shearwaters. Waiting all day, then long into the night, for a switch to go off. I started to imagine what the shearwaters' arrival might do to the place. How might they change it? Would they come in smelling of the sea? As they dipped into their burrows, would the scent of the ocean follow them into the dark?

Even before the shearwaters arrive back at the colony at night, their presence has already transformed the mountain. The ocean *does* follow the birds when they come into land. Their guano is a rich marine fertiliser, transforming the mountain by supporting plants and insects that would otherwise be absent in this nutrient-poor habitat. The shearwaters create herb-rich mossy gardens around their burrows, oases on the mountain, that attract not just the red deer, but beetles, moths, earthworms and other invertebrates, which, in turn, attract birds such as wheatears, ring ouzels, even migrant song thrushes. The shearwaters' presence here, in such large numbers, gives the mountain a pulse of life, a vibrancy that would otherwise be lacking.

One component of this fauna that has gathered around the shearwater colony on Rum is notable not so much for its absence as its lack of prevalence. Brown rats are present on Rum, though they have not become established around the shearwater colony and have therefore not negatively impacted the birds' breeding in the way they have done on neighbouring colonies, such as the ones on Eigg and Canna (though rats have recently been eradicated from Canna and the shearwater colony there shows signs of re-establishing). There is a sense with the colony on Rum of it being located on an island within an island; the mountains are as much a barrier as the sea. And it is perhaps this high-altitude remoteness of the colony which has made it difficult for brown rats to become established there.

Rain impacts the shearwater colony on Rum much more than rats. Burrow flooding, caused by Rum's exceptionally high annual rainfall, is possibly the main factor in limiting the size of the colony on the island. The best sites for burrows, on the free-draining, sandy soils, and where there is a steep gradient to assist the shearwaters in getting quickly airborne, are already taken, so new burrows risk being built on areas prone to flooding. And the importance of gradient, in enabling the shearwaters to launch themselves as swiftly as possible into the air, was brought home to me by the small explosions of black and white feathers I sometimes came across outside the burrow entrances. These were the remains of shearwaters that had been caught – most likely by a gull or eagle – before they had time to take off.

As it grew darker, I became fidgety with anticipation, my ears seizing on every sound that wasn't the wind. I kept hearing the ravens making soft croaking calls to each other. At 10.05 p.m. a strange, mournful *wee-eee-ey* noise drifted up from the cliff below, and it took me a while to realise it was coming from a pair of red-throated divers I'd seen on a loch at the foot of the mountain. The divers' calls had an uncanny habit of drifting up the mountain to my camp when I was least expecting them, and I was always surprised at how far they travelled. One morning I was sheltering in a shallow cave on the side of the mountain when the divers started calling, and the sound echoed off the rocks around me. A long, wailing, mewing sound, full of sadness, like a drawn-out, muted trumpet note.

At 10.45 things began to sound a lot stranger. The ground underneath me started gurgling. A soft *chucker-err-err* was uttered a few times, then stopped. What on earth! It was the weirdest noise, a muffled, coughing gurgle, like a thick soup bubbling and spurting beneath me, as if the hill were releasing something gaseous. It was so close, too; I jumped when I heard it, thinking that whatever made the noise was complaining about my presence, as if I'd trodden on its sleep. A throaty, tummy-grumbling sound, an underground belch, the very ground itself farting. A shearwater! Calling from deep in its burrow, it was the first shearwater I'd heard in almost 12 hours of being on the mountain. And that subterranean call was like a starting pistol, an intimation that the mountain was waking up.

Shortly afterwards the first shearwater of the night flew in low and fast over my head in a whoosh of air. Over the next hour more birds started to arrive, and I was amazed how fast they came in to land, rushing out of the cloud and the dark. There was a charged nervousness to these arrivals; I had a strong sense of the birds running a gauntlet, as if they felt exposed away from the sea and needed to get down to their burrows as quickly as possible. Often, it was too dark to make out the birds themselves and I was only aware of them as a rush of air as they swept past me. The noise was like a tearing sound above my head, and sometimes I would flinch, thinking that one was about to collide with me. After the whirring swish past my ear, I'd hear a crumpled crashing sound as the birds hit the ground. Less of a landing, more like a last-minute ditch into the side of the hill. One bird landed close beside me with a series of bumps and clatters, as though it were falling down a chimney. The effect, as more birds started to come in to land, was like hearing small ordnances going off all around me. By 11.45 the mountain had really woken up, with shearwaters flying in from all over. I noticed how some birds came in silently, in a rush of air; others called as they flew, chuckling and coughing. The combination of thump-landings and wheezy chuckling calls made me think of an accordion being dropped down a flight of stairs, the instrument exhaling wind and squeaky notes with every downwards bump.

By midnight the whole mountain seemed to be talking to itself. Everywhere I could hear the strange cackling and coughing of the shearwaters. As birds approached the colony, their calls speeded up, became louder and more urgent, the noise reverberating off the rocks. The calls reminded me a little of a red grouse's chuckling call, but the shearwaters sounded more wheezy, more squelchy; there was something viscous and marshy about their song. Something rusty too, a squeaky rustiness, like an exhausted bicycle.

Seton Gordon detected an amalgamation of other birds in the shearwater's song. In a chapter from his 1931 book *In the Highlands* he describes climbing 'through dog-rose, crimson orchis, and milkwort, to the foot of a gloomy cliff', where 'in the shelter of a small hazel copse' he 'awaited the wakening of the shearwaters'. Gordon doesn't say exactly where he is; he's not at the colony on Rum, but he's somewhere nearby on one of the neighbouring islands, his line of sight suggesting to me he is below the cliffs at Cleadale on Eigg. He describes 'dark clouds, ragged and rain-filled' drifting across from Rum, and the Cuillin of Skye 'hidden in rain'. I could see Eigg and the Cleadale cliffs from where I was sitting on Rum, and I liked to think of Gordon in his twilight vigil, waiting for the shearwaters, perching somewhere within my own line of sight. Gordon recorded the birds sounding at their peak that night at around 1.25 a.m.:

> Invisible birds made weird music. Shrill pipings, squeakings, gruntings, moanings, the hooting of owls, the cawing of rooks, the crowing of cock pheasants – all this weird shearwater talk mingled with plaintive far-carrying cries that might have been the calls of gulls.

In another encounter with shearwaters, he captures the experience of sitting in a colony, with the birds suddenly appearing then disappearing in the dark:

> At times through the dusk the swift, wheeling flight of a shearwater is seen, but as soon, almost, as noticed the bird is swallowed up in the gloom.

Gordon's description rang true; I experienced similar encounters all through the night on the mountain on Rum, a displacement in the air as a shearwater shot close by me and 'crossed the vision like a meteor', as Gordon put it, before the bird vanished into the dark.

Between 12.30 a.m. and 1 a.m. a continual stream of shearwaters flew into the colony. Birds seemed to pass over my head every second, the whole mountain popping, squeaking, chuckling with their calls. It was hard to think that this was the same mountain that just a few hours earlier had been so quiet. I could hear shearwaters calling from the ground close to their burrows, some from underground, and many were calling as they flew into the colony. How to untangle this cacophony?

Who was calling to whom? What were the birds saying? What was the purpose of their raucous coughing?

I'd noticed some birds flew in silently, while others called as they came in over my head. The silent birds were most likely breeding adults, returning to their burrows to feed their chicks. These adult shearwaters had little need to advertise their presence. They had done their calling earlier in the season, from late March all through April, defending reclaimed burrows, re-establishing pair bonds. Having bred successfully, they were now preoccupied with provisioning their chicks. Through June, July and August the soundscape of the colony is given over to non-breeding immature shearwaters. These are birds that may be a year or two away from breeding themselves but nevertheless congregate around the colony during the middle part of the breeding season, prospecting for burrows and mates for when they are ready to breed.

Male shearwaters do most of the calling from the ground, while the females do most of the aerial calling. What appears to be happening is that immature male shearwaters call to females passing overhead, advertising their presence and the burrow they have potentially secured. The females answer these calls, and their answering often prompts other males to call, so the noise builds up and the mountain reverberates with the sound. Male shearwaters are able to recognise females calling, and vice versa, because, despite the melee of calling, male calls are distinguished by being made up of a combination of clear and harsher-sounding notes, whereas female calls are made up entirely of the harsher notes. Both sexes finish their respective series of notes (which last for around a second) with a throaty gurgling sound. Without this vocal dimorphism, the birds would struggle to find and pair with each other in the dark. Once the female shearwater lands and selects a calling male, she will approach him and the pair will duet together, the male's clear notes ringing around the female's more guttural song. Then, when the pair bond has been established, courtship moves to the burrow, where male and female duet together for long periods underground, testing the acoustics of their chamber. Actual mating and egg laying are still at least a year away (Manx shearwater courtship is a long-term thing). If both birds survive the winter, they will return to the same burrow where they sang together the previous summer.

Rain came in after 1 a.m. and I headed for the tent. All through that night I kept waking to hear the shearwaters calling. At 2.30 the noise was still very loud, echoing around the cliffs, the loudest, most frequent noise being a chuckling *kek-ker, hurr-hurr ... kek-ker, hurr-hurr*. I tried transcribing the sound a few times in my notebook, but the transcription slipped and morphed each time I heard another bird passing overhead. I tried as well to listen for the distinction between the male and female calls, but I couldn't tune my ear to the difference; either that, or the sheer noise of the colony made it virtually impossible for me to isolate individual birds with confidence.

The best phonetic interpretation of the shearwater's call I have come across is in an article in *Country Life* by John Warham from 1950. His version of the call was:

er-kuk-kuk-coo-er
kuk-kuk-coo-er
kuk-kuk-coo-er ... kuk-coo

Warham suggested that the '*er*' portions of the call were produced by 'a sharp intake of breath through the tubular nostrils and the second, third and fourth repeats of the main phrase are pitched rather higher than the first'.

But everyone hears slightly differently. I heard a *kek-ker, hurr-hurr* to Warham's *kuk-kuk-coo-er*. I've also seen the call transcribed as '*cack-cack-cackcarr-hoo*'. Seton Gordon's phonetic sonogram was more of a '*koch koch koch–aah; koch koch koch–aah ...*'. And he added that, as well as birds such as owls, rooks and pheasants, he could detect the 'screaming of cats' in the shearwater's call. Also, memorably, when he visited Lockley on Skokholm, he described the shearwaters passing over the house as he lay in bed as sounding 'like wandering spirits', although the calls I heard from my tent that night, tugging at my sleep, sounded more like the wheezy, phlegmy coughing of trolls.

And trolls were precisely what the Norse settlers in the Hebrides in the eleventh century thought shearwaters were. The Vikings ascribed the weird sounds the birds made at night to trolls, and they named one of the mountains on Rum, where the shearwaters have their burrows, Trollval – 'mountain of the trolls' – providing a useful indication of the shearwater colony's longevity on Rum. Evidently, the birds must have bred on the island in the eleventh century, and in the sort of numbers sufficient to make the kind of nocturnal din that would put the fear of trolls into the Vikings. There are similarly named sites – Trøllanes and Trøllhøvdi – where shearwaters still breed, in the Faroes.

I found it difficult to sleep, up on the mountain that night. It was not so much the noise of the shearwaters, more a sense of agitation that I was missing the sound of the birds at its peak. And I wanted, despite the rain, to absorb as much of the night as I could, knowing the colony would fall silent by the morning. So I put on my jacket and boots and trudged back up to the nearest slope. I was wary of climbing much higher in the dark and wet, but even this close to my tent there were shearwaters calling everywhere. Some were still flying in and flumping into the ground, the noise of their landing like someone kneading a cushion with their fist.

Some male shearwaters will call from the area in front of their burrows, others from inside the burrow itself. It must be the case that calling from within is a safer option, in terms of avoiding predation, than calling from outside, where the bird is more exposed. On the flipside, male shearwaters calling from outside are likely to reach a wider audience of passing females, although burrow-callers, while they may not have as wide a catchment for their song, are able to use the burrow like a megaphone, projecting their call out in front of the burrow entrance. The architecture of the burrow will also affect the quality of the call; whether the burrow's substrate is comprised of earth or rock amplifies, or attenuates, the call differently, depending on where the listener is situated in relation to the burrow. Each burrow, then, possesses its own acoustic properties, each being tuned slightly differently.

Sitting opposite the slope that night, I faced an orchestra of megaphones, each with its own pitch and reach. It was a blur of noise to me, but female shearwaters can recognise an individual male's call by the pattern in his frequency range and the duration of the different sequences in his call. As is the case for male nightjars, each male shearwater sounds sufficiently like themselves not to be confused with other males. Sonograms of individual male shearwater calls back this up, each bird having its own sonogram signature, its own unique call.

There is an anecdote concerning Cory's shearwaters, the species of shearwater that breeds around the Mediterranean and the Canary Islands, that relates to the bird's role as a sort of harbour detective. Fire a shot into the air, and if Cory's shearwaters suddenly rush into the area searching for food it's a good indication that illegal dynamite fishing is being practised nearby. Shearwaters are sometimes referred to as an indicator or sentinel species; that is, a species at the top of the food chain that can provide a useful indication of the health of their habitat through the presence of pollutants such as toxic metals and organochlorine pesticides in their organs. So just as they can reveal illegal fishing in a particular area, shearwaters also carry the evidence of the harm we do to the sea within them.

In recent decades, one of the ways we have most harmed the ocean is by polluting it with plastic; as of 2014 there was an estimated minimum 5.25 trillion particles of the stuff, weighing a staggering 270,000 tonnes, floating in the sea. As indicator species, Manx shearwaters, and the Procellariiformes in general, show us how pervasive plastic has now become in the ocean. A study in Brazil in 2009 that sampled 25 Manx shearwaters as part of a wider study of petrels and albatrosses found 60 per cent of Manx shearwaters had ingested plastic. The percentage was even higher for other shearwater species in the study, with 89 per cent of great shearwaters found to have ingested the material and 100 per cent of Cory's shearwaters. In the Manx shearwaters dissected it was discovered that 83 per cent of the total volume of items found inside the birds was plastic, with only 17 per cent being natural prey items. Plastic was virtually all that the birds had inside them.

Shearwaters are especially susceptible to plastic ingestion. Mistaking the floating items for prey, both visually and olfactorily (plastic debris left in the sea for less than a month emits a similar chemical profile to their marine prey), the shearwaters lack the ability to regurgitate the material once ingested. The plastic can lodge in the bird's ventriculus, a part of its digestive tract, and remain there for months, even years, on end, causing problems with digestion that can lead to a deterioration in energy levels and ultimately the bird's ability to feed, migrate, breed and survive.

Of course, it is not just seabirds that are affected; many species of fish, marine mammals and sea turtles have been found to have consumed plastic. But birds appear to be especially vulnerable; a recent model predicted that 'plastic will be found in the digestive tracts of 99 per cent of all seabird species by 2050, and that 95 per cent of the individuals within these species will have ingested plastic by the same year'. In less than 30 years it will be almost impossible to find a seabird that has not ingested plastic.

A year later I returned to Rum and walked back up the mountain to the shearwater colony, this time with my 11-year-old son. We set off a few hours before dark and were soaked before we even got halfway there. The rain was not that heavy, but as the wind picked up it blew the rain straight through us. I hinted we could still turn back several times, but my son was having none of it; he was determined to spend the night up at the colony, so we kept going. Huge boulders loomed out of the mist and loose stones made a clattering sound as they shifted under our feet. We reached the plateau, got the tent up in record time, then scrambled inside, relieved to be out of the endless rain and wind. My son burrowed deep into his sleeping bag and scrunched himself in its warmth. We huddled there, red-nosed from the cold, beads of water dripping from our hair, waiting for dark.

I was worried that the noise of the wind would drown out the shearwaters. But around 11 p.m. we started to hear the first birds coming in. Soon, the shearwaters' curious chuckling sounds and their quizzical hiccups were bouncing off the side of the tent. The two of us giggled and shivered there in surprise and delight at this otherworldly sound, as though we were eavesdropping on something paranormal. I mentioned to my son that the birds have been known to collide into the side of tents in the dark, so we held our breath and flinched at every gust, as if the tent were about to be pummelled by ghosts.

At 2.30 in the morning the calling became very loud. My son was by then asleep and had rolled in his sleeping bag to take over my side of the tent. I eyed the pile of wet clothes in the corner, which we'd tried to shove as far away from where we slept. The prospect of heading back outside into the storm was not appealing. But I had that same agitated feeling I'd experienced the year before, of not wanting to stay in the tent, of missing the birds at their peak if I did. I put my head torch on its red light setting, grimaced into my wet clothes and quietly unzipped the door of the tent.

Outside the wind was scraping the plateau and I could see a white gash above me where a waterfall was crashing through the dark. I walked away from the tent towards a slope where the birds were calling. At the foot of the slope I found a tall boulder and crouched in its shelter. There were shearwaters just a few feet above me calling from their burrows, and the hillside was crackling with their weird sounds. A bird flew over my head in the darkness, calling as it passed above me, and I thought I heard another shearwater answering it from somewhere on the slope. Once or twice the wind seemed to catch a call just at the moment it was uttered, flinging it away, so that it sounded as though the call itself had taken flight.

By 3 a.m. I was back in the tent, peeling off sodden clothes. My son woke up and pulled himself up on his elbows to blink at me. 'I heard them, Dad – a cackling sound, they're really loud! They sound like cackling bandits! Goodnight, sorry if I've taken up too much room!'

By the morning the rain had stopped. We crawled out of the tent and it was suddenly very cold. We put on hats and gloves, and shook our arms and stamped our feet to keep warm. We got the tent down, packed our rucksacks and then set off around the colony, inspecting the flushed areas of grass in front of the burrows. Water was still pouring down off the mountain and the rocks were slippery after the rain. I wanted to show my son an area with a high concentration of burrows, so we clambered around till we reached a patch of green pockmarked by holes. We knelt in the wet grass to take a closer look and my son put his hand into one of the burrows. He flexed his fingers in there, as though he were trying on a glove. A little further on he spotted a white feather outside the entrance to one of the burrows. I watched as he bent down, picked up the feather, waved it at me, smiling, then tucked it safely in his pocket.

III

The Blacksmith of the Stream

Dipper

A bright, cold morning in February. I'm in a steep valley high in the Welsh hills. Small farms, large tracts of forestry, a raven calling overhead. I park the car and walk down towards the river. Everything is draped in moss: walls, trees and fence posts are soft to touch like fur. I go through a gate then cross a field, making a trail through the frost. When I reach the river I pick up a thin path and follow it upstream. Hawthorn branches reach across the trail, ash trees lean over the water. After 10 minutes or so I come to a wide pool with a waterfall behind it. The banks around the pool are thick with spongy moss, the rocks beside the falls dark with spray. Perched on a rock at the edge of the pool, bobbing and feinting as though always on the point of diving in, is a dipper.

I could see the bird opening its bill, its white throat vibrating as it sang. A fast, soft song; bubbling, trilling phrases with scratchy, squeaky notes like little yelps in between. It was like listening to the compressed repertoire of a song thrush, all the phrases bunched together, speeded up, but much quieter than a song thrush, as though the thick moss around the pool were cushioning the dipper's song. The stance of the bird, perched there, looking down at the water – and the rippling flow of its song – made it seem like the dipper sang to the river, and the sound and movement of the water inflected its song.

I stood there listening, about 20 ft away from the pool. Then another dipper appeared from out of the mossy bank. It saw me and gave out an alarm call: *chit*, *chit*, *chit*. Both dippers took off together and flew low down the river. Five minutes later they were back, the larger male arriving first, landing on a rock just downstream from the pool. I could see his feet gripping the rock, the sunlight on his wet back. When he shifted out of the sun his feathers appeared darker. The dippers' colours were often changed by the angle of the light and by the prism of water beading over their feathers. Sometimes their bellies gave off a coppery glow, and when the sun lit the droplets of spray along their backs the birds shimmered silver.

About 6 to 7 inches long, dippers have a compact, bulbous shape. Perched on a rock in the middle of a river, they have a squat, puffed-out appearance, as though they could just as easily roll off the rock as dive into the water. Their short tail, often cocked at an upright angle, gives the impression of an oversized wren, as if a wren had swallowed a snowball.

Dippers have a distinctive white bib, or gorget, that hangs below their bill and fills their throat and breast. Their belly is a red-brown colour, merging to darker brown where it meets the bird's legs. The gradient of reds to browns across its belly is like the light and dark polish of a conker's sheen, and where the white bib meets the chestnut belly the two colours are demarcated by a curved line, so that the breast resembles a small moon under partial eclipse. The head is brown, the wings and back have a sooty grey, almost black appearance, and there is a faint arrow-like patterning over the plumage of the dipper's upper wings and back where the grey feathers are marginated with a dark outline. This patterning gives the bird a scaly appearance and is most pronounced when its feathers are wet. Each block of colour in a dipper's plumage is accentuated by the white bib that borders the four darker colours, so it looks like the bird is made up of four distinct segments. If you rotated a dipper 90° so its breast faced upwards, it might resemble a Christmas pudding with a splash of cream on top.

This splash of white is the dipper's most striking feature. One origin of the dipper's old Russian name, *oblyapka*, comes from the verb *oblyapat*, meaning to splash with something. The legend is that a dipper, to avert a minor sacrilege, puffed out its chest just in time to prevent a drop of milk from the Virgin's breast hitting the ground, a gesture that left the dipper's breast 'splashed' permanently white. The gorget shows up some distance away against dark water and is noticeably whiter than the white water of the rapids. Often, it was seeing this flash of white against the backdrop of the river that helped me to locate the birds.

There are five species of dipper (family Cinclidae) globally. Their generic name, *Cinclus*, derives from the Greek word *kinklos*, meaning a bird that habitually moves its tail. The white-throated dipper is the species endemic to Europe, the Middle East and Central Asia, with geographical variations in size and colour leading to several recognised subspecies across its range. In the British Isles there are two resident subspecies, *Cinclus cinclus hibernicus*, found in Ireland and the west of Scotland, and *Cinclus cinclus gularis*, resident across the rest of Scotland, together with England and Wales. *C.c. hibernicus* shows a slightly darker head and a narrower and darker chestnut band along the lower breast than *C.c. gularis*, as though less of the Irish-Scottish dipper's chest has been eclipsed.

Dippers are birds of fast-flowing upland streams and rivers; 'young streams', as this steep, plunging stage of a river's life is termed, where there is sufficient gradient for coaxing rapids and hollowing shallow pools. These streams run with clear, calcium-rich water, and are brimming with invertebrates, with mayfly nymphs and caddis larvae (the dipper's favoured prey) lodging among the riffles. Dippers can nest anywhere between sea level and 2,000 ft, and can be found foraging at even higher elevations (Seton Gordon frequently observed dippers in a hill burn in the Cairngorms at an elevation of 3,500 ft, and he suspected the birds nested beside a waterfall 500 ft below this).

The dipper's relationship with gradient – with fast-flowing water – means their distribution in the British Isles is largely confined to upland areas. Dippers live in a world of tumbling, rushing turbulence, and the ways they have adapted to this habitat make them a unique and remarkable bird.

When dippers are underwater, they seem to change colour; air bubbles get trapped in their feathers, turning the birds a silvery grey. Photographs of dippers taken underwater reveal a ghostly sheen, as though the bird's brown and black feathers have been bleached. This effect may serve as a type of underwater camouflage, diluting the bird's colours so that a hunting dipper becomes less visible to its aquatic prey; dippers, by changing colour when they submerge, can hide themselves inside the water itself.

Air bubbles dress the dipper in a ghostly wetsuit. But dippers appear to want to hide inside the river even when they are not submerged. Out of the water, perched on a boulder, dippers are backlit by the movement of the river; the bird's background is never still. So one possible explanation for the dipper's characteristic bobbing is that the movement serves as a type of river-camouflage, mimicking the tumbling water. To stay still against a backdrop of such turbulence would be to risk appearing conspicuous to predators. Other small riverine birds appear to adopt a similar fusion with their background; grey wagtails flick their tails like a speeded-up metronome, common sandpipers bob to the rhythm of the river. Dippers dip all the time, a movement accentuated during courtship and in territorial skirmishes, although dipping is not exclusive to these events. Dippers dip when resting, perched on a rock, between dives, and before and after bouts of preening and feeding. The movement is such an integral part of what the dipper is that it has become its name. It is as though the dipper's bobbing is less a conscious gesture, more a muscular reflex, provoked by the movement of the water. A muscle memory of the river.

Another way that the dipper conceals its presence beside a river is in the patterning of its plumage. It has been suggested that the purpose of the bird's conspicuous white bib – much like its bobbing – paradoxically serves to render the dipper less conspicuous, as the white patterning breaks up the bird's outline against the white water of fast-flowing rivers. Dippers, then, inhabit both the movement and the texture of the water. To my eye, however, the dipper's gorget usually stood out against white water because the colour of the bib was a denser, glossier white than the water. But the bib also helps to break up the bird's outline when seen from below by their aquatic prey, so that a dipper perched on a rock, peering into a pool, is less conspicuous. Other birds that hunt over water, including ospreys and auks, share a similar white patterning down their breast, which helps to break up the bird's outline against the backdrop of the sky.

Because the dipper's white breast is so noticeable, especially over short distances, it is likely that this flash of white also plays a part in the bird's repertoire of signalling. As well as the characteristic bobbing, dippers also blink frequently – the birds I observed on the river combined their bobbing with near-constant blinking. When they blinked, I saw a flash of white flick down across their eye. These are the white feathers of the dipper's eyelid, the same brilliant white colour as their bib. The bobbing and blinking were so constant it felt as though the two actions were linked, a jerking muscular mirror of each other. Dippers have been recorded blinking up to 50 times per minute, sometimes in both eyes, sometimes in just the one. Dippers blink in different ways; there is the distinctive vertical shuttering of their white eyelid, which I frequently observed; also, far less easily seen, there is the rapid flickering of the bird's nictitating membrane, or third eyelid, a milky-coloured membrane that fills the eye like a sudden mist, rinsing it clean of dirt and water droplets. The nictitating membrane, unlike the white eyelid, is drawn horizontally across the eye. So, as well as blinking in different colours, the dipper also blinks both vertically and horizontally, its eye moving like a knight in a game of chess. I found the dipper's display of blinking and dipping mesmerising to watch. These are birds of such restless, quivering energy that it sometimes felt as though they were caught in a loop of constant curtseying, bowing and blinking to the river, with the river reflecting it back.

What emerges from all this movement – from the flashing white of the dipper's eyelids to its dipping and bobbing – combined with the beacon light of its breast, is the sense of a bird that has evolved several ways to communicate besides its song. There is a risk, living in such a loud, rushing habitat as an upland river, that the river drowns the bird's song, or steals syllables from the song so that communication is impaired. The blinking, bobbing and flashing is backup, part of a complex repertoire of communication at the dipper's disposal. To make themselves heard above the sound of the water, the birds use a sign language; dippers sing with their body and eyes, as much as they do with their voice.

I spent a good deal of time in the valley on a small wooden footbridge with views up and down a stretch of the river. Downstream was the waterfall with a series of smaller falls and pools beneath it. Upstream was a long stretch of rapids with a wide pool at the top.

I tended to grade the depth of the different pools along the river according to whether the dippers were submerged when feeding in them – swimming pools and paddling pools, some shallow enough for the dippers to wade through, others into which the birds would dive and disappear beneath the surface for seconds at a time. I often timed the birds on these dives. Usually they were underwater for no more than 3 or 4 seconds, sometimes even less than that. Dives were repeated in quick succession, up to 5 or 6 dives per minute, with just a brief pause on a rock between each submersion. The longest dive I timed was 8 seconds. The length of this dive was unusual, and I thought I had lost the bird until it suddenly popped up out of the water and onto a rock.

The longest dipper dives on record have been timed at up to 30 seconds. There are claims of dives lasting longer than this, of up to a minute, though this seems doubtful, with most researchers agreeing on an average length of somewhere between 4 and 20 seconds. Overall, the dippers I observed spent much more time wading in shallow water than they did diving in the deeper pools. Diving is high-energy activity for the birds; it becomes more necessary when water levels in the river are high, but dippers usually revert, when conditions allow, to the more energy-efficient method of foraging through the shallows, pecking for prey among the stones. When they do dive, the depth of the water tends to be no more than 2 ft, though they will sometimes be forced to dive deeper and for longer – dippers have been observed diving in lakes to a depth of 15 to 18 ft. They can dive straight from a rock into the water or swim out into a pool before diving down. They will even dive into the river from the air, suddenly dropping down into the water out of flight, a movement that dippers also occasionally employ to evade predators such as sparrowhawks (as a reward for preventing the Virgin's milk hitting the ground, it's thought, according to the Russian legend, that God granted the dipper the ability to dive underwater to escape danger). Returning from a dive, dippers will either pop back up onto a rock, or occasionally fly straight into the air from out of the dive, flying, without pausing, from one element into another.

For some time it was thought that dippers, after they dived and reached the bottom, would walk along the riverbed, headfirst into the current. It's a striking image; a bird walking along the bottom of a fast-flowing river, angling its body so that the force of the water kept it submerged. It was also suggested that, in order to stay submerged, dippers must have a particularly high specific gravity (that the bird's mass was denser than the equivalent volume of water), especially if the current was not strong enough to keep the birds submerged.

Dippers *can* move along the riverbed but, crucially, they only do so with the aid of their wings. And there is no evidence that dippers possess a denser mass than the equivalent volume of water. Nor is there evidence, as is sometimes suggested, that dippers possess solid bones throughout their skeleton (as opposed to the hollow bones of most birds). The dipper's leg bones are solid, but so are several other passerines' leg bones, and this is therefore unlikely to be an adaptation that enables the dipper to reduce its buoyancy.

Primarily, dippers move underwater, and stay submerged, with the aid of their short, powerful wings.

They use these to propel them through the water, not unlike the way that a penguin uses its wings to swim. The dipper doesn't fully extend its wings underwater, as they are not sufficiently rigid (unlike a penguin's, having dispensed of its flight feathers) to form an efficient surface of resistance for propulsion through water. Instead, the dipper partly extends its wings so that the more rigid parts, around the bone and the firmer sections of the outer primaries, serve to resist the water. The downward tilt of the anterior edge of the dipper's wings helps to move the bird towards the riverbed, while the backwards sweep of the wings propels the dipper through the water. Rather than walking, dippers 'fly' underwater. It's a different way of flying, a different technique, to how their wings move through the air, as though, underwater, dippers are flying through a constrained space and need to angle their wings closer to their bodies to pull their way through. The dipper adapts its wings according to whether it needs to accommodate gravity, in the air, or the density of water, when it dives. As the dipper leaves the water and plunges into the air, its wings adjust, extend, taste the air's lift.

It might have been this 'swimming' position of the dipper's half-opened wings that led to the belief that the birds walked underwater without the use of their wings. It's more difficult to appreciate the role of the wings if they are only partly extended. And it can't have helped observers that dippers usually disappear into the water in a blur of bubbles, before diving at a rapid rate. Once on the riverbed, the bird's feet are extended and used either to paddle with (so that it can seem as though the dipper is running along the bottom), or to grip the rocks, as the dipper probes for prey within the substrate with its bill. In this way, feet and wings work in conjunction to propel the bird along the bottom and to enable it to swim in any direction, including into the current. In fact, dippers tend to dive facing the current, then switch direction, if needed, when underwater.

That the dipper does not, strictly speaking, walk along the riverbed, is no less remarkable than how it does move underwater. Its wings are almost as efficient underwater as they are in the air. The two elements are interchangeable to the dipper; this is a bird that can fly through water, just as it flies through air.

It was bitterly cold in the valley that day. The sun was bright, but it never got high enough to touch the valley floor. At midday I decided to clamber up the steep hillside to find the sun and warm up a bit. Halfway up the side of the valley I walked over the frostline. Everything below me – the bracken bank, the small field beside the river – was white with frost. Above, the hill steamed in the sun. There seemed to be more birds up here in the sunshine: blue tits sparked the branches of an oak; a nuthatch seemed to cool a pine cone's reds with its blue-grey back. The thin warmth was lovely, and I was reluctant to head back down to the cold of the valley floor. But I also wanted to get back to the dippers. And the perspective, of looking down from the relative warmth of the hillside to the valley bottom, locked in shade and frost, made me think about the dipper's resilience, this small bird's ability to survive in such an extreme environment, spending all day in and out of the freezing water.

Dippers have several adaptations that enable them to survive and hunt in such an environment and that, significantly, have allowed them to occupy a habitat niche with little competition from other birds. In particular, dippers are able to exploit an abundance in their invertebrate prey that occurs in late winter and early spring during the insects' larval stage, before these insects take to the wing, and before other insectivorous birds arrive on the river.

Foremost among the dipper's adaptations is the extent of the bird's plumage. Dippers possess a thick downy layer between the feather tracts (where most birds have naked skin), as well as a substantial down cover over their head and an extensive covering of down over their wings. Dippers also have a higher density of contour feathers (the feathers that form the bird's outline) than any other passerine, perhaps any other bird. One study of 5 dippers counted between 3,700 and 5,300 contour feathers per bird (an average of 4,200 feathers), with no more than 3,000 contour feathers counted on other passerines of a similar size. By comparison, dippers have six times higher a density of contour feathers than a resident of even colder waters, the emperor penguin (the penguin makes up for this deficiency by having about four times the number of downy plumes per contour feather than the dipper). The dipper's exceptionally dense plumage means it can maintain its body temperature in conditions at least 40°C below the bird's lower critical temperature. Conversely, dippers can struggle to keep themselves cool on hot days; when the air temperature is above 29°C, dippers are usually found skulking in the shade, reluctant to fly, trying to keep cool by standing in the water so heat can escape quickly through their uninsulated legs.

Despite spending most of their day in the equivalent of a washing machine spin cycle, dippers are also remarkable for their ability to keep themselves dry. They possess a particularly large oil gland (about ten times larger than birds of a similar size), called the uropygial gland, located at the base of their tail, which the dipper utilises for preening, coating its feathers with oil to waterproof its plumage. I found it captivating to watch dippers preening; the action was so vigorous, it looked like the bird was trying to tug out its feathers with its bill. And each time its bill passed through a clump of feathers, a brief path opened through the dense plumage, revealing streaks of darker feathers beneath the dipper's white bib. So effective is this waterproofing, a dipper can dive several times and remain dry. When the bird pauses on a rock between dives, water droplets bead like mercury over the feathers, and slide off the dipper's wings and back.

Dippers also seem to need the river itself to retain their waterproofing. Dippers removed from their river and held in captivity quickly lose their water-repellent capacity. There are several reports of dippers from zoos and elsewhere, days after their capture, being placed in a tank and becoming soaked, their plumage wet and bedraggled. I think of the dippers I watched – the way droplets of water slipped off their necks, the way they dived headfirst into the current, then dived back out onto a rock, their plumage intact, gleaming in the sun – then of those birds in captivity and the humiliation of their drenching. Take the dipper away from its river and you break the bird's integrity.

When a dipper dives, the impact of hitting the water causes a flap of skin, called the operculum, to close across the bird's nostrils (known as nares in birds) to prevent water entering their nasal cavity, a bit like a swimmer donning nose clips before they dive. Also like a swimmer fixing their goggles, dippers have a much more developed iris sphincter (the muscle that controls pupil size) than other birds of a comparable size; the cross-sectional area of a dipper's iris sphincter is at least two and a half times larger than a robin's. The sphincter acts on the bird's iris by increasing the curvature of the lens, enabling the dipper to focus on objects at different distances, giving the bird greater visual accommodation when it is underwater. The dipper's power of accommodation in its eyes is similar to that of other diving birds such as cormorants and guillemots.

Dippers can also control their heart rate when they are underwater. When it dives, a dipper undergoes a sudden and pronounced drop in heart rate, which then continues to fall more gradually over the course of the dive. Its heartbeat rapidly increases again as soon as the dipper surfaces. In this way, like other diving birds, dippers can shut down the blood supply to tissues and organs superfluous to the bird while underwater, and therefore conserve oxygen. Dippers also have a higher concentration of haemoglobin in their red blood cells, and so they carry more oxygen in their blood than most other non-diving birds. This adaptation also equips the dipper for periods underwater, providing oxygen to the heart, as though the bird is rigged with its own internal aqualung.

Over the months that followed my first trip to the valley, I returned to the same small stretch of river several times to observe the dippers there. On all those visits I never ceased being amazed by the dippers' ability to survive in such a place, plunging all day into the freezing water; that a bird was here at all seemed extraordinary. The adaptations dippers have evolved to survive in this riverine habitat – from their unique plumage density to their immaculate water-repellence – make them a fascinating bird to study, and I experienced such a sense of absorption watching these birds.

From my vantage point on the wooden bridge, I saw the dipper pair shooting past me. They flew fast, sometimes at the height of the hawthorn trees that lined the bank, sometimes so low they only just cleared the tops of the mid-stream boulders. A dipper flying straight at me was a white ball filling the field of vision of my telescope; the dipper's white chest was mostly what I saw. The bird bore down through layers of magnification till it looked like I was going to be hit by a supercharged snowball.

Searching for dippers along the river, I found my eyes attuned to any flash of white. The first intimation of a dipper was always something white; the bird's distinctive bib, which lit up against the backdrop of the river; even rocks splashed white with the bird's droppings caught my attention, and reassured me, when I returned to the river after months away, that the dippers were still here. Once, I caught both signals at the same time; I saw the flash of a bib, and the moment I focused on the bird, out shot a white excretion to chalk the rock where the dipper stood. Sometimes I'd follow a dipper into one of the steep-sided banks, which were like caves with dense clumps of moss overhanging them. As the dipper merged into the darkness of the overhang, I lost the outline of the bird and all I could see was its white bib, moving like a lamp through the dark.

The white bib, set against the darker colours of the dipper's plumage, is the root of many local names for the dipper. This pied patterning is reflected in names like 'piet', 'pyot', 'water pyot' and 'river pie'. There is also the lovely Scots name, 'burnie baker': the baker of the burn, evoking both the bird's plumage and habitat. Other regional names include 'ess cock', 'water peggie', 'water colly', 'water crake', 'water thrush', 'Bessie ducker', 'Willy fisher', 'water blackbird', 'water crow' (*feannag-uisge* in Gaelic), 'water ouzel', 'wee waterhen' and the wonderful 'little peggy dishwasher'. In some parts of England, the dipper was referred to as 'kingfisher' because it was believed that the dipper was the female kingfisher, with the bright-coloured turquoise bird being the male. The two species share a similar low-level, fast-and-straight flight over water, and they do sometimes overlap along their river territories, though kingfishers tend to be associated more with slow-moving lowland rivers, with dippers occupying the fast-flowing upland stretches.

Some of the most evocative names for the dipper are in languages other than English. Two other Gaelic names for the dipper, *gobha uisge* and *gobha dhubh na alt*, translate in turn as 'water blacksmith' and the beautiful 'blacksmith of the stream'. Irish has the similar *gabha dubh*: 'blacksmith'. Welsh has several names for the dipper; the wonderfully evocative *bronwen y garw*: 'whitebreast of the torrent'; *bronwen y dwr*: 'water white-breast'; *wil y Dwr*: 'water willy'; *trochwr*: 'plunger'; *iar ddwr*: 'waterhen'; *merwys*: 'dipper'; and *mwyalchen ddwr* and *aderyn du'r dwr*, both of which translate as 'water blackbird'. Several languages have variations of 'water blackbird'; Latvian has *ūdensstrazds*: 'water starling'; Swedish, *strömstare*: 'stream starling'; while the French (*merle d'eau*), German (*Wasseramsel*) and Spanish (*mirlo acúatico*) names all translate as 'water blackbird', as if blackbirds held their own secret aquatic lives. In Norwegian, the dipper is known as *fosse konge*: 'king of the waterfall'; and also *fossekall*: 'waterfall fellow' or 'voice of the waterfall'. Polish has the imitative *pluszcz*: 'splash'. In neighbouring Estonia the bird is known as *vesipapp*: 'water priest'. And across the Baltic, in Finland, the dipper is *koskikara*: 'pick-axe of the rapids'.

* * *

'Pick-axe of the rapids' brilliantly describes the way a dipper forages through the river, the phrase capturing the constant jabbing of its beak into the water as the dipper searches for prey. There is a frenetic pace to this feeding, a continuous drilling, probing and sifting as the bird interrogates the river. It reminds me of the way some wading birds, such as oystercatchers, aerate the ground with the rapid probing of their bill. Dippers also forage above the waterline, over rocks, in vegetation and along the riverbank. They pick at stones and boulders with sudden quickfire taps of their beak, as though prising apart a fissure in the rock.

I found it remarkable how dippers retained their balance when they were foraging through rapids. They seemed impervious to the strongest of currents, as though carrying their own unique ballast. I watched dippers wading through rapids, holding their position in the most turbulent part of the river, the water appearing to have been instructed to flow around the bird. Occasionally, the dippers did slide a few inches with the current, but the action always looked controlled, a way of repositioning themselves, of moving efficiently through the rapids. If they entered deep water and were forced to submerge, I noticed that the birds usually let the rapids carry them a little way before hopping out onto a rock. Sometimes, the force of the water did cause the birds to momentarily lose their balance, but they invariably checked this by holding their wings out, flapping them briefly to steady themselves and retain their poise, their extraordinary inertia, within the current.

Watching dippers foraging through the river, I was struck by the way water moved around the birds. I loved seeing the patterns created by the bird's displacement. When a dipper ducked its head underwater, it formed an arc of water that flowed over the bird's back. And where the current parted around the dipper's submerged neck, the water rolled into two symmetrical columns. When the dipper's back was turned to me, and it was foraging like this, I noticed how camouflaged the bird was against the river. The dipper's dark back blended with the water, while the bird's movements were obscured by the wider disturbance of the river. The bird became just another rock, another eddy in the river. It was easy to lose the dipper against this backdrop. With their arched back, their head underwater, the birds folded into the river, and I had to scan every inch of water to locate them again. It was easy, as well, to misread the river, to think I had spotted a dipper moving its head in and out of the water, when it was just the river jerking round a stone.

The way a dipper can merge with the river, become inseparable from it, meant that I often had to unpick the bird from the water. The same applied to the dipper's song. I had to listen carefully to pick out its song against the noise of the river. Sometimes the sound of the river was so loud, I could only tell a dipper was singing by the way its beak was moving, so the impression I had was of the bird talking to itself. I thought, then, of a description of the dipper's song I'd come across, and liked, by the naturalist Herbert Edward Forrest (1858–1942). 'Somewhat lark-like are the notes,' Forrest wrote, 'but subdued, as though the bird were singing to itself.' Other times I found the song was strangely loud and clear, as though the river had suddenly hushed itself. It seemed to make a difference where I stood in relation to the bird; if I could not hear the dipper clearly, I would walk slowly along the riverbank till the song came into focus. The noise of the river was still there, but it settled into the background, like the sound of traffic on a distant road.

Dippers sing within a narrow frequency belt of 4.0 to 6.5 kHz. Their song is at a higher pitch than the low background rumble of the river, which has a frequency of less than 2.0 kHz. This difference in pitch means the dipper's song can carry for some distance above the sound of the water. However, the song can still be compromised by the noise of the river and thereby lose some of its complexity. And dipper song is markedly complex; one dipper that had 22 of its songs recorded and analysed was found to produce more than 157 distinct syllables. Unpaired male dippers sing the most complex songs, more complex than males who have already paired with a female, indicating that mate attraction drives and lends nuance to the male dipper's song repertoire. Some of that intricacy will, inevitably, be lost against the background noise of the river, which is why dippers supplement their song with other forms of communication, blinking and bobbing being the most prominent of these. It's possible that dippers also try to preserve the integrity of their song by seeking out quieter parts of the river in which to sing, suggesting that they carry within them an acoustic map of the river.

I found the dippers' song was loudest when they were flying up and down the river. I'd stand on the wooden bridge and watch the birds shooting past me. Sometimes, they saw me standing there and would flinch mid-flight, suddenly darting upwards to clear my head, rather than swoop under the bridge as they often did. I almost knew the birds were coming before they arrived; their song seemed to rush ahead of them. The birds in pairs, one close behind the other, tearing round a bend in the river, dashing past me, singing loudly as they flew. It was a surprising context for birdsong, breakneck speed bringing with it this clear, liquid song.

I'd tended to think of birdsong as something that the bird delivered from a perch, whether from a branch like a robin, or perched on a column of air like a skylark. To fly fast and sing at the same time seemed such a difficult, energetic juggling act, like learning to circular breathe while playing a wind instrument. But the dippers had mastered the technique. Perhaps they relied, to some extent, on this way of singing for their song to be clearly heard above the sound of the river. I certainly found these flypasts were among the clearest moments to listen to their song. There was little interference from the noise of the river, and the songs were preserved and accentuated within the slipstream of the birds' flight.

Both the male and the female dipper sing. Once the pair starts breeding, it is the male who sings the most, with the female largely silent once she begins laying her eggs. Analysis of their respective songs suggests that the male's song is more associated with mate attraction, the female's with territorial (and mate) defence, as female dippers tended to sing more often during encounters with birds – usually other female dippers – who had encroached on their territory. Female birdsong is more common in non-migratory, sedentary, largely monogamous species like the dipper, for whom joint territorial defence by both male and female may be a more efficient way for the pair to hold their often extensive territory throughout the year (a dipper's territory, for instance, stretches between 300 and 2,500 metres along a river). Defence responses tend to be intrasexual, with the male bird responding to incursions by other males and the female to other females. Several observers have suggested that the female dipper's song is less sweet-sounding than the male's, with the female's being made up of a series of whistles and disconnected units, although analysis of both sexes' songs found no structural differences in their respective complexity, frequency and temporal characteristics.

Pair-bonding seems to be another important function of the dipper's song. The male and female will often sing together when they meet each other mid-stream on a boulder. These duets are a thing of great beauty. The pair also sing in flight, as I saw, chasing each other up and down the river. Some observers have also witnessed a distinctive display flight, performed by the male and female dipper together. This particular flight seems to be a rare occurrence, or is rarely witnessed. The pair is seen to rise to a considerable height of about 100 ft above the river, flying together just a few feet apart, sometimes in a wide arc that carries the dippers over 300 ft away from the river, sometimes flying parallel to the river, singing continuously. It is a rare thing for a dipper to leave the vicinity of its river, so conjoined are they to their habitat; to witness dippers flying so high above a river that the pair, as one observer noted, 'were lost to sight as they moved into the glare of the sun', would be an almost uncanny sight, as though the birds had strayed beyond themselves.

An equally strange sight, and just as wonderful as this display flight, must be when dippers occasionally fly at great heights over watersheds. These are not birds that have become lost; rather, they are birds, most likely young ones, moving between river systems. Even watersheds in the high Alps will be traversed in this way by juvenile dippers, more often female birds, looking to find a territory for themselves. Most juvenile dispersal occurs along the birds' natal river and its tributaries. But if these territories are already occupied then young dippers will follow their natal river upstream and fly over the watershed into a neighbouring river, or beyond. There is a frequent exchange of young dippers between stream systems across the hills. Mountains are not a barrier to the birds; to a dipper, a watershed is merely a doorway into the next river.

* * *

Over the course of my visits to the valley in Wales, at different times of year, I began to build up a spatial sense of the dippers' territories. On some visits, however, I found that these territories blurred, became fluid and disjointed, with encroachments and overlaps from birds that were not the resident pair. A common sight in February was to witness a single dipper fly downriver, singing loudly, followed a few seconds later by a pair, seemingly in pursuit, sounding their alarm call: *chit, chit, chit* … all of this while flying low over the water at high speed. The pair would then fly back up the river a few minutes later, singing together. I assumed this was the resident pair seeing off an encroachment from an unpaired, possibly male, bird.

In winter there is a tendency for dipper territories to contract a little as birds migrate downstream, increasing population density along the river. These migrations occur if the weather turns particularly severe in the uplands and are more common on high-altitude streams. Exceptionally cold winters can result in dippers congregating in high densities around estuaries. The freezing winter of 1879, for example, saw an extraordinary gathering of a hundred dippers on 31 January on a mile stretch of the River Ewe in the north-west Highlands.

As the breeding season approaches, territories stretch out again along the river and pairs defend these territories vigorously. Dusk, however, sees a truce descend on the river, and there is an opening of gates between territorial boundaries during the autumn and winter as dippers pass through the territories of other birds to gather at communal roost sites. These roosts are often under stone bridges, or somewhere sheltered and out of the wind, where the birds can conserve energy. Dippers approaching a roost will often start to sing, so that the stone arch of the bridge becomes a brief echo chamber for their song.

In October I spent most of one day trailing a dipper slowly up the length of its territory and back again. I knew when I had reached the downstream boundary of the territory as I frequently met another dipper there, distinguished from the first bird by a slight yellow stain, like sun-bleached paper, on the white feathers of its neck. There was a point at the top end of this territory where the dipper invariably turned around and started to work its way back down the river again. Top to bottom was roughly 800 m in length, and it always took me a long time to walk from one end of the territory to the other, stopping, as I did so often, to scan the river for dippers.

I never had much inclination to explore further up or down the river beyond that 800 m stretch. Downstream, the banks were more densely wooded and it was difficult to find good vantage points to observe the water. I was content to spend the whole day on this one short stretch of the river. The dippers were here, and that was all I needed. Two spots along this stretch appeared to be significant foraging areas. If I lost the bird I was tailing, I'd usually locate it again in either of these spots. One of them was the series of pools below the waterfall; the other, the shallow rapids by the corner of a pine wood.

The dippers spent long periods feeding here, working their way across the river, seeming to sieve the rapids with their bill. The picture I began to build of the territory was that it comprised a few prime feeding spots, more often shallow water, linked by stretches of river that the dippers used as flyways between these foraging areas. It seemed like the extent of these shallow feeding areas was an important factor in governing the size of the dippers' territory.

I sometimes caught up with one of the dippers just below the waterfall. The bird would often be perched on a rock at the edge of the pool, preening its feathers, as though the pool were a mirror for its grooming. Below the waterfall a cave had formed under the overhanging clumps of moss and matted bramble. On one occasion the dipper kept looking up towards this cave, then slipped under the brambles and began to move about in the darkness. I could see its white bib, then a sudden flash of white excretion lit the cave like a spark. When it emerged out of the cave, the bird continued jabbing with its bill at the moss and rocks below the falls. The dipper was seldom at rest, and I had this sense of a bird driven by an intense metabolism, constantly feeding as it went along. After it emerged from the cave, I watched the bird hop up the side of the waterfall, then perch on the lip of the falls, the current eddying round its feet as it stood there. It dipped its head into the water, as if peering over the edge of the falls, and, as it did so, the current parted its feathers to cut a pale streak down the bird's forehead. I'd hoped to witness the dipper actually passing through the waterfall, but this bird preferred to forage around the side of the falls rather than behind them. Dippers will occasionally build their nests in the rocks behind a waterfall, in the dripping, roaring acoustics of the cavern, flying through the curtain of water to reach their young as though disappearing through a rent in the air.

Seton Gordon, who loved dippers and watched them diving under ice in the high Cairngorms, described the dipper's song as one of 'extraordinary sweetness, resembling to a certain extent that of the wren, but being much purer and more liquid'. Other listeners have detected hints of nightingale, in the clear way dippers can be heard above the sound of the river, and song thrush, as both species tend to repeat phrases and notes. To me the dipper has a wren-like, burbling song, with traces of song thrush, skylark and blackbird in there too. There are squeaks, beeps, electric pulses, throaty trills, notes that sound like they are being squeezed, and notes so crystal clear they remind me of water dripping in a cave. I can also hear the movement of the river itself in the dipper's song, in the bird's rippling, plunging, dancing notes. One of the distinguishing features of the dipper's song is that it is one of the few birdsongs that can be heard in the depths of winter; even on a freezing day in January it is possible to encounter a dipper performing its beautiful song. And, for this reason, as Gordon wrote:

> One should owe a debt of thankfulness to the dipper if only for the fact that he is one of the few, the very few, of our birds to utter his song during the dead of winter, and how melodious his song is, those who have listened to it can testify.

I once watched a dipper perched on a rock while a robin sang nearby. It was a rare moment of dipper inactivity, and it almost seemed as though the dipper had paused to listen to the robin's song. When I heard the dipper singing a little later it sounded like a zany robin, as though it were playing the robin's song back to itself at twice the normal speed, those long robin-pauses compressed into milliseconds. When this dipper began to sing I was briefly unsure whether the song was in fact coming from the bird I was watching. The sound was so clear and loud, and yet the bird on the rock didn't appear to be opening its bill wide enough to generate the volume of its song. Instead, it looked like the dipper was talking quietly to the river, murmuring, not throwing out this song that carried above the sound of the rapids and up the river to where I stood 30 ft away. I was in one of those curious dipper vacuums, where the river mutes itself and all you hear is dipper song.

The dipper, like many songbirds, also has a quieter song. This is, predominantly, the song the juvenile bird sings when it is learning to sing, known as the bird's subsong. It is most common in first-year male birds in early spring, though it can sometimes be heard in older birds too. The subsong is a warm-up, a rehearsal, a trying out of notes and phrases the young bird has absorbed from its parents' song, as well as from other birds. These rehearsals are done quietly, the bird seeming to sing to itself, practising, retuning, finding its way into full song. Listeners who have heard the dipper's subsong, which is said to be delivered in a lower tone than the main song, have detected phrases that sound like they have been borrowed from the sand martin, chaffinch and greenfinch.

I suspect the dipper's subsong may also borrow from the wren's trills and rattles, the spotted flycatcher's scratchy notes and the high-pitched fiddle music of the common sandpiper. All three species can be neighbours – sometimes tenants – of the dipper. Seton Gordon once found a dipper's dome-shaped nest with a spotted flycatcher's nest built on top of it, like a bobble on a woollen hat, a 'double nest', as he described it. Wrens construct nests that are the same dome shape as a dipper's, though a wren's nest is so small it could fit inside a dipper's nest, as occasionally they do, with wrens building their own nest inside an abandoned dipper's nest, as though constructing a version of a Russian doll.

Wrens will also use old dipper nests to roost in during the winter, and in a delightful echo of the dipper – in its appearance resembling an oversized wren – as many as ten wrens will sometimes squeeze into a dipper's nest to keep warm on cold winter nights. The wrens choose their squat wisely; a dipper's nest is an immaculate construction. The interior is a bowl of woven grasses, lined with dry deciduous leaves. The walls and base are made from moss (heavier mosses around the base, lighter mosses from the entrance hole upwards). The moss is collected by the dippers from the surrounding trees and rocks, and, if dry, the birds dip the moss in water before wedging it into cracks in the nest as though applying a mortar. When finished, the nest is as waterproof as the dipper itself.

Grey wagtails are another close neighbour of the dipper on its summer river. There are even reports of dippers helping to feed grey wagtail nestlings and vice versa. So the wagtail's sharp-sounding, quickfire notes may be another component of the juvenile dipper's subsong. All of these acoustic influences – grey wagtails, wrens, common sandpipers, spotted flycatchers, as well as others – the young dipper may sift through in its subsong, tuning its audible memory until it settles on the right notes and phrasing and recognises itself in its song.

Dippers, like other bird species, learn their songs in the first few weeks of their life. All that time in the nest, waiting for the next meal, is also time spent listening to their parents' song, learning and storing the soundtrack for their adult lives. As the nestlings grow, the song-learning nuclei in their brains develop and connect with each other. There are two principal nuclei associated with song, one nucleus that is associated with learning and production, the other with the structure of notes and syllables. The latter nucleus functions as a sort of fine-tuning of the former's 'first take' stage of the song, and the connection of these two nuclei in the brain is what initiates the bird's first rendition of subsong. It is the nucleus associated with production and learning, called the HVC nucleus, that sends out neuronal projections to connect with the nucleus associated with the structure of notes and syllables, known as the RA nucleus. It is as though the orchestra and score are in place, and by connecting the two nuclei the orchestra is then paired with a conductor.

There has been some interesting research into the relationship between the quality of a bird's song and the bird's condition during its first weeks of life. This is the crucial period when a bird learns its song, investing in its brain's ability to memorise. The theory is that the more energy invested, in terms of nutrition, when the bird is a nestling, the greater its ability to memorise song and therefore the more robust, accurate and complex its song will be in adult life. By the same token, if the nestling suffers stress during this critical stage of song learning, the bird's song will be diminished accordingly.

This theory is known as the 'development stress hypothesis', and it has been tested and shown to occur in several species, including blue tits and great reed warblers, as well as dippers. It's as though by listening to the quality of an individual dipper's song you can glean the conditions of the bird's first few weeks of life, whether it was stressed, either through lack of food, the weather, parasitism, pollution or disturbance. A dipper's song, therefore, can bear the imprint of the bird's early life. And it follows from this that a dipper's song can also be a marker for the health of the river itself. For example, if adult dippers struggle to procure sufficient food from the river for their young, this can be an indication that the river's ecosystem is in poor health. So, following this theory of 'development stress', a dipper that sings a poor-quality song could well be singing from a poor-quality river.

This, crucially, is what dippers are: indicator species for the health of a river. Just as their song can indicate the stresses the bird endured as a nestling, so the dipper's presence or lack of, its territory size and population density are all indicators of the stresses the river itself has been put under. If dippers are not where they should be, if they are suffering breeding failures, then there is usually something wrong with the river.

The wrongs we do to rivers are numerous, and many of them are well highlighted by environmentalists, fishermen and local groups. Fertiliser runoff and sewage discharge persist as two of the most significant forms of riverine pollution. Both contaminants increase the levels of nitrates and phosphates in rivers, boosting algae growth, depleting oxygen and suffocating the dipper's invertebrate prey. Other forms of pollution that also affect dippers include acidification, exacerbated by the presence of large conifer plantations in the uplands, whose needles trap sulphates and other pollutants in the atmosphere and convert them to a weak sulphuric acid. This acid eventually enters the river system, and the subsequent reduction in calcium content in the water, so critical for the dipper's invertebrate prey as well as for the birds themselves, who require calcium to form their eggs, makes these acidified rivers a difficult place for dippers to survive. Increase in flooding due to climate change, and made worse, for example, by the removal of natural tree cover from the river's basin, is another issue that negatively impacts dippers across their range. Swollen, flooded rivers become onerous for dippers to hunt in, and, in times of flood, the birds may be forced to forage in tiny rivulets, like a reserve larder, and even out of desperation in watering troughs or guttering. A dipper foraging in such unusual places would indicate that the river has become unmanageable for the bird.

Perhaps the most insidious of the harms we inflict on rivers, however, was revealed in a study published in 2020. This examined the transfer of plastics between the dipper's prey and the birds, sampling regurgitates and faecal samples from dippers across 15 sites in South Wales. The study found that dippers were ingesting around 200 plastic particles a day from the invertebrate prey the birds consumed. The closer the study sites were to urban areas, the larger the concentrations of plastic particles. Overall, 50 per cent of dipper regurgitates and 45 per cent of their faecal samples were found to contain these particles. Just as shearwaters have shown us how pervasive plastic is in the ocean, dippers have provided evidence that it is now endemic in our rivers as well.

There is an account, published in *Country Life* magazine in 1979, of intriguing dipper behaviour observed on a tributary of the River Dee in Aberdeenshire. The incident took place during a long spell of freezing weather and the boulders in the river were all fringed with ice. The dipper was seen landing on a mossy log and, as the observer noted, 'his next gesture was puzzling … he began picking up hailstone-like frozen droplets from it [the log], and, walking solemnly to the water's edge, dropped them into the river.' I love this account because it conjures the image of a bird attending to its river. For some reason, the dipper felt the ice droplets belonged in the water and not on the mossy log. But in that small gesture of attending to its environment, of 'tidying' the ice from the log, of icing the river, it is almost as though the dipper was showing us how to attend to things better, how to care.

IV

Up in the Lift Go We

Skylark

I hear the skylark field before I see it. Walking up the path, just inside the wood, I become aware of a wall of sound on the other side of the trees. The noise is muted on the path itself, but each time I pass a gap in the trees there is a swell of song and I have a sense of the air above the field trembling.

After a steep climb to the top of the wood the path begins to level out. I sometimes come across a robin here, perched in one of the smooth-barked cherry trees. The long pauses in the robin's song make me think he is listening out for his own echo. Occasionally, a nuthatch's loud whistling notes ring out from the bank below. And I often hear snippets of wren too, their songs running ahead of them through the brambles like fast-flowing water. There is a low, tumbledown shed here, just off the path, virtually hidden by blackthorn bushes. One winter the wind blew snow into the shed and, a week after the storm, when all the snow had gone, there was still a small, yellowing patch just inside the entrance. The snow had been so compacted by the wind it remained in the shed for several days, looking like a ball of dough left there to prove.

This stretch of the path, just beyond the shed, is where the noise coming off the lark field begins to pulse through the trees. It's almost a humming, insectile sound, the way so many lark songs seem to trip over and fuse with each other. I turn off the path, past the hollow trunk of an old beech where one cold morning I disturbed a fox curled up inside the hollow, wrapped in the tight ball of its brush. Once past the old beech, I pick my way over a bank of hazel, and I am out of the wood and into the sudden brightness of the field.

I spent four months, between the end of March and the end of July, visiting the skylark field as often as I could. It was such an immersive experience observing these small, graceful, energetic birds through their breeding season. There were some mornings when so many larks were singing above the field, I thought the sound must carry for miles. Other days there was little to see or hear, when I coincided my visit to the field with what I came to term a 'lark-lull', when the field slept and occasionally stuttered into song. The weather conditions seemed to determine these lulls, but not in the way I anticipated. Mornings of thick mist or rain, when I traipsed up to the field expecting to hear little, were in fact full of singing skylarks. Wind seemed to be the main factor in impeding the larks' song flights. If it was very windy, they tended to keep low to the field, sometimes perched on top of the swaying crop, occasionally singing from the ground instead. And there were some days of clear, still skies when I'd arrive at the field expecting a deluge of song, and there was not a lark to be heard. I'd wait and fidget and grow increasingly anxious at the silence, until a lark would suddenly shoot up into the air just a few feet from me and all felt well again.

It was an absorbing experience, those few months spent watching the field. The feeling I had at the time was of being locked into the place to the extent that if I had to miss a morning there, I felt the absence strongly. I find it difficult to explain the pull the field had over me, but it grew beyond my initial goal to observe the birds as carefully and often as I could into something more involving than that. I felt such a compulsion to be there, and most mornings I found myself walking, as though being led, along the muddy track through the wood towards the field.

* * *

What sort of bird is a skylark? Just as the nightjar can fold itself into the woody floor of a heath, the skylark blends into the clays and stony greys of the ground it lives on. Its breast and back are streaked with the buffs and browns of the stubble, crops and grasses it feeds and nests among. The lark inhabits two different spheres: the one in the sky, the familiar backdrop to us, where the males sing high on their columns of air, and the other, their more unobtrusive life on the ground, where the birds feed and nest and hide from predators and are so camouflaged there we rarely see them.

Some local names for the skylark reflect this duality; besides 'rising lark' and 'sky-flapper', there is also 'field lark', 'clod lark', 'clod hopper' and 'ground lark'. And that ability to fold itself into the ground, so that the bird becomes almost impossible to locate, is rendered in another local and widespread name for the skylark, 'laverock' (found in many place names), a word that may have its origins in the Anglo-Saxon word *laferre* or *lawerce*, meaning one who is guilty of treason, such is the lark's reputation for deceiving the searcher as to the location of the bird and its nest. There is a species of lark, the 'desert lark', so attuned to the ground it inhabits that the colour of its plumage varies markedly between different populations over reasonably short distances, so that, chameleon-like, these larks replicate shifts in the colour and texture of the ground. It's even been suggested that of the hundred or so lark species in the world, some must bathe in the dust where they live to achieve such crypsis, though it's more likely to be a reflection of the predation pressures these small, ground-nesting birds face that the laverock has evolved such nuanced means to deceive.

Skylarks inevitably invite us to look up, to search the sky for the distant singer, but some of the most fascinating activity to observe among the birds happens at ground level, or just a little above the ground. It took me a while to fully appreciate this. Initially I'd spent most of my time blinking at the sun, trying to follow the larks through their song flights. But more and more I became aware of these fast-paced pursuit flights between birds as they skimmed low over the field, chasing each other at incredible speeds, sometimes fusing together in a mid-air tussle, rising a few feet above the crop in a frantic coil of legs and wings. From then on I began to watch the ground as much as I did the sky, alternating between the vertical and horizontal, the song flights and the ground flights of this captivating bird.

Around 7 inches from the tip of their bill to tip of their tail, a skylark could make its nest in the cup of your hand. They have a small crest on the crown of their heads that, when raised, resembles a neatly combed quiff. The birds also possess a long hind claw, the purpose of which is not entirely known, though like the belief that nightjars wounded cattle with their beaks, skylarks were once thought to use their claws to strike at the eyes of sheep, inflicting a poisonous wound. There is an old Scottish rhyme that proposes another purpose of the skylark's claw – to test the skill and patience of shoemakers everywhere. The rhyme appears to imitate, in its fast, shifting tempo and diction, the song of the skylark itself:

> Larikie, larikie, lee!
> Wha'll gang up to heaven wi me?
> No the lout that lies in his bed,
> No the doolfu' that dreeps his head.
>
> Up in the lift go we,
> Te-hee, te-hee, te-hee, te-hee!
> There's not a shoemaker on the earth
> Can make a shoe to me, to me!
> Why so? Why so? Why so?
> Because my heel is as long as my toe!

Skylarks are birds of wide, open spaces: coastal marshes, large arable fields and set-asides. Around 70 per cent of the UK population is found on lowland farmland, with 50 per cent on arable land (sheep don't need to worry too much about being spurred by a lark's claw, as the birds are at their lowest densities on heavily grazed grassland). What matters to skylarks is the structure of a habitat. Intensively grazed pasture restricts their numbers because there is insufficient vegetation cover for the birds to conceal their nests. On the other hand, vegetation that is too tall or dense crowds out their nests and impedes the birds from moving around. Vegetation at around 60 centimetres high is about perfect for skylarks; when arable crops grow taller than a metre, the birds tend to relocate to nest in shorter-length sward.

The wider structure of the landscape also matters to skylarks. The birds prefer to keep a distance – around 200 metres – between their nests and the nearest woodland or tall hedgerow. Even in winter, skylarks concentrate their feeding in the centre of large fields, only moving out towards the edge as food diminishes. Any structure that affords an avian predator the opportunity to perch and survey the skylarks' nesting area is shunned by the larks. This aversion applies to electricity pylons, buildings and other tall structures; the only vertical thing a lark tolerates is its own song flight. For the same reason skylarks will, where possible, steer clear of kestrel nest sites. Interestingly, however, skylarks will sometimes breed in the vicinity of raven nests, perhaps in a similar way to how red-breasted geese have been observed to nest close to peregrine falcon eyries; ravens, like peregrines, are highly effective sentries, hustling other would-be predators away from the area. There are also a few rare examples of skylarks, in extremis, ditching their aversion to all things vertical by seeking shelter next to people in order to escape a merlin's pursuit.

Besides tall structures, skylarks also prefer to nest away from roads, especially busy ones, where the noise of traffic can pollute the birds' song. This buffer zone between a road and the bird's nesting territory appears to be particularly significant among skylarks, with a study showing that their densities adjacent to roads were only a third of what they were in fields 3 kilometres from a road; every busy road, it seems, depresses the skylark's ability to sing and be heard.

These, then, are the skylark's basic habitat requirements: suitable length and density of vegetation, somewhere unimpeded by noise pollution, and an expansive panorama that provides the birds with both a sense of security as well as, crucially, the space to launch their song flights. The field I watched over those four months had most of these features. The hedges along the field's boundaries were low, there were no pylons or telegraph poles, and though a wood bordered one side of the field, the skylarks kept their distance from it, with the majority of nests congregated at least 200 metres from its edge. The soil was free draining, so the birds' nests did not succumb to waterlogging after heavy rain. The nearest road was a mile away and there was even a raven's nest close to the skylarks' field, in a tall pine in the centre of the wood. During their nesting season I often heard and watched the ravens noisily escorting red kites and buzzards, in particular, out of the area.

One of the best places to view the field was from a hedge along the field's eastern boundary. There were several toothy gaps in the hedge that I could slot into, giving me a good perspective of the whole sweep of the field. Sometimes when I stood in one of these gaps, the sun coming up behind me spilt my shadow across the field. In May the hedge became a corridor for whitethroats and yellowhammers. I'd listen to the whitethroats' scratchy song, watch the hedge twitching with the birds' jerky movements. Perched at intervals of around 12 to 15 ft, the yellowhammers glowed like streetlamps along the top of the hedge.

It was often quiet when I arrived at the hedge in the early morning and settled into my gap. Skylarks must be one of the first birds to usher in the dawn. 'To be up with the lark' is really to be up while it is still dark, and some mornings I tried, not very successfully, to get to the field before first light. Skylarks will not only sing well before it gets light but also, when conditions allow, after it becomes dark in the evening, so that their song seems almost to bypass the bird's circadian rhythm. The ornithologist Eric Simms conducted a beautifully conceived survey in June 1951 that recorded the times skylarks began to sing across the British Isles, 'to present a sound picture of the birds awakening', as he described the project. The recordings were broadcast on radio a few days later with the aim that 'listeners could imagine themselves suspended above our islands and with powers of hearing that would bring all parts within earshot; thus the birds of Aberdeenshire would be heard equally with those of Dorset or Antrim.' In the Cairngorms the first skylark began singing at 01.30 GMT; 21 minutes later, at 01.51, a skylark went up in the Tweed valley in Berwickshire; in Lancashire it was 02.33; in South Wales, 02.36. Like a network of fire beacons signalling to one another across the land, that lark in the Cairngorms set in train a wave of song that spread south and west across the country, pre-empting the dawn.

Skylarks seem to anticipate the dawn a long way out, well before other birds begin to sing. Simms also recorded the song thrush, robin and blackbird in his survey, and the skylark pipped them all, with the lark starting to sing, on average, 1 hour 25 minutes before dawn. It is as though the skylark, through the height it gains in its song flight, has foreknowledge of the dawn, can see the light approaching around the curvature of the earth. Interestingly, the lark near Southport in the Lancashire Plain rose to sing later than Simms anticipated, and he speculated that this may have been due to smoke from nearby factories inhibiting the light, depressing the dawn itself.

Through April I watched the rapeseed crop in the adjacent field begin to yellow. There was a density of light in the middle of the crop that faded towards the field's margins, such that when a skylark flew low over the centre of the field its white breast was lit by the yellow light beneath it. The first skylark of the morning to go up always made me feel glad, and I never stopped being amazed by the display that followed. Up it shot on its steep, flickering climb, singing as soon as it cleared the crop, as though its song were helping to propel it. When the lark reached the top of its climb it made a tight loop around the circumference of its column, then steadied itself in the air, wings flickering, hanging there, pouring out its song. Often there would be a slight pause, a moment when the lark's wings ceased their rapid whirring, and the bird would then begin to glide, wings held out, tail straight back, maintaining its height.

At that moment, when the lark switched from flickering to gliding, its song changed, became slower, with an increase in longer notes. I always thought of this gliding stage of the song flight as being the moment when the lark started to think about coming down. The bird would glide like this for perhaps 20 seconds, still singing, before I noticed it slowly begin to tilt downwards, dropping incrementally out of the glide. Then suddenly I was watching the bird plummet out of the sky, the white in its plumage streaking through the air, pulling up out of its dive just a few feet above the ground, before gently landing in the field.

That dive back to earth was, for me, the most exhilarating moment in the display. The lark pulled its wings back, tilted towards the ground, then suddenly cut its song. The silence and speed of the drop was what I found so mesmerising; after all that surge of song, to have the song cut so abruptly, then to see the lark drop with such meteoric speed. I kept thinking the bird was going to hit the ground, then somehow, in the last few seconds of the descent, the lark pulled out of the dive to float the final few feet and touch down on the field. Diving like this with folded wings is not the lark's only form of descent, but it is the fastest and most dramatic to watch. Sometimes it will descend more gradually on flapping wings, and, more slowly still, it can also glide down in a parachute-like descent, usually singing as it does so. But there is something in the silence of the fast, diving descent that, paradoxically, draws attention to it; the air is full of song – and then it's not. It's as though the song has been snatched away and the lark is desperately flinging itself downwards to retrieve it. The end of a skylark's song flight is the moment the song itself takes flight.

The blackthorn blossom came on in April, and the mud dried and hardened along the path through the wood. I found that the colour of the sky made a difference to how quickly I could locate the singing larks. On overcast mornings it proved easier to find the birds; I'd hear a lark singing and look up to see a black dot backlit by grey. On clear bright mornings those dots were more difficult to find as they shimmered and became frayed in the sun's glare. One cold wet morning I watched a lark climb so high I thought it would freeze up there in the rain. But the bird kept climbing higher, still singing as its wings brushed the low cloud. Sometimes I thought that tiny dot in the sky must be as high as the larks ever went, only to see another singing above it, as though the birds were stacked in a holding pattern.

How high *do* skylarks reach during their song flights? Victorian naturalists thought it could be as high as a mountain (over 2,000 ft). And I have watched skylarks over the field soar so high some mornings, the birds seemed to disappear. The reality is maybe not quite as dramatic as those early naturalists gauged, but the heights the birds can reach are no less remarkable for such a small bird that propels itself straight up by flapping its wings, not rising on a thermal like many high-soaring birds do. About half of all skylark song flights go above 160 ft, not many go beyond 650 ft (one study showed an average height reached of 400 ft). Most skylarks, therefore, easily clear Big Ben (310 ft) on their ascents. And the birds go straight up at an extraordinary rate of 3 ft per second, their wings beating at around ten to twelve beats per second as they climb; even the lark's rapidly delivered song can't keep pace with the rate at which the birds beat their wings when they ascend like tiny rockets into the sky.

The energy expended in such an ascent must be substantial, and it is the reason male skylarks have longer wings – and a lower wing loading (the ratio of body weight to wing area) – than females, giving the males more aerodynamically efficient wings to assist with the climb. But the climb, and the descent, despite the energy costs and the sheer drama of these flights, are not really what it's all about. From the perspective of the female skylarks, and rival males, watching a male's song flight from the ground, what counts is how long he stays poised, singing in the air. It is the stage of the song flight where the male reaches the top of his climb, and levels out to sing and hang above the field, that provides the most information about his endurance and fitness as a potential mate or rival. The sheer rapidity of the ascent and descent implies that their main purpose is to get the lark to and from his platform in the sky as quickly as possible. It is this podium in the sky, the apex of his song flight and, importantly, how long he occupies that podium, how long he holds himself in level flight while singing, that matter most, that convey the most information about the singer to his audience far below.

How long the lark stays in level flight depends, frequently, on the height it achieves on the ascent; the higher the lark goes, the longer it spends singing in level flight. The majority of song flights last between 2 and 4 minutes; more than 10 minutes is rare, though there have been some flights recorded lasting over half an hour. The length of the song flight has a tendency to decrease as the breeding season progresses, as the demands on the adults of raising their brood increase (those exceptionally long song flights are most likely performed by unpaired males, unencumbered by a brood of chicks to protect and feed).

Once the lark reaches the culmination of its climb, it switches to the equivalent of a vehicle's eco mode, with the bird adopting the most energy-efficient means of staying in the air. The lark stabilises its speed at around 20 ft per second, and the bird is held in the air by the force of the wind checking the lark's momentum, just as a kestrel holds itself in the air while hovering. If the wind speed drops below 20 ft per second, the lark is forced to tack around its platform, circling about to maintain its height. Conversely, when wind speed increases it can be difficult for the lark to retain its poise in the air for very long, and song flights are curtailed or abandoned altogether if the wind becomes too strong.

The ubiquity of the skylark's song flight belies its complexity and sensitivity. The song flight is a finely tuned, delicate feat of balancing, of judging the wind against the bird's own momentum. To sing and, at the same time, tread the air with its wings, to float in the air as the lark does, is a remarkable spectacle. According to Pliny the Elder, the lark's Latin name (and the scientific name of the genus to which the Eurasian skylark belongs) *Alauda* had its origins in the Gaulish words *al*, meaning 'great', and *aud*, a 'song'; thus, *Alauda* means 'great singer'. The skylark's song is mesmerising, and it possesses one of the largest repertoires of any bird, with over 300 syllables. But for me the lark's 'greatness' derives from the way it uniquely balances song and flight, delivering its music from that platform in the air.

There is some fascinating research that complements this notion that it is the period of singing during level flight – the apex of the lark's song flight – that conveys most information about the lark's fitness. A study that looked at the relationship between skylarks and one of their principal avian predators, the merlin (the bird capable of prompting a lark to seek shelter next to people), showed that skylarks will sing in order to evade a merlin. It is a striking thought; the larks sing, literally, to survive. Merlins will often pursue skylarks in flight for several minutes. So a skylark that sings vigorously and complexly, while having a merlin hot on its tail, is informing the merlin that it is fit and has the stamina to fly higher and faster still. Rather than expend unnecessary energy on the pursuit, the merlin takes the decision to give up on that particular individual; both merlin and skylark benefit from this communication exchange, as both are not needlessly exhausted by the pursuit. The study showed that singing skylarks – both male and female – escaped merlin attacks more frequently than non-singing skylarks. So, the skylark's song conveys information not just to other skylarks, to potential mates and rivals, but also to potential predators. Just as some grazing animals such as gazelles and some species of deer stott, or leap, into the air to signal their fitness to deter predators, so a skylark's song is its version of such a leap. A lark's song can stop a merlin in its tracks.

As soon as I see one lark drop out of its song flight, and parachute the last few feet to the ground, I notice another bird start to rise, as though their flights are choreographed so the air is never empty of song. When there are lots of birds up and singing at the same time I get a sense, too, of one song triggering another, of multiple echoes reverberating. A lark singing on its own in the far distance has a special quality; you miss some of the intricacy of the song, but there is a flow, a softness, to the sound that I love.

I try to listen to one of the birds singing close by, to unpick the notes from its song. I can just about catch the first few whistling notes, but then the song accelerates away into itself, and I find it impossible to keep pace beyond a sense that the range of squeaks, ricochets, trills and whistles is extraordinarily diverse. Sometimes the lark conjures a note from such a surprisingly low frequency that it sounds like it belongs to a different bird altogether. Skylarks are great imitators of other birds, and they will enrich the repertoire of their song by dropping in sounds from many other species. Wading birds, perhaps because they have such distinctive vocalisations, seem to be a particular favourite, with curlews, redshanks, oystercatchers and others often making an appearance in the skylark's song. Many of these waders – notably curlews and lapwings – are now absent from large swathes of the country where, just a few decades ago, they were once common. And so, in some places, all that remains of these birds is the trace of their voices in the skylark's song.

That ability to imitate other birds has not always been cherished in the skylark. In the nineteenth century, when caged songbirds were in high demand, dealers in these birds tried to make sure skylarks were not influenced – or corrupted, as they saw it – by the songs of other birds. The dealers kept the larks in a sort of song-quarantine whereby the birds were only exposed to other larks that had recently been caught. This procedure was known as keeping the larks 'honest'. There is a peculiar logic at work here; at the same time as conditioning the birds to only hear the songs of other wild skylarks, by stacking the larks in cramped, fetid cages in appalling conditions, their wildness was crushed out of them. But it was a profitable business, with a 'good singer' – often blinded because it was believed that blind larks sang better – costing more than 15 shillings in the 1850s, the equivalent of over £60 today. Larks were traded in their thousands each year in the London markets, either as caged songbirds or as meat for a fashionable dish, lark pudding, *mauviettes en surprise aux truffes*. There was also a trade in skylarks for use in the fashion industry, where the subtle, earthy shades of the lark's wing feathers were dyed bright colours to give them an exotic sheen; even the wildness inherent in the lark's crypsis was crushed, by a garish dye.

By mid-May the field was alive with larks, their song flights going higher and lasting longer. There was so much flickering activity over the crop. Some birds hovered, patrolling low over the field, hesitating, thinking about a place to come down, briefly alighting, before hovering up into the air once more. Others were perched on the tops of the plants, some of them singing quietly. Most days I found myself staying late into the morning, absorbed by the sheer bustle of the place.

One morning I watched an individual lark perched on top of a bean plant for 15 minutes or so through my scope. I could see its yellowy, pink-tinged legs, the white trim highlighting the sides of its tail. It had a dusty yellow patch across its cheek, a white eye-stripe just above its bright black eyes and a bill full of insects that hung in a gluey ball from the corner of its beak like a cigar stub. Every few minutes the bird flicked up from its perch and flew low over the crop before alighting on another plant, all the time calling quietly as it flew. The call was subdued, anxious-sounding, a short, jerky *teet-teet*. I wondered if it was searching for its chicks, which disperse from the nest soon after they are born and can sometimes become lost and difficult for their parents to locate. When perched on top of the plant, the lark often adopted a crouched, bobbing posture. It would bob its head down so that it was hidden by the depth of the crop, as though it had suddenly ducked to avoid something. It reminded me of watching the dippers on the river and their constant bobbing movements; the white flowers of the bean crop also made it look as though the skylark had briefly assumed a dipper's white chest. Sometimes, when a breeze got up, the lark flickered its wings to keep its balance on top of the plant. And every so often I watched it run a short distance over the crop, hopping from plant to plant; the crop swayed beneath the lark as it moved, so that it looked like the bird was running over water.

The next morning the wind was stronger and most of the larks kept close to the ground. I watched one bird, again perched on top of a bean plant, swirling about in the breeze, singing from its perch. Its song didn't sound as fast and fluid as when the birds sang from the air. This ground song seemed more hesitant, slower, with frequent pauses for breath. I had a sense of the lark trying out its song, testing notes and variations, a kind of ground rehearsal, a warm-up, before the wind dropped and allowed it to sing from the sky again. Those larks that did take to the air were flung across the field by the wind, fast as swifts. I then watched them as they slowly made their way back, flying into the wind, keeping low to the field, one after the other, as though hauling themselves along a rope.

Those caged larks in the squalid dealers' shops of the nineteenth century, who were kept 'honest' to preserve the integrity of their song, would, in fact, have sung a different song to the recently caught birds they were exposed to. Unless the fresh birds were caught in the same field as the other larks, they would have almost certainly possessed another song, distinctive enough for those caged birds to know they were not from their patch. The difference in their respective songs, rather than producing a musical harmony between the birds, as presumably the dealers hoped, would more likely have caused tension between the larks, if there was not already sufficient tension in such a place.

Birds with complex song repertoires, combined with a wide geographical range and a habit of breeding in the same place – such as skylarks – tend to show a marked variation in their songs across neighbouring locations. Birds in one valley will sing with a different 'accent' to those in adjacent valleys. In skylarks these differences can be so pronounced they are more like distinct dialects than accents. Variation in song occurs over distances as little as a mile, with the differences increasing the further apart groups of skylarks are from one another. It's not so much that these separate groups cannot understand each other, more that they identify the differences in the structure between each other's songs and thereby establish whether the singer is a resident or non-resident bird.

Another way of thinking about these differences is that they are less like an accent and more like a set of grammatical rules. Skylarks in one location learn and use a distinctive temporal arrangement of syllables (the grouping of notes) within their song. So, separate communities of skylarks may share a song phrase, but within that shared phrase the precise ordering of the syllables, or notes, may differ, depending on the community. If the grammar is different, if the arrangement of syllables differs, then this identifies the singer as belonging to a different group. This is where that tension comes into play; once identified as belonging to a separate group, the singer is treated as an intruder by the resident birds. The shared grammar of their songs – the ability to recognise the correct syllable order within a song phrase – additionally allows the resident birds to recognise one another and therefore not waste energy on responding aggressively to each other's songs.

If the mechanics of the skylark's song flight are both subtle and complex – and the range of their song's repertoire seems immensely complicated too – then the lark's ability to arrange and learn a sequence for the syllables within its song also seems dizzying in its subtlety and intricacy. Not only is it an indication of the skylark's cognitive skills that they can learn and process such complex song arrangements, it is also a reminder of what we do not hear when we listen to a skylark's song. We lack the ability to comprehend what is being communicated within the song, to identify those syllables, the pauses that last around 11 milliseconds, where the bird may snatch a tiny gulp of air between notes. We are always partially deaf around birdsong, and our human ears miss almost everything of the lark's song. What we can glean from it is, of course, still beautiful, and made more so by the knowledge that it is infinitely more rich, complex and multidimensional than we can hear.

One morning I came across a lark on the track beside the field. It was foraging along the path, picking at the grass for insects. I could see its delicate pinkish legs, its spiky, wind-ruffled crest. The bird seemed browner, duller-looking on the ground, though once or twice it shook its feathers and there was a ripple of white through its plumage. It felt strange to come across a grounded lark after being so used to watching them in the air, but it was also thrilling to meet one like this, as though I were being given a brief glimpse into a hidden part of its life.

Just as the male and female nightjar have their own tremulous, secretive ballet, shivering around one another, lowering and folding their wings, so a skylark pair perform something similarly graceful, balletic and hidden as part of their bonding display. During this display, the male skylark stages a strange hopping dance in front of the female; crest raised, head held back, his whole posture – legs and body – is held very stiff and upright, like a soldier standing to attention. Retaining this stiffness, the male then proceeds to bounce up and down in front of the female several times, hopping a couple of centimetres above the ground and often singing as he hops. Sometimes, this hopping performance will also include a beautifully tender gesture, where the male lark holds out one of his wings to the female until it touches, or almost touches, her; he then shivers his wing softly beside her.

There is a description of another unusual performance by skylarks when they are on the ground. Though rarely witnessed, it involves the male descending from a song flight then running to a tuft of grass, where the bird turns around repeatedly in the same spot, stamping the ground with his feet, flattening the grass until he has made a cup in which he often settles down. This performance is possibly an extension of the display flight, though it has been so little observed it's not exactly clear what its purpose is. The trampling of the grass to make a nest, or a form, has its echo in the form that a hare makes when it scrapes the grass to make a shallow depression for itself on the ground. It is interesting that both skylark and hare are largely inhabitants of open fields, and not only do both have a preference for wide, unenclosed spaces to feel secure, but they also appear to share this habit of pressing the grass to make a form, a mould in which to fit themselves to the ground.

The actual nest of the skylark is itself usually just a scraped cup on the ground. This can make the nest, with its exposed location in the open, especially vulnerable to predation. To counter this risk, skylarks incubate their eggs and raise their young in a hyper-speed version of the shearwater's nesting cycle. The less time eggs or chicks are in the nest, the less the probability a predator will locate them. The incubation period therefore lasts no more than 10 to 14 days, and skylark chicks disperse from the nest well before they can fly, or even feed themselves. This period, when the chicks scatter but are still dependent on their parents for food, is still fraught with risk; sometimes, particularly if they have been disturbed, the adult larks have difficulty in locating the chicks to feed them; sometimes, the chicks will fall into a drought-crack in the ground and starve to death.

Skylark nesting is immensely precarious; so many nests – often as many as three-quarters – fail through predation, starvation, being crushed by machinery or trampled by livestock. All these pressures mean that skylark pairs need to raise around three broods per season to maintain their population. And so, not long after the first brood disperses from the nest, the adult pair will start preparing for the next.

The last days of May were warm, with blue skies and thin streaks of cloud. The skylarks sang high above the field, their song fizzing like electricity pylons crackling in the rain. I'd often go from hearing a song thrush in the wood, then step through the hedge into the field and think the skylarks sounded like high-speed song thrushes. If I hovered near the edge of the wood, I could sometimes hear both birds at the same time, and I wondered if the skylarks borrowed notes from the song thrush too, accelerating and reinterpreting the thrush's freestyle repertoire. Sometimes, the skylarks' song reminded me of the sound an ancient dial-up modem made, processing its thoughts in beeps, clicks and rattling trills.

By June it was already warm at 6.30 a.m. The heat shimmered over the far side of the field and the hedge became blurred in the haze. Many larks were singing on the ground, some perched on the bean plants, some hidden inside the crop, so it felt as though the field itself was singing. The perched birds were like pale beacons swaying on top of the plants. Some of these perched skylarks appeared to be overlooking nest sites, keeping watch, bobbing nervously, then dropping down from their perch into the crop. I watched some of the larks singing from the tops of the plants, and their songs had a hesitant quality that distinguished them from the aerial songs, as if that crouched, bobbing nervousness among the perched birds influenced the timbre of their song. I watched one bird perched very close to me and, as it opened its beak to practise its song, I could see the yellow lining of its bill, the orange gape inside.

Some mornings there were unexpected visitors to the field. As the crop grew taller, passing fallow deer became submerged, so I'd see just their necks, heads and the bucks' velvety antlers poking above the plants, moving through the crop in a line, as though the deer were swimming. If the deer were disturbed, however, they bounded through the field, spraying larks in their wake. One morning a brown hare loped slowly along the path towards me, pausing to browse the bean plants, its long, soft ears twitching as it moved. In the middle of July, just as I was about to leave for the day, something caught my eye – a scuffle above the field – and I saw a lark being pursued by a sparrowhawk; sharp-angled carpal joints on the hawk's wings, a long, narrow tail. A sudden burst of speed and it was over in seconds; the lark flew away, and the sparrowhawk abandoned the pursuit and slunk back towards the wood. One day a yellow wagtail suddenly appeared on the bean crop like some exotic apparition. I'd never seen one there before and for a moment I thought one of the rapeseed flowers from the neighbouring field had come loose and been blown across on the breeze.

Through most of May and into early June I heard a cuckoo calling, and I'd listen to it moving through its call along the bracken bank and into the corner of the wood. The 'cuckoo bank', as I started to call it, was a wonderfully overgrown, brambly place, fidgety with linnets, dunnocks and chiffchaffs. I often stopped there on my way back from the field to listen to the linnets' quiet, spinning song and watch the males with their blood-orange breasts glowing among the brambles. The dunnocks always looked as though they had slept in a patch of winter bracken, with their reds and browns and greys; their song was fast and rippling, delivered in short bursts from the mossy elders and hawthorn bushes.

4 June. I watched a skylark perched 30 ft away on the top of a bean plant, balancing in the breeze. When it hopped across to another plant its white undertail flicked up as it adjusted to regain its balance. The bird gave off a plaintive *pee-ee* call. Then it crossed to the other side of the path and brushed its feet over a bean flower, before suddenly shooting upwards into full song. It climbed to about 20 ft, then levelled off and hovered above me. I watched it there for a couple of minutes, then it started to come down out of its song and, as it did so, another

lark joined it. The pair began to chase each other in a wide circle around me, skimming the top of the field. After 30 seconds of this fast pursuit a third lark joined them, so there were now three skylarks spinning around me in a dizzying gyre.

I noticed that as soon as one of the pursuing birds started to gain on the bird in front, the lead bird would speed up to maintain the gap – about 6 ft – between them. It was an extraordinary display to witness, and the whole thing was conducted at incredible speed; I thought of electrons chasing and repelling each other around a circuit. The way the birds responded to each other by speeding up then slowing down, tuning the distance between each other, made it seem as though the display had its own rules, its own pre-arranged symmetry.

It was hard to tell what was going on with this three-way display – a courtship flight that had melded into a territorial dispute? It was common to see these low-level flights over the field trigger a reaction from other birds on the ground, prompting them to spring like jack-in-the-boxes out of the crop and occasionally pursue the bird that had flown over them. Sometimes, so many larks would spring up out of the crop in the wake of another lark's cruising flight, the birds reminded me of popcorn spitting and jumping above the rim of a pan. The courtship flight itself is a spectacular low-level, rapid, twisting pursuit, where the male skylark chases the female, singing as he does so. If you could sketch the flight path of these courtship dances, the air would be a whirl of vortices and hairpin turns. Territorial disputes similarly involve fast, frantic, acrobatic pursuits through the air, with rivals often locking claws and tumbling over each other in a furious mid-air spin. And I occasionally witnessed a lark suddenly drop like a stone out of its song flight, levelling out at the very last second to shoot across the tops of the bean crop in pursuit of another lark.

Both the courtship chase and these territorial skirmishes remind anyone lucky enough to witness them that skylarks are among the most agile of birds, and that the vertical ascent and descent of their song flight are just a fraction of what these birds are capable of in flight. Both displays also involve song, with adversaries also frequently bursting into a loud song as they bash each other's wings and lock claws. Perhaps, in the same way that skylarks signal their fitness to merlins through their song, rival larks convey their fitness to one another by singing, such that a quick burst of song is as forceful as a wing slap or claw scratch. And perhaps, ultimately, song trumps violence, as male skylarks occasionally revert to 'song duels' to settle territorial disputes. These duels involve both birds rising together to perform a song flight, but instead of the usual distance between singing skylarks, the rivals ascend and sing together very close in the air, usually only a few metres apart. What decides the outcome of these sing-offs? Volume, complexity of repertoire, mid-air posture? Whatever the answer, after a while one bird folds, admits defeat and floats away, while the winner climbs higher, keeps on singing.

* * *

17 June. The hedge line was a dark blur in the mist, as though the heat haze of the previous days had boiled over and made a soup of itself. Two cock pheasants were fighting in the bean field and every so often their long tail feathers shot up above the crop. The pheasants made a strange, muffled, squeaking noise as they fought. The mist hadn't subdued the larks and the field was full of song. The sun was beginning to break through, making small pools of light over the field. There was a brightness behind the mist, too, and spots of vapour sparkled in the air. Lark song everywhere and, because I couldn't see the birds hidden in the mist, the sound over the field took on its own background hum and flow, like sleeping beside a river at night.

Of the numerous methods employed to kill or capture skylarks for those nineteenth-century markets, one of the more curious was a practice known as 'low-belling'. This involved a group of men dragging a wide net over the skylarks' nesting ground and capturing the larks as they flew up into the net. The quirk was that the men wore, or carried, bells that they tolled as they walked; the idea being that the men deceived the larks into thinking they were cattle, which also wore bells around their necks, and which the skylarks would have been used to hearing as the cows lumbered around the field.

In some ways, we are still tolling bells for skylarks, though it seems that we do so now, not to deceive the birds, but to mark their passing. Skylarks are listed on the UK's Birds of Conservation Concern Red List. The skylark population in the UK is now less than half of what it was in the early 1980s; that's a loss of between 1 million and 1.5 million pairs. In the skylark's preferred habitat of farmland, the species declined by 75 per cent between 1972 and 1996. Paul Donald puts this loss into perspective when he writes in his monograph on the species that 'the abundance of skylarks means that British farmland may have lost more individual skylarks than individuals of all the other species [of farmland birds] combined.' It is not a problem confined to the UK either, as skylark numbers have been declining across over half of all European countries. In some of these countries the situation is exacerbated by the continued hunting – legal and illegal – of skylarks; an estimated 3 to 4 million birds are harvested each year (partly for food and partly as a cultural and leisure activity), around 5 per cent of the European wintering population.

What has been happening to skylarks to cause such a dramatic decline in their numbers? To understand the problem, it's helpful to return to the premise that it is the structure of a habitat that is so important to skylarks; the height and density of vegetation are critical to the species' breeding success. One of the principal ways the bird's habitat has been altered over the past few decades is the shift in agriculture to planting cereals in winter rather than spring. Sowing earlier, in winter, gives the crop a head start, so that by the time skylarks are at the peak of their breeding season in late spring, the crop has grown too dense and high for skylarks to nest in; winter-sown cereals crowd skylark nests out. The birds may have time to raise one, possibly two, broods, but that critical third brood – so crucial for maintaining the population – is rarely possible where the larks' habitat becomes swamped by the crop's density. This alteration to the skylark's habitat through a shift in planting times, combined with an intensively sown crop, is seen as the most important factor driving the species' decline.

While lowland farmland has witnessed the bulk of the decline in the skylark population, the species has also seen declines across other habitats. Frequent cutting of their grassland habitat gives the birds hardly any chance at all to breed successfully. And both upland and coastal breeding populations of skylarks have also seen significant population declines. It's possible that these populations, which breed away from lowland farmland, have declined because their winter feeding grounds – particularly stubble fields – have also declined in extent, as these fields are not left fallow through the winter months, instead being ploughed for early sowing. It is a complex picture, but it underlines the subtle and intricate relationship skylarks have with their habitat. We may see it as just a field planted with crops, but for a skylark the difference in sowing time, by just a few months, can mean that field is either a refuge or a calamity.

Another of the methods employed to hunt skylarks in the nineteenth century was the use of a lure called a 'lark mirror'. The lure, though it varied in design, usually comprised a small block of wood decorated with pieces of glass. Beneath the block there was a longish pole, spiked at the bottom, to enable it to be fixed into the ground. The whole thing, in its shape and profile, looked a bit like a shooting stick, one of those walking sticks whose handle unfolds to form a seat. The decoy was designed so that if you pulled a long string attached to the pole, then the block with the glass inserted into it would rotate like a spinning top. Something about the way light reflected off this spinning glass would entice migrating skylarks to come down and take a look, and the birds could then be easily shot by a waiting hunter.

The lark mirrors are something of a puzzle. Why are skylarks, in particular, attracted to the spinning glass? Is it because it resembles water, or even other skylarks? Nobody quite knows what is so inviting about the design to the birds. Nevertheless, they were brutally efficient devices, often luring hundreds of larks to their death in a single day. Lark mirrors may only show up occasionally in antiques sales today, but the skylark's helplessness in the face of our manipulation hasn't gone away. If anything, the ways we manipulate the bird's habitat are far more devastating and impactful to the species than these fatal lures the Victorians set spinning to coax the larks from the air.

Late into July there were hints the season was coming to an end. The bean crop was looking brown and withered, and the plants crackled in the warm breeze. I would no longer hear the field from inside the wood. Skirting the hollow beech, as usual, to pick my way through the hazel, the sky above the field was hot and still. I'd scan the top of the bean crop with my binoculars, back and forth, checking the tramlines' hollows.

The last skylark I heard singing, over the course of those four months I spent with the birds, was at the end of July, perched on top of one of the plants, its breast like a pale moon. I could see the lark's beak moving rapidly as it sang, and I noticed how its bill opened wider when the bird held its longer notes. The pale patch of feathers around its throat vibrated while it sang, and I could see its throat trembling, as though a heart were quivering in there. Then the lark flew up from the field and was singing above me in the air. It didn't stay up there for long, maybe 20 seconds, before I saw that movement I had come to love so much while watching these birds: the lark gradually lowered itself out of its song, wings spread wide, gliding; then its song was suddenly cut and the bird dived straight down in silence, before it levelled off and slid like an envelope into the field.

I still walk up to the field, along the path through the wood, as often as I can. If a lark is singing up there, I invariably continue along the narrow footpath that bisects the field. There is a section of this path, halfway along, that pools out into the crop. It is a good place to stand and listen to the birds. This part of the field is not intensively sown, and there are small clearings, plots, deliberately left undrilled for the larks. Apart from late summer, when the larks enter their period of quiet moult, I have heard skylarks singing up there almost every month of the year, even in grey November and on a dark morning in January. Through February, I hear the birds more often every day. By March, it feels as though there is always some part of the field that is singing. Then there is that morning in April when I look up to see a lark rising, clearing the horizon, climbing higher and higher, until it is just a speck, hidden behind its song.

V

Xylophone in the Trees

Raven

Late summer, the breeding season is over, and there are white splash marks on the tall nettles below the ravens' nest. The nest itself is large, about 2 ft in diameter, and another 2 ft in the accumulated cone-like depth of sticks and twigs that forms its base. It sits in the dark green crown of a Scots pine in the middle of a wood. Two large branches of the tree cup, and partly conceal, the nest. There is a long piece of orange baler twine, frayed, hanging below the nest like the pull cord for a light switch. I once saw a squirrel hanging from this cord, gripping the orange twine, and the bowl-like shape of the nest above made it look as though the squirrel were holding on to a balloon of sticks.

Below the nest tree a steep bank falls like a wave through the wood. The heavy clay of the bank is pitted with the hoof prints of deer and streaked with a network of badger trails. Some of the taller trees have lost their footing on the bank and fallen at a right angle to the gradient, so there are sections of the bank that look as though they are being supported by a series of beams. The best place I found to watch the ravens' nest was from one of these fallen trees. It was a huge spruce, blown over in a gale; its branches made an ideal hide into which I could slip unseen, and from where I could see the top of the nest. I could stand among the thick-needled branches and use a mossy log in front of me to rest my notebook and binoculars on. If I ventured any closer to the nest than that, or if I stuck my head above the parapet of the branches, the adult ravens would usually spot me and wake up the entire wood with their loud *krark*, *krark* warning.

There were some wonderful moments in that hide. Early-morning fog, the air soft and cool; a fallow buck coming out of the trees, its antlers tangled in mist. A roe deer in the snow, browsing the brambles near the hide, its warm breath in the cold air. Mornings spent watching the young ravens, glossy black in the sunshine, wing-exercising, frantic flapping from the top of the tree, as though signalling from a ship's mast. Seeing one of the nestlings pick up a white-splashed branch in its bill, holding it curiously, as though considering it, then pointing the branch at one of its siblings as if casting a spell with a wand. Watching the adult ravens circling above the tree, calling softly, and the young ravens in the nest jerking their heads to follow their parents' calls; the young birds' bills already huge and shiny, and a sense of the nestlings' bulk as they shifted awkwardly through the branches around the nest, making soft gurgling noises in response to the adults' calls.

There were mornings, too, spent listening to the adult pair conversing in the mist, a soothing, throaty *ker-runk* call, like the sound of a stone being plopped into a bucket of water, answered by a deeper, softer *ker-ronk*, as though the stone had then been dropped into a deep well. And strange popping, percussive noises, mixed in with low growls, gurgles and coughs. Sometimes it sounded like the ravens had a makeshift xylophone up there in the trees and were experimenting with different objects – rocks, sticks, pine cones – they could tap and scrape across the instrument. I found it fascinating how inflected the ravens' voices could be, how much it sounded like I was listening in on a conversation between the birds.

Do ravens sing? The many different vocalisations they use to communicate with each other are types of song: resonant, rhythmic, sometimes even soothing. I know that I loved hearing their strange music, and there is a soft, mournful, almost tender, gulping song the ravens sing that is among the most beautiful sounds I know.

Winter and early spring were the best times to sit in the hide. Towards the end of April and through May, the oak trees either side of the Scots pine thickened with leaf, so that each day, as though a curtain were gradually being drawn, the nest became less visible.

Some days in the hide the ravens were quiet, and I would tune in and out of the other sounds in the wood. Two robins singing, answering each other either side of a clearing, so that the usual pauses in their song were filled by the other bird, a constant robin refrain. Marsh tits sounding their rapid *dee-dee-dee-day* calls, like the sound of fat spitting in a frying pan. A great-spotted woodpecker's loud monosyllables: *teet*, *teet*, *teet*. A jackdaw's soft chuckling call, the notes bumping against each other, sounding like a wobbly chord. But by far the weirdest noise I heard didn't sound like it came from any bird. It started with a loud tapping, and at first I thought it was coming from a woodpecker, before the tapping culminated in an explosive squawk. More loud, frenetic tapping followed. There was then a burst of hysterical cackling. It sounded as though a Punch and Judy show were taking place in the tree above my head: tapping, bashing, chuckling, squawks of laughter ... I scanned the branches with my binoculars until a brightly coloured jay hopped into view, then another, and suddenly there were five jays dancing about in the top of the tall ash tree, talking, arguing, shrieking at each other's jokes. Finally, one of the jays noticed me and all five birds gushed out of the tree with a loud collective shriek. After the jays had gone, it felt, for a while, like the whole wood was in a dazed stillness, trying to absorb what it had just heard.

Despite the intimacy of the hide in relation to the ravens' nest, I never felt entirely comfortable there. Entering the wood often felt like an encroachment of sorts into their territory. I also felt more constrained in the wood, less able to observe the adult ravens when they were away from the nest. To be inside the wood, particularly during the summer months when there was so little visibility, was about just sitting quietly and tuning in to the ravens. And I continued to do that throughout the year, to sit on a fallen tree below the bank and listen to the ravens talking to each other somewhere in the canopy above.

But I also wanted to find a different perspective, somewhere I could see more of what was going on with the birds, as well as listening to them. The best location I found for this was in the field below the wood. There was a solitary oak in the middle of the field, and if I stood beneath it and put my scope up I could observe the ravens' nest site and also keep track of the birds as they moved about the environs of the nest. It took me a while to familiarise myself with this new perspective. At first I wasn't entirely sure which was the nest tree; I was so used to seeing it from inside the wood. So, I drew a sketch of all the prominent trees along the top of the bank then went into the wood and climbed the bank to check my bearings. This way I was able to confirm which tree held the nest, how many trees to the right of it was the ravens' preferred perch and also which trees the young ravens liked to hop across to when they had fledged. I came to relish this view from the field. I felt more comfortable with the added distance, that buffer between myself and the birds. And I especially loved watching the ravens over the wood, how they moved through the trees and how the sky backlit their dark shapes as the birds perched, preened and called to one another from the tops of the trees.

Of all the birds I went in search of for this book, the raven was the one most likely to turn up anywhere. I saw ravens on Rum at the shearwater colony, over the dippers' valley in Wales, and I often saw their shadow passing over the skylarks' field, as well as coming across them in several other locations I visited. The raven's expansion and recolonisation of many parts of the British Isles after decades of persecution – sometimes returning to the same nesting cliffs abandoned for over a hundred years – mean the bird's loud, percussive notes are now an acoustic backdrop to many different habitats, from lowland farmland to mountain top. The scale of that expansion is emphasised by the situation a hundred years ago when Seton Gordon noted, in the 1920s, that 'so wary has the raven become from much persecution, that only in the Outer Isles is there any hope of finding a raven's nest in an accessible spot.'

Ravens are both omnivorous in their diet and in their range of habitats. The diversity of habitats ravens can be found in across the British Isles is a small sample of the great range of habitats they occupy across the Northern Hemisphere; ravens can be found over the ice of the Arctic and over the sands of the desert, in the tundra and the savannah. They are perhaps unparalleled among birds in the range of climates and temperatures they can endure, and the different habitats to which they can adapt.

Ravens build their nests on both coastal and inland cliffs, in quarries, on electricity pylons, on buildings and in trees. They are among the earliest birds to nest, with some ravens in Britain laying as early as February, and the majority of females, in all parts of the British Isles, sitting on eggs by the last week of March (there is a Gaelic proverb that translates as: 'Nest at Candlemas, egg at Shrove-tide, bird at Easter; if the raven have them not, death then is his lot'). The nest is lined with a bedding of usually wool or hair, which helps to keep the eggs and chicks warm. Female ravens have been observed tenderly arranging this lining around very young chicks for the hatchling's comfort, and also burying the nestlings deep in the wool's warmth in cold weather. Similarly, when the temperature becomes too hot, the female will sometimes bore a hole through the bottom of the nest to increase ventilation. In hot weather the female raven has even been observed to wet her underparts in a stream or pool, then fly to the nest to cool her young with her damp feathers. When egg collecting was rife, ravens who'd had their nests robbed were sometimes observed to have torn out the wool lining so that it was strewn around the side of the nest, as though the birds had been searching through the wool for their eggs in desperation.

I often wondered with the ravens in the wood what they fed on, how far they travelled to feed and what sort of food they brought to their young. Ravens are, across their range, opportunist scavengers. That omnivorous diet includes everything from carrion to small mammals, eggs, insects, seeds, fruit and grasses. I occasionally came across a raven pair foraging over the fields, walking back and forth in that upright, strutting, slightly swaying gait they have, stopping every now and then to peck at the ground. I couldn't identify what they were eating, but assumed they must have been feeding on invertebrates, perhaps worms, moths or grasshoppers, all of which ravens are partial to (large black slugs also appear to be a favourite).

Carrion, though, is perhaps the most important component of the raven's diet. Its availability is likely to be the main reason ravens nest so early, to benefit from the abundance of late winter mortalities. The author and biologist Bernd Heinrich posited the interesting idea that 'perhaps the cold storage of winter allows food to accumulate so that ravens can nest before meat decays in the spring.' This is perhaps more applicable to the colder winters of Heinrich's study area in New England; in the British Isles it has also been suggested that ravens time their nesting to coincide with the lambing season, when there is an abundance of placentas, as well as lambs that have inevitably not survived. A study conducted in the Welsh uplands found there was a positive correlation between the number of eggs ravens laid per year and the availability of carrion in winter and spring. Perhaps, as the ornithologist and artist Donald Watson suggested, the question should not be why ravens nest so early, rather, why they don't nest earlier still, in order to feed their young on winter mortalities? The answer being, Watson conjectured, that there was insufficient daylight much earlier than March for the adult birds to find enough food for their young.

One morning in early November I was fortunate to come across the ravens at a deer carcass, the incident proving interesting for the insight it gave me into how the birds fed and behaved around a large source of carrion. I was walking towards my usual spot beneath the oak tree just before 7 a.m. It was cold, with a thick mist hanging over the field. The fallow deer were in rut and I was expecting to hear their hoarse, throaty roars coming from the wood. The previous week I had listened to a strange duet between the deer and one of the ravens; the raven was perched on a tree close to its nest, and there was a fallow buck roaming the hazel grove beneath the bank. Both the raven and the deer were calling at the same time, both making a gruff, rasping sound, though the deer's call was deeper, more like a belch, as if the noise were coming from further down its throat. I noticed how both the raven and deer also adopted the same posture when they were calling, their long, thick necks thrusting out in front of them. Sometimes the deer called, and the raven answered, and sometimes it was the other way around, like listening to a slightly distorted, interchangeable echo.

That morning in November I didn't hear the deer, but as I entered the field I was immediately aware of ravens moving and calling through the mist. Every so often I caught a glimpse of a black shape banking out of the fog, and all the time I could hear heavy wing beats – *whup, whup, whup* – circling around me, coming closer, then receding across the field. When the noise of those wings was close by, I had a sense of each downdraught disturbing the air, making wakes through the mist. It was a similar experience to being in the shearwater colony at night, that whoosh and brush of invisible wings and voices in the dark.

I immediately sensed something was different about that morning. For one thing, I had never seen the ravens behave this way over the field. I was also beginning to think there were more than just the resident pair of ravens present; there was so much movement and noise, though it was difficult to be sure exactly how many ravens were flying about in the mist. Several red kites were also there, adding to the mix, and I heard a buzzard calling over the field. I was lucky with the fog that morning; it allowed me to walk, hidden, slowly out across the field without disturbing the birds. When I reached the oak the edge of the wood shimmered into view, and as I stood watching from beneath the tree, I started to get a clearer sense of what was happening with the ravens, and why so many birds were present.

At least four ravens were concentrated around a small area just inside the wood. I could hear their calls bouncing off the trees, the birds making high-pitched *quark-quark* calls, occasionally punctuated by a deep glugging sound. The ravens were moving between the branches of an oak and the fence that marked the boundary between the wood and the field. When the birds were perched on one of the fence posts I could see their long, black tails hanging beneath them, trailing over the fence like tailcoats. The ravens kept dropping from the fence to the ground just inside the trees. There was a constant flow of birds from the ground to the fence and then up to the bronze leaves of the oak, and, given all this activity, I started to think there must be more than four ravens present. There were lots of magpies about too, flickering back and forth among the trees, as though dislodged by the movement of the ravens.

I decided to give the spot where the birds were gathered a wide berth and circle back into the wood to approach the ravens from a different angle, to try to get a better view of what was happening. Clearly, there must have been a food source inside the wood, but I couldn't identify it from the field, nor could I see the ravens once they had dropped from the fence to the ground. Once I was inside the wood I walked slowly and quietly towards the feeding spot, anxious not to disturb the birds. I kept pausing to listen out for any change in the ravens' calls that might suggest the birds had spotted me. It was like playing Grandmother's Footsteps; as I froze beside a bramble bush, a tiny goldcrest shivered over the brightly lit spiders' webs strung between the bush's leaves, the small fire of its crest making sparks every time the bird moved. I got closer and closer to the sound of the ravens, and I started to make out their dark shapes perched in the oak.

There was such a plethora of noise coming from the birds – knocking, clicking, coughing, gurgling – it felt as though I were passing a house party, everyone talking at once, the hum and noise of the chatter spilling out into the street. The birds sounded louder inside the wood than they had done in the mist over the field, as though the fog had muffled their calls. I was anticipating that at some point one of the ravens would clock me and they would all then disperse in a noisy exodus. But, perhaps because the birds were so preoccupied, and because the noise they were making meant they didn't hear me, I got to around 30 ft from where they were perched and hid myself in a stand of hazel. I was even able to put my scope up, and still the ravens went on with their clamour, oblivious to me, darting up and down from that spot on the ground just inside the wood.

It didn't take long before I noticed the splash of red and the upturned hull of ribs. There were two ravens over the carcass, feeding vigorously, probing and tearing. There were occasional lunges to push each other off the deer; the raven on the left did most of this shoving, with the other bird hopping backwards off the carcass at each lunge, before quickly hopping back on again. Magpies darted in and out, grabbing a piece of meat then retreating a foot or two. The ravens looked massive, hunched over the carcass, their thick necks and broad shoulders above the curve of their wings especially prominent. Their bills also seemed huge, as though too heavy for their heads. There was a slight grey sheen to their beaks, like murky, tarnished silver. Despite their size, their bills worked rapidly, snipping and tugging at the meat, as though the ravens were working to stitch the carcass back together, as much as to unravel it.

The two ravens left briefly to hop up into the oak tree above. Straight away, seven magpies moved in, as though till then they had been held in check by the ravens' presence. I then heard the sound of heavy wingbeats right above my head, and a few seconds later five ravens descended on the carcass and all the magpies scattered. This flow between ravens and magpies continued through the morning; the ravens would suddenly be spooked by something and leave the deer for the safety of the tree, and the magpies would then wash in like a wave. The magpies were quiet and appeared far less nervous than the ravens. There was also little sign of squabbling among them; occasionally one of them made an odd squeaking sound, and there was a brief flurry between the caller and another bird before the dispute seemed to be quickly resolved. The ravens' size dwarfed the magpies, but it also gave the magpies a nimbleness, a fleet-footedness to dart in and out and snatch a morsel from between the ravens. I loved the sense of contrast the magpies brought; their whites against the ravens' black, their manoeuvrability, their lack of timidity. A raven with several magpies escorting it resembled a black knight on a chessboard surrounded by white pawns.

Ten minutes later I counted six ravens over the carcass, covering it, as though a coat had been draped over the deer. The magpies stood a foot away in a white semicircle around the ravens. There were occasional squabbles and adjustments of positions among the ravens, but mostly they worked quickly and methodically at cleaning the carcass. I watched one raven pulling at a long white thread of sinew, as though tugging at some elongated worm. The sinew appeared a vivid white against the raven's dark face and chest. The bird next to it had a bead of flesh at the end of its bill, as though a rowan berry had stuck there. Later in the morning the sun broke through the mist, and I caught a glimpse of the bright purplish sheen over some of the ravens' cheek and wing feathers.

The next morning, I was back in the wood just as the light was coming up. I walked down the track to the hazel trees where I'd hidden the day before. I got my scope up and scanned the ground in front of me, but there was no sign of the carcass. So I walked down to the spot and after some searching found the deer had been dragged about 40 ft in the night. There was not much left – some skin, hooves, ribs and sinew all held loosely together. I dragged the remains by one of the hooves to a spot where I could watch it through my scope.

Just as I was walking back up the slope to the stand of hazel, I heard two ravens calling, flying overhead, making soft *cronking* calls. I cursed myself for being out in the open when they flew over. The ravens didn't stop but kept flying east, and I continued to hear their low contact calls as they flew up the valley. I then settled down to wait and keep watch. A crow called loudly from somewhere further up the track and several deer moved heavily through the trees behind me. I waited an hour, two hours. Nothing came to the carcass. Even the magpies didn't show.

I wondered if, yesterday, the magpies had been attracted to the spot by the ravens calling, and if those other ravens had similarly been drawn in from the wider area by calls from the resident pair. Were the other four ravens this year's young, who might still be in the area, or were they adults from other territories who had come to share the bountiful meal? I wasn't sure, but I was aware how fortunate I had been to catch and observe such unique behaviour by the birds. That none had yet visited the carcass on this second day made me realise how lucky it was, the previous day, that I'd decided to head out to the field that morning despite the mist. Just as I was preparing to dismantle my scope, a lone magpie tripped and flicked its way through the trees and landed next to the carcass. I watched it cock its head, shake out its wings, then hop up onto one of the grey ribs.

That winter I settled into a routine of heading out to the field in the early morning, and then again in the evening, as often as I could. If I timed it right in the morning, both adult ravens were usually perched on a curved branch high up on a larch overlooking the Scots pine. Even during the nesting season, there was usually one raven on the larch at dawn, while the other, the female, was incubating the eggs. The view of the ravens on that perch was always striking, with their profiles outlined against the sky, the great wedge of their tails hanging below the branch. Often, the birds would be preening when I arrived, running their bills along their wing feathers as though checking a pocket in there. Grey winter skies backlit the dark outline of the ravens beautifully. Sometimes, one of the birds would stretch out its long neck to call and, from where I stood several hundred metres away in the field, there was a slight delay between the raven opening its bill and the sound of the call itself, as though the noise reached me a fraction of a second late.

The pair usually staggered their departures from the perch. One of them would leave first and circle over the wood, calling to its mate. Only after a minute or so would the other bird stretch out a wing over the edge of the larch, then drop from its perch to follow its mate with a brief *quark*, which I read as, 'Okay, okay, I'm coming now!' Occasionally, standing beneath the oak tree, I would hear slow, heavy wingbeats above me, almost swan-like in the heave and *whup-whup* sound they made through the air. I knew straight away it was one of the ravens, but I never dared to look up in case my movement spooked the bird. I loved those moments, hearing the raven's wingbeats just a few feet above me; the sound their wings made was as much a part of the birds' soundtrack as their calls.

While ravens are remarkably adaptable with respect to the range of habitats they have colonised, there is one structural aspect of a landscape that, as with skylarks, is extremely important to ravens – a habitat's openness. Ravens need wide, open spaces over which they can forage. They are able to do this in woodland that has a reasonably open aspect, but where blanket afforestation occurs, as it does over many parts of the British uplands, this tends to have the effect of squeezing ravens out, just as it does many other bird species.

Studies of raven territories in the Cheviots and Southern Uplands made in the 1970s, for example, where extensive afforestation had occurred, found a decrease of 50 breeding pairs of ravens from a population of around 90 pairs in the 1950s. By the 1990s it was clear that many of these territories had become permanently deserted, with the greatest decline occurring in areas of greatest afforestation. Ravens are resilient and adaptable birds, and, where these conifer plantations are smaller and more fragmented, offering ground for the birds to still forage over, ravens are often present. But a landscape that is smothered wholesale in densely packed conifers usually has the effect of pushing ravens out.

* * *

Towards the end of January it snowed on and off for several days. At night the snow froze hard, and in the morning I would crunch across the field, following the frozen dent of my footprints from the previous evening. Fieldfares often gathered in the oak and, as I approached the tree, twenty or so birds would shake out of the branches with their squeaky chatter and I'd catch a glimpse of their ash-coloured necks, the reddish glow of their breasts. With little to eat, the deer had taken to browsing the bark on fallen branches and on some of the smaller trees; the patterns their gnawing made looked like a kind of writing, like the faded graffiti people had carved onto the larger, smoother beech trees in the wood. The snow made the wood quieter, so the ravens' calls sounded closer. Standing in the field, I'd find myself wanting to enter the wood, to listen to the ravens in that new stillness the snow had brought.

Bernd Heinrich recounts a vivid experience of listening to a raven singing. He describes finding the song so 'uplifting and exuberant' that he got out his tape recorder and started recording the bird. This particular raven, a male, sang for hours, just 15 ft from where Heinrich sat, 'gurgling, chortling, yelling, trilling, bill-snapping, *quorking*, and making sounds like water rattling pebbles.'

I never heard the ravens in the wood sing for as long as Heinrich's bird did. But I have heard them make just as eclectic a range of sounds – *crunks*, clonks, low whistles, quizzical-sounding *kar-arks*, the last syllable inflected, so that it sounds like the raven is asking a question. The times, though, that I've most felt like the ravens were singing was when I heard them make a more subdued, softer, more rhythmic sound. I called it their 'gulping song' because to me it always sounded like the birds were making a pronounced deep gulping noise, like the sound a gluggle jug makes when water is poured from it. *Glunk–glunk* – a pause of about 10 seconds – then the raven would call again, *glunk–glunk*. The song had a relaxed, soothing quality to it, making me feel that the ravens were relaxed themselves and the call, if it had a meaning, meant something along the lines of 'All is well.' I heard this song at all times of the year, but most often during the long evenings of mid-summer; still, cool evenings in the middle of the wood, song thrushes singing along the top of the bank, large brown hawker dragonflies hawking along the paths. Then one of the ravens would start to sing, close to the nest tree, soft, plosive gulps: *glunk–glunk*; *glunk–glunk*, like listening to a slow heartbeat.

The ravens Heinrich studied in Maine would almost certainly have sounded different to the pair I listened to in the wood. Even across the United States there is a marked variation in regional 'accents' among ravens, and Heinrich describes a trip he made to a part of Yellowstone National Park in Montana where the knocking sounds the ravens made sounded 'more wooden than the more liquid and rapid calls of those with the Maine accent' that he was used to. Heinrich added that he heard 'distinctly different calls' among ravens in 'every area outside New England' where he had been, and on a visit to the Canadian Arctic, in a community where there were large numbers of ravens, Heinrich writes that he 'heard sounds or nuances of calls almost every day that I had never heard before'.

A study in Switzerland, published in 2002, that recorded ravens in an area of 1,000 km², found an amazing 79 different call types being used among a sample of 74 ravens, with some of these calls found to be specific to individuals, some to the sex of the bird and some to the geographical area. As with skylarks, the greater the distance between raven territories in the Swiss study, the fewer call types were shared between birds, and there was a notable geographical boundary in the study area across which call types were less frequently shared. Interestingly, those ravens that occupied territories along this boundary tended to be 'bilingual', sharing call types that were used on either side of the border. Established raven pairs will sometimes communicate using their own personal variation of an innate call, and it has been suggested that this may enhance the emotional bond between the pair – a bit like the way some human couples use baby talk – as well as helping them to locate and identify one another over distance. Additionally, if one of the raven pair becomes lost or separated from the other, the remaining bird will call to its lost mate using a call phrase that its partner, rather than itself, habitually used. It is an intriguing and moving gesture; by adopting its partner's voice, the remaining bird seems almost to be articulating its sense of loss: I have lost *you*, the *sound* of you.

Through February and into March a large flock of bramblings – around 30 birds, with rusty orange breasts, flecks of white down their wings, thick yellow bills like arrow tips – took up residence in the trees along the edge of the wood. The male bramblings' heads were starting to blacken, sharpening the orange of their breasts. In the evenings, a blackbird sang from the dead branch of an oak, and it sometimes felt as though the whole wood was listening to its song.

The raven pair were spending more and more time around the nest tree. In early February I saw one of the birds carrying a stick up to the nest, and now every evening one of the ravens would perform a fast, patrolling flight around the vicinity of the nest just before it got dark, rushing through the trees, skimming the top of the wood. I wondered if the pre-roost gathering of the rook and jackdaw flocks, which swirled over the wood like a restless cloud, set the ravens off on their own swerving flights. If the other raven stayed near the nest during these dusk sorties, I would often hear them making a cork-popping sound, while its mate flew back and forth over the wood. Eventually the pair would settle in the top branches of the pine for the night, and I would pack up my scope and call it a day. By then, the fallow deer had usually drifted out of the wood and were grazing in the dusk not far from where I stood.

Something I noticed during the winter months was that the ravens were often perched in one of the evergreen trees, either the Scots pine, where they had their nest, or one of the neighbouring tall spruces. It meant that it sometimes took me a while to locate the birds, especially if they were silent; I'd scan the trees with my scope until I picked up a dark shape among the branches. I wondered if the ravens preferred these evergreens (as opposed to the deciduous oaks and ashes) to perch in during the winter because they were more hidden against the dark needles of the pines. I also wondered if that's why they had selected the Scots pine for their nest (a tree that ravens frequently nest in), for the same reason that it offered their young a safer, more camouflaged refuge; certainly, I noticed that once the fledging ravens were hopping about in the pine around the nest, they were well hidden among the dark foliage. Sometimes the first I'd know of a raven being in the tree was when its head and broad neck popped right out of the flat canopy from one of the topmost branches. It always struck me, when this happened, that the bird had climbed up to poke its head through a trapdoor in the tree's ceiling.

As well as spending more time around the nest in February, the adult ravens had also started to display more frequently over the wood. There were two kinds of display that I observed. One was a type of bowing display, which usually started with one of the birds calling from a perch. When its mate joined it in the same tree, the bird that had been calling would hop down to join its partner on the same branch. Frequently, there followed a fair bit of bill-scraping, running their beaks over the branch and preening. The most common behaviour I observed in the ravens was this bill-scraping; the action is similar to the way you might run a blade over a whetstone, back and forth, constantly turning the blade over to hone its edge. The ravens may well have done this to sharpen their bills, as well as perhaps, more obviously, to clean them after feeding. That I witnessed the pair often bill-scraping next to each other on the same perch also suggested that there might be a display element involved in this behaviour. After about a minute of bill-scraping, the bird that had called (I assumed this was the male) would face its mate and begin a series of bobbing, bowing movements, its neck feathers puffed out. After this bowing performance both birds would briefly touch bills, and that final gesture – the bill 'kiss' – seemed to mark an end to the display, as one of the ravens would then fly off.

The other display the ravens performed was a beautiful aerial manoeuvre. I usually witnessed this when one of the birds was high above the nest tree. The raven would be flying along and then suddenly flip over onto its back so that, for a brief second, it was flying upside down, before righting itself again. I didn't witness these rolls often, but when I did catch one of the ravens performing these tumbling, playful flights it was such a joy to see. These roll-flights occurred most frequently in the last week of February, and they coincided with what felt like peak activity around the nest. That week I saw constant comings and goings from the nest, and on several occasions I saw one of the ravens retrieve food from a nearby cache to bring to a branch near the nest, where it then fed its mate. During this period, the male raven also spent a lot of time perched on a tree next to the Scots pine, overlooking the nest, calling loudly, *kark*, *ka-aark*, throwing out his whole neck as he made each call, his crest feathers raised in a spiky quiff.

By the middle of March, the male raven had become extremely vigilant and vocal around the nest. I assumed this meant that the young had either hatched or were close to hatching. On one occasion I watched the male flinging himself after a crow, beating hard in pursuit, looking like he was intending to seize the crow mid-air, before the raven tipped out of the pursuit and tumbled back down towards the wood, calling a short, sharp *kark*, *kark*, *kark* as he dropped. He then performed a series of tight loops, very quickly, above a felled area of the wood. As I watched him, it felt as though he was now in a state of hyper-alertness, patrolling the area around the nest, displaying, relentlessly driving off any potential threats. Two days after the encounter with the crow, I heard a raven calling loudly in a harsh rasping call I'd sometimes heard them make around buzzards. I looked up to see two ravens flying fast towards the north. One bird was clearly pursuing the other, calling vigorously. I watched them fly like this for over a mile, then the pursuing bird suddenly turned and began to fly back towards the wood, much more slowly, making a soft, deep *ker-uk* sound as it flew. I assumed that what I had witnessed was the adult male driving off another raven from a different territory. What was fascinating was the contrast in calls between the outward and return flight over the valley; from that furious, rasping call to a much calmer, softer call the bird used as he drew closer to the wood. I had the sense, on the return flight, that the raven was talking to his mate back at the nest, as though informing her that all was well, that the interloper was gone.

The playfulness that seems inherent in the raven's rolling display flight is something that manifests itself in other aspects of the bird's behaviour; ravens appear to be innately playful birds. They have been observed 'sledging', sliding down roofs and banks of snow; bathing in the spray that is shot into the air through the nozzles of irrigation hoses; hanging and swinging upside down on branches and on power lines; even, in a quirky adaptation of the roll-flight, flying upside down for at least a hundred metres. Other typical playful behaviour includes tugging at each other's tails, playing with stones and sticks, and passing these among each other. The birds also seem to enjoy gathering objects such as bits of turf or sheep dung, flying up with them, then letting go, and shooting down to try and catch the object before it hits the ground.

Dropping things from a height extends to some other unusual behaviour witnessed in ravens. They have been observed, for example, dropping tufts of dried grass onto nesting kittiwakes on a cliff below to dislodge the birds from their eggs. And two unfortunate ornithologists in Oregon had the unnerving experience of rocks 'the size of a golf ball' being dropped on them by a raven from a cliff above. At first, the ornithologists (who were studying raptor populations) had assumed the initial rock had been accidentally dislodged by the raven, but when they looked up, they saw a raven with a rock in its beak, and with 'a slight flip of its head' the bird then tossed this second rock down onto the two men. Six more missiles rained down on the pair, who were struggling to find shelter on the cliff, with one of the rocks hitting one of the men on his leg. This particular raven appeared to be protecting its nest on the cliff, and in a separate incident a bird ringer had pine cones thrown at him by a raven who was also protecting its nest.

'Tugging at tails' extends to other animals, with sleeping dogs and cats, in particular, being a favourite target for ravens. Seton Gordon once observed a raven baiting a collie dog by allowing the collie to rush excitedly across a field after it:

> The raven allowed the dog almost to reach it, then rose into the air, to fly a little way and then settle once more, looking hopefully back at the dog. The dog, annoyed and excited, again rushed to the attack. The raven again waited, then did the same thing as before. The dog, now considerably out of breath, again pursued and the game (a game at least from the raven's point of view) went on for some time.

Was the raven that Gordon witnessed teasing the collie simply, as Gordon surmised, being playful, having a 'game' with the dog? Or was it perhaps trying to draw the dog's attention to something, to a potential source of food, for instance? Ravens are known to behave in a similar way around wolves (and other predators such as bears); they will signal to the pack, usually by calling, where prey can be located, so that the ravens then benefit when the wolves open up the carcass or make a kill.

The relationship between ravens and wolves is a particularly fascinating one. Bernd Heinrich, who has studied this relationship and subtitled one of his books about ravens *Investigations and Adventures with Wolf-Birds*, posed an intriguing question: is the mutualism between wolves and ravens so deep-rooted that it causes ravens to behave 'shyly' – to be distrustful – towards any food source that has *not* been killed by wolves (behaviour that Heinrich frequently observed among ravens in Maine), given that ravens seem to display no such hesitation when it comes to feeding on a carcass that *has* freshly been killed by wolves? In other words, are ravens and wolves so interdependent that ravens can seem uncomfortable, as Heinrich put it, feeding on a carcass where wolves are *not* present?

And does such mutualism sometimes also extend to the raven's relationship with humans? Many Inuit communities believed that ravens indicated the location of game to hunting parties by dipping their wings, then tucking in a wing so that the bird's body tilted to the side, pointing out the direction the hunters needed to follow. If the hunt was successful, the choicest titbits would always be left for the raven by way of a thank you. In a more modern twist on this human–raven relationship, game wardens in the US have found that if they go to a spot where ravens are circling, there is a good chance they will be able to catch poachers literally red-handed.

Whether the raven Gordon observed was playing or signalling to the dog, either behaviour would suggest the bird possessed a high level of cognitive skill. Exactly how high is something that was tested in a 2020 study that specifically looked at the physical and social cognitive performance of ravens. The study tested the birds for their performance in spatial memory, counting, problem solving and communication, and concluded from these tests that ravens not only have 'developed, sophisticated cognitive skills', but that their skills are at the same level as chimpanzees and orangutans.

As well as clearly being playful and highly intelligent birds, ravens have also, perhaps most interestingly, been observed to show sensitivity towards the emotions of other ravens. A study in 2010, which posed the question 'Do ravens show consolation?', found that ravens who witnessed other ravens (with whom they shared a valuable relationship) being attacked by dominant birds appeared to console the victim after the attack by making gestures such as sitting beside it, preening and touching bills. This demonstrates another parallel with chimpanzees, who have also been observed to console each other when one of their number is distressed.

A bright morning, frost over the field. When I reached the oak tree, I noticed a pair of foxes sitting in the field close to the edge of the wood. One of the foxes was grooming itself, while the other was rolling on its back and sliding through the frost. I watched them for a few moments until the fox that was rolling had drawn a series of swirling patterns through the frost. A raven flew over the wood to the east calling loudly, its mate following in its slipstream. I decided that morning to head into the wood and listen to the ravens from the fallen tree beneath the bank.

A blackbird flustered and scolded when I propped myself against the trunk of the fallen tree. I could hear a song thrush singing from the top of the bank. The ravens had settled on a perch near the Scots pine, and I could hear them talking softly to each other. One of the pair was making a quiet, hollow-sounding *clock*, *clock* call, like someone tapping on an empty barrel. I could see the raven perched high up in the larch overlooking the nest tree, and I watched its grey bill opening as it called. I couldn't spot the other raven, but it was answering the *clock*, *clock* calls with a very deep, soft, pronounced *glunk*. I put my binoculars down and listened.

Sometimes it sounded like one of the ravens was asking a question of the other by making a gruff, upward-inflected *quaa*, *quaa* call, to which its mate would answer with a muffled *crump*; '*quaa*, *quaa*': '*crump*'. Other times, it sounded as though they were talking to each other underwater; a low-pitched, gloopy-sounding *clunk-clunk* was immediately answered by a slightly higher-pitched *clink*. Then one of the ravens would revert to the hollow *clock-clock* calls, its mate keeping time beneath with those soft, deep gulps. I loved hearing these exchanges; I could have sat on the log all morning listening to the ravens' xylophone music, their strange, tender-sounding, underwater songs.

In all those months I spent watching the ravens I sometimes wondered if the birds were able to recognise me. Heinrich's ravens in Maine recognised him, even when he dressed in a neighbour's clothes to try to dupe the birds (the ravens were also not deceived when the neighbour dressed in Heinrich's clothes with a mask on, the birds flying about in fright when the neighbour approached them). I always wore the same clothes when I went out to the wood, a different coat in winter being the only anomaly. I never sought to get too close to the ravens, but on several occasions one of the birds flew low over my head and paused there, for no more than a couple of seconds, looking down at me. The ravens were always silent when they did this. I can't, of course, claim this as any kind of recognition on the part of the ravens, but I have never experienced that unsolicited proximity with any other wild bird, nor the sense of being looked at by a bird, as I did on those occasions with the raven.

Do ravens possess a theory of mind? That is, are they capable of attributing mental states to other animals, to other ravens? The study that looked at consolation responses in ravens suggests that they possibly do. Another study, conducted in 2016, that observed how ravens behaved around food when a peephole in their cage was open or closed, and when they could hear other ravens calling nearby (but not see these other birds), found that ravens guarded their caches of food when the peephole was open, but not when it was closed. This observation suggested to the researchers that ravens have the ability to recognise the possibility of being seen by a competitor, despite not actually observing that competitor gazing at their food. So, the paper suggests, the ravens are inferring the possibility of being seen by another bird, rather than confirming it through observation.

As well as the findings of that 2016 study, there are numerous anecdotal reports of ravens behaving in a way that suggests they possess a theory of mind. One particularly interesting account came from a trapper in north-west Saskatchewan in 1995, who came across a raven feeding on a carcass. Every so often this raven would stop feeding, roll over and lie still for a few minutes. The trapper noticed that the raven did this whenever a flock of ravens flew by, and he concluded that the bird must be playing dead, misleading the other ravens into thinking that the carcass was poisoned and therefore should be avoided.

Heinrich also addressed the question of whether ravens are conscious and emotional. He pointed out that ravens have the largest brain cephalisation – the size of a brain that is greater than would be predicted by body size alone – of any bird (most passerine birds have an encephalisation index of between 4 and 8; a raven's is 19), and that their intelligence relates to the complexity of the social world they live in. Heinrich's own view, which he sums up elegantly, and which stems from his close observations of the birds, is that they 'are able to manipulate mental images for solving problems' and that 'they are aware of some aspects of their private reality, seeing with their minds at least some of what they have seen with their eyes.'

One afternoon in early spring I was cycling with my two sons back from their school along a track that runs beside the top of the wood. The boys had reached the age where they could easily, fearlessly, shoot ahead of me on their bikes, while I puffed and dawdled in their wake. It had been dry for several weeks and the boys' bikes kicked up clouds of dust as they raced ahead. I suddenly noticed they had stopped and were leaning their bicycles against a tree.

When I caught up with them they didn't say anything, just nodded, and one of them pointed at the tree above them. I looked up and there was the raven, huge, sitting on a wide branch just a few feet above us. The bird was scraping its bill along the branch, arching its long neck each time it leant over. We could hear the scratchy, sandpaper sound its bill made against the bark. Then the raven stopped and looked down at us, feathers puffed out around its head, bill open, as though about to call. But it didn't make any sound, just sat there watching us, blinking, occasionally turning its head with stiff, jerky movements. The boys were completely silent. Why didn't the bird fly away? I had never encountered a raven as close as this; I'd never been looked at by any bird in the way – and for the length of time – this raven looked at us. I could tell the boys were transfixed, awed by the proximity of such a huge bird. I had a strong sense that the raven was waiting for us to leave. And after a while, we picked up the bikes and began to wheel them away.

VI

Rather like the Howl of a Dog

Black-throated Diver

The first loch had so many small islands dotted over it, you could almost have crossed it by leaping from one to the next. I thought it looked perfect for divers; the loch was shallow, with lots of islets to choose from for the birds to haul up and lay their eggs, and enough of a runway between the islands for the divers to taxi and take off into flight. I sat in the wood and scanned the loch below me with binoculars, checking each island in turn.

There was a pair of Canada and a pair of greylag geese, and several mallard on the water. But no sign of any divers. Beyond the loch, the low hills were pale and brown from winter, and beyond them the tops of the mountains were white with snow.

I walked on through the wood to the next loch, and again sat down and scanned the water. There was just one small island in a sheltered bay close to the wood, with a few tiny islets, no more than a couple of metres or so across, scattered around it. The loch was shallow, with rocks sticking up out of the water some distance from the shore. It was less sheltered here, the surface of the loch dipping and rolling in the breeze. Again, there was no sign of any divers, but the small, dark waves in the centre of the loch played diver-shaped tricks with my eyes.

It was getting late, so I found a sheltered spot inside the stone walls of an old sheep fank and put up my tent. I cooked some supper, then washed up in the freezing water of the river. Between my tent and the loch was a large area of bog, and I could hear snipe in among the reeds, making a squeaky, flapping *chick-aa–chick-aa–chick-aa* call. Like the ventriloquial nightjars, the snipe seemed to throw their calls across the bog, giving the impression that they were constantly on the move. I could never predict where a call would come from next, and it was quite disorientating listening to the snipe, like trying to follow a game of acoustic pinball.

I wanted to take another look at the loch and thought, given how still the evening had become, there was a chance I might at least hear the divers if they were present. I found a wobbly, leapfrogging route across the bog, and reached a dryish mound overlooking the loch. A thin layer of mist had gathered over the water, and I could no longer see the wood on the far shore. I waited till it was almost dark but heard nothing besides the snipe mislaying their calls in the mist. Perhaps the divers weren't here after all, and I would have to move on in the morning and explore some different lochs in the area. Returning to the tent, I watched a barn owl flying slowly up the glen. Earlier, a curlew had been displaying close to the fank while I prepared supper, and I caught a glimpse of its long, curved bill and the white above its tail like a cornice of snow.

That night was very cold, the temperature dropping below freezing, and I found it difficult to sleep. Several times I heard snipe drumming through the long twilight above me; a strange, whirring, rubbing sound the snipe make by vibrating their two stiffened outer tail feathers when they dive during their display flights. The timbre of the sound is a bit like the one a mobile phone makes when it twitches and vibrates on a table in silent mode, but the snipe's drumming is much faster, more quivering, as though the phone's vibrating has gone into overdrive. At 3.30 a.m. the sound of drumming was so loud I went out in the pre-dawn light to see if I could spot the bird. The tent was white with frost, and the frozen grass in the fank crunched when I stepped on it. I could hear the snipe drumming all around me, but it was still too dark to properly make out the bird. I stood there waiting for the dawn to come up over the pine forest to the east, listening to the snipe's whirring song.

What does a black-throated diver sound like? These are some of the descriptions of the bird's call that I have read, and, if they have something in common, it is that hearing a black-throated diver appears to have a great impact on those who experience the sound: 'perhaps the weirdest, most awesome sound ever to break the stillness of the mountain scene'; 'swelling from a guttural twanging to a trumpeting wail; a maniacal sound'; 'as if a lost spirit was bewailing its fate'; 'strikingly like the unavailing cries of a human mother'; 'dismal and melancholy'; 'weird, strident, metallic calls'; 'like those of a large lost cat'; 'no more unearthly bird sound one could hear on Scottish lochs than this'; 'strange goose-like sounds, a grinding honking noise with an occasional high wail, though the wails were much shorter than usual – more like a very loud metallic double curlew cry'; 'a loud yelp, rather like the howl of a dog'; 'a strange and powerful clamour'; 'very like the howling of a wolf'; 'weird and discordant cries'; 'a remarkable and far-carrying goose-like clamour'; a 'strange hollow call'; 'mingled laughter, howling, and every other earthly and unearthly cry'.

Black-throated divers have several different types of call. The most striking, and the one that the majority of the descriptions above try to convey, is a kind of yodelling. It appears to be a territorial call, performed mostly by the male diver, often in response to calls from divers in neighbouring territories or if another diver flies over a pair's nesting territory. Its haunting, otherworldly quality arises from the way the bird's initial low, whistling note lurches into a higher-pitched, longer note, thus producing a pulsing, wailing effect that does, in a way, resemble the howl of a wolf, or possibly a ghostly ambulance siren whose battery is on the wane. Perhaps because of the acoustics of the water, the diver's call has a quivering intensity to it, and it is much weirder, more echoey than a wolf's howl. Added to this, the noise is incredibly loud, 'dominating all other sounds over tundra or taiga, both by day and night'. On a clear day it can be heard over 6 miles away.

Besides this strange, beautiful 'yodelling', the divers also have a 'moaning' call that is a little like a human humming loudly, with a slight rise in pitch around the middle of the sequence; its function is probably as a contact call, to locate young or an absent mate. There is also a short, deep, frog-like call, a cross between a woodcock's 'burp' and a raven's croak. This call is often heard at night, is sometimes given in an alternating duet by both the male and female diver and has been heard in flight and when a diver has been disturbed. There are also variations on these calls; the 'moaning' can be abbreviated to a single 'humming' note, and the 'yodelling' can lack the distinctive rise in frequency and sound instead more like a 'wailing' call, with a prolonged falling note. This 'wailing' call, essentially a low-intensity form of yodelling, also seems to be adopted in territorial encounters and between neighbouring pairs of divers.

All of these calls have an unusual and evocative quality. To me, the black-throated diver's calls – especially the 'yodelling' song, but also the grunts, yelps and moans that make up the bird's repertoire of sounds – remind me of the recordings of the songs of humpback whales I've listened to; the diver's calls, at least, possess that same curiously hypnotic, reverberating quality that whale song has. To hear a black-throated diver for the first time can be disconcerting in the way that it's not immediately obvious the sound has been made by a bird. The Victorian naturalist Charles St John mentions that he could scarcely persuade a companion he was with, who was not used to the birds, that the sounds black-throated divers made 'did not arise from a number of people shouting and laughing'. Seton Gordon – who *was* used to the birds – once mistook the not dissimilar (though more anguished-sounding) call of a red-throated diver for the cries, Gordon speculated, of a 'solitary hiker', who 'had perhaps met with an accident and, wading in the lochan, had been trapped in the liquid peat'. The ornithologist Edward Armstrong, in his study of magico-religious traditions involving birds, points out that the diver's voice 'has a very human quality', making it relatively easy for people to imitate the bird's 'quasi-human wails'. Perhaps that's another way to describe the diver's call; like the sound of a person speaking through the syrinx (the vocal organ) of a bird. The diver's song – that haunting, echoey wail – is not like the songs of other birds.

* * *

After listening to the snipe in the early morning, I went back to my sleeping bag for an hour or two, then got up and started to make some porridge. While the porridge was cooking I sipped a cup of tea and watched a lapwing displaying near the edge of the bog in a crazy, twisting, electric dance. A skylark landed in the grass close to the fank, and I had a fine view of the low crest on the lark's crown, the buffs and whites of its plumage. I swung my binoculars over the bog towards the loch where several greylags were making a clamour in the shallows. Something low in the water, behind the geese, caught my eye; larger, and sitting much lower in the water than the mallard the previous night. It was too far out in the loch to identify clearly, even through binoculars, but I had an inkling what it was. I hurriedly assembled the scope on its tripod, rose the tripod's legs above the height of the fank and got it focused on the loch. And there it was, the unmistakable colours and outline of a black-throated diver.

The dog Seton Gordon observed being teased by a raven was called Dileas, and she appears in his writing about birds on several occasions. In fact, Dileas comes across, in her various cameos, more like an ornithologist's assistant than just a faithful companion (she even receives a dedication at the front of Gordon's 1931 book, *In the Highlands*). And it is Dileas's role during Gordon's work with black-throated divers where her collie intelligence and resolve come to the fore.

Two incidents stand out, both of which Gordon wrote about at length. On the first occasion he was observing black-throated divers from a rowing boat out on a loch. Two days earlier he had landed on the divers' nesting island and discovered two diver chicks that had just hatched, appearing 'like small balls of sooty down' in the nest. The adult divers called anxiously to the young, and one of the chicks, in response, entered the loch. Though it was the chick's first time in water, it swam strongly out to its parents and even dived with them. Gordon heard the male diver making a loud yelp, 'rather like the howl of a dog', and he observed the bird make a great splash before diving, presumably, he thought, to distract attention from its young. The female sometimes made a wailing cry, and both adult birds called to the young with 'a soft grunting note' (I assume this was the 'croaking', frog-like call I mentioned earlier).

As Gordon was rowing back towards the island where the divers had their nest, he noticed one of the lesser black-backed gulls, who were also nesting on the island, suddenly swoop down on the diver chick, which had momentarily drifted away from its mother. Just a few minutes earlier the chick had been riding in safety on its parent's back, but now it was exposed, and in 2 seconds the gull would have grabbed the chick and carried it off. Quick as a flash, Gordon yelled at the top of his voice, and Dileas, who had been sitting patiently in the boat with him, joined in by barking as loudly as she could. The gull took fright and swerved away from the diver chick. But that wasn't an end to it; the female diver, with all the noise they were making, now saw Gordon and the dog as the threat, and she 'sprang out of the water with a wild cry', flying straight at them with that long, sharp beak, passing just a few feet from the boat. Gordon, no doubt a little shaken by this charge, still managed to herd the diver chick away from the reach of the gulls, and once he felt the chick was safe he rowed quickly away.

Dileas saved the day with her barking, of course, but the account is also interesting for its ornithological observations: the range of calls Gordon heard the divers make, and the different context of these calls; that the divers carried their young on their backs, as some grebes also do; that the hatchling took to the water so confidently and skilfully, and was able to dive at only a few days old; the splashing distraction display of the male; and that the adult female diver was so fearless in defence of her young. Perhaps Gordon's most unusual observation, though, is that the adult divers momentarily allowed such a young chick to drift away from them, as, typically, they are very protective parents, closely attending to their young at all times.

Young divers, in fact, are dependent on their parents for over three months, with the family remaining on the nesting territory till they migrate in the autumn to the sea. The diver's year is therefore split almost equally in two, with pairs arriving on their breeding lochs in April (in Scandinavia, black-throated divers return on the day the ice thaws), and then departing for the sea, usually sometime in September. The eve of this September departure appears to be a particularly vocal occasion for black-throated divers, as Gordon's evocative description suggests:

> The air was mild and still, and a strange and powerful clamour was wafted up to them from the loch far below and already indistinct in the shades of approaching night. This was the excited discussion which each year is carried on by the divers the evening before their departure. The next morning the birds had gone; they had exchanged the small waves of their loch for the ocean swell.

After I had spotted the diver on the loch, I finished breakfast and tidied up as quickly as I could. The first thing was to try and get a little closer to the loch without the birds knowing I was there. The low mound on the other side of the bog, which I'd walked to the night before, was, I felt, a good place to aim for, as I could lie down and observe the loch from there without being seen. I could peer over the top of the mound with my binoculars, and even the vigilant greylags didn't notice me lying there.

I found the diver again out on the loch. The bird was sitting low in the water, constantly dipping its head below the surface as it swam. Its colours and the patterning over its plumage were remarkable; Donald Watson, with his artist's eye, wrote that the black-throated diver's pewter head appears 'smoother than seems possible for feathers', adding that the pattern of black and white lines on the bird's neck 'seems to have been drawn by a fine brush'. I loved the way the diver's soft grey head contrasted with the dark grey water of the loch, like the different shades of a rain cloud. I found the patterning down the bird's neck mesmerising in its subtlety, and there was a striking zebra crossing of black and white stripes along the diver's back, which also stood out against the dark background of the loch. As the bird glided through the water, it opened its bill wide, as though yawning, and made a soft *yonk-yonk* call, which reminded me more of a woodcock than a raven, and which I took to be the diver's 'croaking' call. The bird kept to the same straight line, swimming across the loch, calling periodically. I glanced over towards the other bank, where the diver was headed, and there was its mate, sitting low and sleek on the nest.

The second instalment of Dileas's black-throated diver heroics is even more memorable than her saving the diver chick from the marauding gull. A few days after that incident, Gordon and his wife borrowed a collapsible canvas boat in order to reach an island in another loch where they had spotted a diver nesting. First, they had to drag the boat across a 'seemingly interminable bog' to reach the lochside. Finally, when they came to inflate it, they found to their horror that the rubber had disintegrated and so the boat could not be inflated properly. With miles to the nearest repair kit, they decided to launch the frail craft anyway, with only one of them crossing to the island in the boat at a time. Gordon's wife Audrey went first, with the camera and plates, the boat sitting less than an inch above the water as she made the precarious crossing. Meanwhile, Gordon paid out a long line, attached to the boat, so that he could pull the boat back across the loch after Audrey had disembarked on the island.

Amazingly, Audrey reached the island without capsizing and Gordon commenced hauling the boat back for his turn. However, when the boat was halfway across the loch, he suddenly realised the paddle was still on the island with Audrey. What to do? Audrey was stuck on the island with a paddle but no boat; Gordon was stuck on the mainland with a boat but no paddle, and the nearest thing to a paddle – a stick – was at least 30 miles from where they were, far out on the moor. Gordon thought about swimming across to the island, but it was too far and the water too cold. Then Audrey had an idea; she whistled to Dileas, who easily swam across to the island. Audrey then tied the paddle to the dog's tail, carried the weight of it to the water's edge, and pushed the paddle off the moment Gordon whistled to Dileas from the mainland. Dileas then swam back to Gordon and the boat, towing the paddle behind her! The dog didn't even notice the weight of the paddle until she reached the shore and was leaving the water.

Thanks (again) to superdog (and Audrey's quick-thinking), Gordon was able to take some remarkable photographs of the diver from a hide he and Audrey built on the island. He was also able to record this wonderful observation of the female diver:

> She gives the impression of possessing unlimited reserve strength, and swims just as easily against the wind as with it. She reminded me of a torpedo-boat

> destroyer as she suddenly, without effort, increased her speed in the teeth of a fresh breeze. By comparison with her, the lightly floating gulls were as sailing craft. Sometimes as she swam she turned almost on her back and preened her beautiful flanks, that were as snowy as the plumage of a sea-gull.

Early twentieth-century black-throated diver research is notable for its unorthodox fieldwork techniques. Besides the Gordons' use of a leaky boat and their oar-towing dog, there is an account from 1925 of recently hatched diver chicks being placed in someone's cap 'to keep them warm' while a hide was constructed close to the divers' nest, from where the birds could be photographed. The resulting black and white photographs, taken by Arthur Brook, are striking portraits of the birds, with one image capturing a rare moment when both adult divers are on the nest at the same time. As an aside, these two chicks, which were kept cosy in the man's cap, appear to have been unusually harmonious, sibling aggression in black-throated divers being common during the first five days after the chicks hatch. These fights appear to diminish once the chicks start to spend more time in the water, as though their brief stint on the nest agitates the young divers, making them restless for the water.

The gold medal for early twentieth-century unconventional black-throated diver research, however, must go to the egg-collecting ornithologist Norman Gilroy, who in a paper published in 1923 describes swimming 'laboriously' to five different islands in a Sutherland loch 'in arctic weather'. Previously, Gilroy had found divers' nests on each of these large islands, and he was sure, that season, that at least one of the islands held a nest. But after searching each island in turn, it wasn't till Gilroy had swum back to the shore that he discovered a nest 'on a grassy spit in a little bay on the mainland'.

It seems that Gilroy thought little of swimming out to islands in freezing Highland lochs. On another occasion, he describes watching a loch, hoping to spot a black-throated diver. After half an hour of waiting, and with no sign of the bird, Gilroy 'decided to strip' and swim out to search the islands. The first island he reached 'yielded nothing but a wigeon and a common gull'. He searched the second island all the way round and was just about to swim back to shore when a diver crashed out from under a bank, bowling Gilroy 'clean over into the water'.

It's tempting to think – both with the birds who bypassed the islands to nest on the mainland and the bird who bowled him over in the water – that the divers had the last laugh with Gilroy (with an added 'splash' of Schadenfreude, as he was an egg collector whom Donald Watson described as 'a most devious character'). Gilroy's escapades did, however, result in some interesting observations. For instance, after being knocked into the water by the diver, he examined the bird's nest closely and described it as being 'very substantially built of grass, heather stalks and weeds on a dry, rather powdery bank of peat, and was well underneath the overhanging fringe of heather – altogether an unusual situation'.

Gilroy then provides this useful summary of the many black-throated diver nests he, presumably, swum to:

> The nest is generally a fairly substantial structure of turf, grass, heather and water-plants carelessly put together, but the whole showing a very decided rim and general formation; it is probably added to considerably in the event of floods, as it is so placed that the sitting bird can reach or leave it with ease and the outer edge is generally almost if not quite in the water, although I have seen at least three nests which were fully four yards from it.

And Gilroy ends his account with the observation, 'when leaving the nest the bird disappears so smoothly below the surface as to leave scarcely a ripple,' a trait of black-throated divers that has struck many observers of the bird.

It perhaps says something about the rarity, and therefore difficulty, of finding these birds in the first decades of the twentieth century that Gordon and Gilroy went to such lengths to observe black-throated divers. Human persecution, egg-collecting in particular, but also breaking eggs and shooting birds to protect angling interests, are widely thought to be the reasons the black-throated diver population was brought to such a low ebb during this period. Gilroy concludes his paper with the judgement that, 'of recent years the Black-throated Diver has steadily and noticeably decreased as a breeding-species in Scotland.' Writing just a few years earlier, Osgood

Mackenzie, creator of the famous garden at Inverewe, came to a similar conclusion for the birds in his area of Wester Ross:

> A few pairs of black-throated divers still float about on our lochs, and sometimes rear their young, but sad to say they are diminishing in numbers, and many lochs where they used never to fail to breed are now without these beautiful and most interesting summer tenants.

I realised why I'd failed to notice the diver on its nest when I was the scanning the loch the previous evening. The reason was that the nest was in the most unlikely place; it appeared to be floating on just a few reeds above the waterline. How on earth there was sufficient dry, let alone solid, ground for the eggs in such a spot was difficult to fathom. It seemed an impossible place to build a nest. And why had the divers chosen that clump of reeds to nest on, instead of the small island in the bay or one of its satellite islets? Charles St John commented that a black-throated diver's nest he knew of on an island was so close to the edge of the water, 'the nest was always wet.' Still, I was perplexed, and apprehensive, about the divers' choice of nest site. Would the nest be flooded if there was heavy rain? It looked as though it wouldn't take much of a rise in the water level for the nest to be swamped, the eggs to be washed away.

I lay there on the mound, watching the diver on its nest through my scope, which I'd rested on a tussock in front of me. Its mate was circling in the water around the nest site and still opening its bill, as though calling, but the bird was now too far away for me to hear. Gordon observed that, close to the nest, the swimming bird seemed 'to speak' to its incubating mate in 'a low voice', and I wondered if the diver was making those soft *yonk-yonk* calls I'd heard it make earlier. Occasionally, the sitting bird preened its breast feathers or rearranged some of the reeds around the nest. Several times it reached into the water with its bill and pulled up bits of vegetation to tuck into the side of the nest, as though proofing it against the loch.

I was overjoyed to find the divers, but I felt anxious for them seeing their nest situated as it was, and that anxiety gnawed at me all the time I spent with the birds, and for several weeks afterwards. Later in the morning I was able to get a better look at the nest from a different angle and could see it was positioned on a tussock of grass sticking up out of the loch, with some reeds growing around the tussock. Whichever of the diver pair was sitting on the nest, they spent a good deal of time tugging and snipping at these reeds, then arranging them around the nest, wedging the reeds beneath where they lay, almost as though they were building the island around them.

Seton Gordon recalled a similarly precarious nesting location, where he observed a female black-throated diver trying to save her eggs from a rising flood. This nest was also on a 'rushy promontory', as he described the site. He watched as the diver snipped off rushes with her bill, 'cleanly cut, as if with a knife', and used the cuttings to build 'a breakwater of rushes' beside the nest. The loch, however, continued to rise and the diver was eventually forced to start swimming once the water reached the nest. Despite this, the bird continued to snip off rushes with her bill, and as she did so she threw them over her shoulder towards the nest, as though in desperation to protect her eggs.

The issue for divers is one of equilibrium. Too much rain and their nests run the risk of being flooded. Conversely, if there is a drought and the water level drops, then the divers can find their nests uncomfortably far from the loch. Gordon, in fact, cites an example he'd heard about where a black-throated diver had deserted its eggs when the loch had shrunk so much the bird could no longer dive from its nest into the water. This diver then laid two new eggs in a different location, closer to the water's edge. The ideal solution for the black-throated diver is to be able to build its nest between about 1 and 3 ft from the edge of the water, and no more than about a foot above the loch. Though this is their preferred zone, black-throats, perhaps because of their larger size and strength, sometimes nest further from the water than the smaller red-throated diver, and one black-throated diver nest was discovered an unusual 12 ft from the loch and 3 ft above the water level.

This need for equilibrium, the tightrope walk between flood and drought that divers face, is ultimately driven by the bird's anatomy. The diver's legs are set so far back on its body to aid propulsion through water (one observer described the position of the legs as being 'like the propellers of a boat') that the bird struggles to walk on land and essentially has to shuffle-flump its way from the water to its nest. There is often a noticeable imprint, a slipway, running between the nest and the water's edge, where the diver has repeatedly hauled itself along the ground. The bird's awkwardness on land may even be the origin of the name used for members of the diver genus in North America, 'loon', a word possibly derived from the Old Norse *lum*, meaning 'clumsy', or the Old English *lumme*, meaning 'awkward' (though another derivation might be the Norse word *lómr*, meaning 'moaning', referring to the bird's call).

For divers, their aversion to land is even more pronounced than it is for shearwaters. Land is an alien medium for divers and the reason they nest so close to water, so they can dive from their nest straight into their own element. I wonder if it is also one of the reasons why red-throated divers are capable of nesting on much smaller lochs than black-throats, as the smaller, lighter red-throats need less of a water-runway to launch themselves into flight, thereby avoiding a crash on land. Even so, on windless days red-throated divers can still struggle to get airborne and their preference, in such still conditions, seems to be to stay on their lochan, rather than try to get airborne. Gordon wrote a useful passage on how a red-throated diver achieves take-off from its nesting lochan, describing how the bird 'swims below the surface to the leeward end, then rises to the surface and "taxis" against the breeze, using wings and feet until, like a flying-boat, it has reached a speed sufficient for it to become airborne'.

It is no exaggeration to say that divers – with the exception of that brief, awkward shuffle from water to nest site – need to avoid coming into contact with land. To touch down on land, rather than water, would in most circumstances prove fatal to the bird as, given the position of their legs, they are unable to use the ground like they do water, as a runway to take off from. Gordon noted that the occasion when young divers leave their lochs for the first time must be a particularly hazardous one; should the fledgling divers crash-land before they can reach the sea, they would be unlikely to survive, as there is little hope of their becoming airborne again. He thought that young divers, therefore, must only leave their natal loch for the first time when there was a sufficiently strong breeze to assist their flight.

I decided to leave the mound, walk back across the quaking bog and find a spot in the wood where I could watch the divers. I felt I would be more hidden among the trees, and, as a result, I knew I would feel more comfortable there. The wood was also on higher ground, giving a better, more expansive view of the loch. As I entered the wood I came across a troupe of acrobats, a large flock of siskins in among the birch trees, many of them hanging upside down from the delicate twigs, their wings flashing yellow. The siskins were an extraordinary burst of colour amid the mauves and greys of the wood, and collectively, as the flock shifted from tree to tree, they resembled a light pulsating through the wood. There were also many chaffinches among the trees; listening to them, I thought the chaffinches here had less of a flourish at the end of their rapid, descending song. The chaffinches I was used to hearing at home often sounded like they signed off their song with a pronounced *I-thank-youuu*. These more northerly chaffinches, by contrast, had a softer conclusion to their song, almost trailing off at the end. Everywhere among the moss-covered oaks and birches I also heard the willow warblers' cascading song.

I found a spot beside some ancient Scots pines near the edge of the wood where the ground was soft with a thick layer of pine needles. Some of the trees were so large I could stand behind them, my back against their scaly crimson bark, and assemble my scope without being seen from the loch. That clump of pines became my office for the next two days, and I walked so often between there and my tent back at the fank that I drew a thin line through the heather.

It had started to rain lightly by the time I had assembled my scope. The wind had picked up from the east and it was still very cold. It was interesting to observe the diver on its nest from this new perspective. The bird kept its head and neck low to the nest, so that, without binoculars, you couldn't tell the bird was present; the diver had made itself as inconspicuous as possible by moulding its shape into the nesting platform. It was almost as though that low profile the divers had when swimming in the water was transposed to the bird's stance on the nest, so that how the divers sat on the nest was an extension of how they sat in the water.

I felt less annoyed with myself that I hadn't been able to spot the divers the previous evening. For such a large bird (just over 2 ft long, with a wingspan of around 4 ft), they seemed adept at making themselves inconspicuous on the loch (one researcher described black-throated divers as being 'surprisingly difficult to locate' on large bodies of water). Another aspect of the diver's crypsis, I noticed, was the way the white markings over the bird's back – what Donald Watson described as 'the extraordinary white domino pattern on its black back' – resembled the white tips of the waves out on the loch. Sitting low on the nest, the arc of the diver's back was the shape of a wave; the white patterning over the bird's back, the wave's crest. So the brightness in the white of the diver's plumage in fact served to blend the bird, with immaculate precision, against the background of the windy loch. Only when the wind dropped, and the water lost some of its choppiness, did the white markings on the divers show up that little bit brighter.

There is a beautiful Gaelic name for the larger cousin of the black-throated diver, the great northern diver, which, though it doesn't breed in the British Isles, is present in autumn and winter around the coasts. Known as the common loon in North America, in Gaelic the bird is called *bun a' bhuachaille*, which translates as 'herdsman of the tide-race', *bun* being the Gaelic for the steep-crested waves that form when wind and tide combine. The great northern diver's summer plumage has a similar white banding over its back to its congener, the black-throated diver, both patterns resembling the white crest of a wave breaking over the bird's back.

Eventually I spotted the other diver further out on the loch, its bill tucked along its back, as though sheathed there, so that the bird appeared to be sleeping. Like its mate on the nest, the diver floating on the loch resembled, in its blacks, greys and whites, another wave out there on the choppy waters. Looking back through my notebook, I see I wrote down the phrase 'birds of the grey loch' to try to encapsulate the divers in their setting, but another description I might have used is 'the bird that hides in the waves'.

Black-throated divers can hide in the waves, but that exquisite patterning on their plumage also serves to conceal the bird on its nest, to break up its profile against the surrounding vegetation. Even on the tiny platform of reeds out on the loch, the divers were difficult to spot when they were lying low on their nest. It has been suggested that there is a marked correlation between the crypticity of nests and the relative solitariness of the breeding species, and that crypticity in birds is an adaptation to reduce predation in the absence of neighbours to warn and help repel threats. One way of thinking about the black-throated diver's beauty, then, is that it is an adaptation that has arisen from the bird's solitariness (the majority of British pairs breed on single-territory lochs). Divers hide in the waves, but they also hide in their own beauty.

How important that crypsis is for divers during their nesting season was highlighted by research conducted in Norway in the 1970s (the Nordic countries hold 99 per cent of the European population of black-throated divers outside Russia). Black-throated divers normally breed on large bodies of water, anything from around 100 m or 200 m across to the largest of the Highland lochs. But in Norway, four black-throated diver pairs were discovered nesting in small lochans, between 0.01 and 0.07 km^2, in other words the sort of bodies of water that red-throated divers prefer to nest in. There obviously wasn't sufficient food in these lochans for the black-throated divers, and it was discovered that while the birds were nesting there, they were flying to the nearest large lakes to feed. Such a split is unusual for black-throated divers, who tend to feed in the same lakes they nest in; the reason suggested for this behaviour was that the larger lakes in the area were characterised by 'very exposed shores with sparse or no marginal vegetation'. Without vegetation to provide cover for the divers' crypticity, the birds had chosen to nest instead beside smaller lochans where there was sufficient vegetation.

When I read this Norwegian research, I thought back to the nightjars on the heath and their extraordinary ability to fold themselves into the heathland floor; it seems that black-throated divers share that requirement to become, like nightjars, part of the background, to the extent that divers will shun their preferred large nesting lakes if they are unsuitable. It is an indication of the predation pressures divers must face that these Norwegian birds chose such atypical nesting sites in preference to the larger lakes, where the divers, presumably, felt too exposed.

A cuckoo called from the edge of the wood; I'd been hearing it, on and off, since early in the morning. I wondered, did I hear the divers calling in the night from my tent, or did I imagine it? I thought I heard a faint wailing, but I couldn't be sure it wasn't just the wind. Apart from the '*yonking*' call one of the birds had made earlier, the divers had been silent since I arrived. I was hopeful that I might hear their 'wailing' song but, more than anything, I felt privileged to be in their company. It was sufficient just to be able to observe these exceptionally beautiful birds in such a place.

I realised, too, that their wailing-yodelling calls were most often provoked by the presence of other divers, and that I hadn't seen any sign of other black-throated divers in the vicinity, despite returning to the first loch to check I hadn't missed the birds there. It is noteworthy that Charles St John's account from Tongue Bay in Sutherland of the 'rocks and hillsides' resounding with the 'singular and wild' cries of black-throated divers occurred when 'great numbers' of the birds had gathered there one May. And bringing things a little more up to date, it is also notable that I was unable to find many recordings of black-throated divers in Scotland on the internet (there are a few more recordings from Scandinavian countries).

So that solitariness – which black-throated divers require during their breeding season – also has a bearing on their song; the less interaction there is with other divers from neighbouring territories, the less they call. I wondered, then, if you could describe the song itself – that distinctive yodelling – as being rare, so that in Britain, which holds less than 1 per cent (around 200 breeding pairs) of the global population of black-throated divers, the song of these birds is as rare, perhaps rarer, than the birds themselves.

The diver on the nest raised its head and looked out across the loch to where its mate was swimming. As it raised its head, I noticed how long and straight the diver's bill was. The bird (I was unable to sex the divers because they appeared identical to me, although the male is slighter larger, with 'a bulkier grey head') then slipped off the nest and dived into the loch. The diver seemed to relish being in the water, dipping its head repeatedly under the surface, then rising up out of the water into an almost standing position, flexing its wings as it did so. I had the sense that the bird was enjoying a much-needed respite after sitting still for so long on the nest. I noticed its mate, who had swum closer, was also now rising high up out of the water, as though pushing itself up on its legs, and then shaking its wings. As the birds rose out of the water like this, I could see a good deal of white showing on their bellies, so that I had a glimpse of the contrast in colours between their dark top and white underside. When they raised their wings to preen beneath them, I also noticed this flash of white below, and, depending on how they tilted themselves in the water, the divers could sometimes appear as strikingly white birds.

After flexing its wings and preening, the bird that had been sitting on the nest proceeded to swim once around the islet, before heaving itself up out of the water onto the nesting platform. The diver looked very peculiar as it did this; I caught a glimpse of its legs, which appeared short and stubby, set far back on its body, and I watched as the bird used them to sort of hop then waddle up to the nest, like a penguin falling off a pogo stick. Once it reached the nest, the diver peered down at it for a few seconds, then seemed to gently nudge the eggs (though I couldn't see them) with its bill, as though delicately rearranging the clutch. The bird then settled down onto the nest, at first facing the opposite direction from where it had been before, but then quickly shifting around to face the same way as earlier. There followed a fair amount of tugging at the surrounding vegetation with its bill, as though tucking itself in to the nest.

I returned to the tent for some lunch in the rain, then went back along the path through the heather for the afternoon shift, settling down under the Scots pine with its crimson, deep-cut bark. The wind had got up, and the trees were shifting and clicking around me. I focused in on the diver on its nest; I could see the narrow black and white stripes down the side of the bird's neck, like an upturned collar. Next to these stripes was the diver's black neck, which held, when the light caught it, a slight purple gloss. The bill was dark and shiny, like it had just been dipped in black paint. The face, around the eye, appeared dark grey, and there was a noticeably lighter, velvety grey over the diver's head and down the back of its neck. At the top of the neck, separating the dark grey head and the black throat, was a thin white band, which I often found myself focusing on, and which has been described as resembling 'a miniature pearl necklace'. Below the black throat, the breast was white, with pencil-thin black stripes running through the white towards the bird's back. These lines appeared almost symmetrical, as though a zebra's wavy stripes had been ironed into straightness. The black and white patterning – the wave crests – on either side of the diver's back was especially striking; these markings were oval-shaped, and resembled two eyes looking out and up from the bird's back. I was unable to detect the colour of the diver's actual eyes; from a distance, even through the scope, I found the eyes sat too dark against the bird's head. But the eyes are a deep ruby red, and rest like jewels in the soft grey of the diver's head.

What I found astonishing about the black-throated diver's appearance was that I had never encountered those three colours – grey, white and black – in such a bright, striking arrangement as on the diver's breeding plumage. You'd think these colours would be a recipe for something drab, but in their subtle juxtaposition, the delicate arrangement of the colours, the effect was breathtaking, and it was difficult to imagine a more beautiful bird.

As the Norwegian study showed, not any old large freshwater lake will do for black-throated divers. To be suitable for nesting, a body of water must meet specific criteria for these birds. Shoreline vegetation is, as the Norwegian study established, one of these requirements; for this reason, lakes impounded for hydro-electric schemes may not be suitable for divers, with their rocky, fluctuating shorelines. The loch must also contain islands, although, as the doughty swimmer Norman Gilroy discovered, not all diver pairs select islands to nest on. Nevertheless, it remains the case that, without the isolated protection of an island as a nesting site, black-throated diver breeding success is almost negligible. Lots of freshwater Highland lochs have islands, but not all of these lochs have black-throated divers.

The reason for this, and perhaps the most important criteria for divers, is that the loch must have a zone of shallow water, no more than 15 or so feet deep, in which the birds can feed. Steep-shelving lochs, whose depths plummet quickly, are, for this reason, not suitable for black-throated divers, as the birds feed almost exclusively in that shallow zone. A survey conducted in the late 1970s found that less than half of the large, island-studded lochs in two extensive areas of northwest Scotland were used by black-throated divers. This suggests that the birds are limited, not so much by the availability of large lochs (of which there are hundreds in the Highlands), but by the availability of lochs that meet the bird's specific requirements. The lack of *suitable* lochs, it has been suggested, is therefore the main reason black-throated divers are so rare in the British Isles.

In the middle of the afternoon there was a sudden panicked scramble among the meadow pipits in the tussocky grass between the wood and the loch. A female merlin swooped in front of me on sharp, sickle-shaped wings. She landed on a branch of one of the dead pines near the shore of the loch, and I had a wonderful view of her brown back and the speckled patterning down her breast as the tiny falcon perched there. There were more agitated calls from the pipits, and the merlin then took off, flying along the shore, before curving around the trees and out of sight.

I looked over towards the diver on its nest and caught the moment a swallow flew low across the loch, gliding over the diver's head. The way the swallow dipped and rose just above the water, it was as though someone had set a stone skimming across the surface of the loch. I studied the divers' nesting platform again and thought it looked even more like a sketchy raft of matted reeds. Perhaps I was unduly concerned; the divers must know what they were doing, and anyway the weather was bound to improve, the level of the loch dropping accordingly. Even if there was a flood, it was still early in the season; the divers still had time to lay another clutch, choose a different nesting site, should this one fail.

Perhaps, too, the precariousness of a black-throated diver's nest site is something that is just implicit in the species. The following Gaelic song, for example, which renders the cries of the black-throated diver into this anxiety-ridden lament, suggests that nest-flooding has always been a common occurrence for the birds:

Mo chreacli! mo chreach! – My sorrow! my sorrow!
M' eoin us m' uibhean! – My chicks and my eggs!
Mo chreach! mo clircach! – My sorrow! my sorrow!
Mo dhith! mo dhith! – My grief! my grief!
Mo linn 's an tuilinn – My brood in the flood
Mo dliitli! mo dhith! – My grief! my grief!
M' urragan! – My chicks!
M' ulagan! – My gifts!
M' eoin! – My birds!
M' uibhean! – My eggs!
M' ulaidh! – My treasures!
M' eislean! – My troubles!

Does flooding present the most serious threat to nesting black-throated divers? It has probably always posed a hazard to the birds, as the song suggests, and as the diver's habit of nesting so close to the water's edge predisposes them. Niall Rankin, in his book on British divers, suggests that the black-throated diver's choice of nesting loch, besides the other criteria I have mentioned, is also determined by those freshwater lochs that have the capacity, through their outflow, to offset a sudden influx in rainfall. In other words, those lochs that rise rapidly from spates in their tributary burns are the least likely to be selected by black-throated divers.

Nevertheless, flooding remains a significant cause of nest failure in the species (causing around 30 per cent of failures), and more recently has most likely been exacerbated by human interference, either through drainage dykes in conifer plantations, which can cause rapid runoff, or where lochs have had their outlets raised and narrowed for the purposes of fishing. One successful scheme to ameliorate these flooding risks for the birds has been the provision of rafts lined with natural vegetation, which the divers seem to readily accept as nesting platforms. A study in the 1980s showed that the adoption of these rafts 'increased the chick productivity of the Scottish black-throated diver population by around 43 per cent'.

Besides flooding, the most significant cause of nest failure for black-throated divers is predation. Otters and pine martens were identified as the main predators in one study, with ravens and hooded crows also causing a small number of nest failures. Human disturbance is also a factor in causing some divers to desert their nests, and as recently as the 1980s a study attributed 13 per cent of nest failures to human egg collectors.

After the nadir of the early decades of the twentieth century, which coincided with Gordon's research, a decrease in persecution led to an expansion in the black-throated diver population through the middle of the twentieth century. Since the 1980s, the breeding population in Scotland has remained stable, though they remain, of course, exceptionally rare birds, with all the vulnerability that entails.

At five o'clock in the afternoon the diver stood up from the nest, tall and stooped, like a monk hunched in his cowl. It slipped off the nest and I could see the reeds parting as the bird swum through them. For the next 10 minutes I watched as the diver appeared to take in water through its bill, before turning its neck around to spray the water over the feathers down its back. It did this repeatedly, dipping its bill in the loch then turning around and spraying the water over its dorsal feathers. After this 'shower', it drifted out in a wide circle away from the nest, periodically rising out of the water and flapping its wings, followed by vigorous preening. Having finished preening, the bird tucked its bill under one of its wings and drifted for a while, appearing to doze.

The diver had now been away from the nest for 20 minutes and I wondered how long it would remain away from its eggs. There was no sign of its mate. Then I noticed it starting to swim slowly back towards the nest (break time over!). The bird got itself into position beside the edge of the islet, then heaved itself out of the water like a seal, legs following behind the bird as if an afterthought. For a few seconds the diver stood upright above the nest, and I had a sense of what a large, tall bird it was. It then pivoted slightly, before settling down on the eggs, gathering the tiny island in around itself.

I had stayed so still watching the diver over those 20 minutes or so, a small herd of red deer had grazed past me among the old pines, their coats dark with rain. When I got up to leave, I could smell the deer's warm, musty scent.

Within that shallow zone in the loch, divers are efficient predators, travelling underwater at speeds of up to 8 mph, outswimming the majority of fish. Trout, char and minnows are typical species of the freshwater fish caught by divers, but the birds will also eat invertebrates, including dragonflies and beetles. During the winter months, when black-throated divers have left their freshwater breeding grounds for the sea and moulted into a whiter, more sooty-grey bird, losing their striking black and white patterning, they feed on shoaling fish such as small cod and gobies. Dives in shallow freshwater lochs can be surprisingly frequent; one observer recorded 48 dives in a 30-minute period. Most of these were successful, averaging around 17 seconds; unsuccessful ones tended to last longer, approximately 27 seconds. Rapid dives, such as these, are likely to be in pursuit of very small fish, with larger, quicker fish requiring longer dives, often over 40 seconds. The birds can remain submerged for around 2 minutes, though the majority of dives last less than a minute, and divers are capable of swimming distances of between a quarter and a third of a mile underwater.

Interestingly, within the genus of divers – *Gavia*, comprising five species – there isn't a great deal of variation in either appearance or behaviour between the species, with the divers being described as constituting a 'very homogeneous group'. I have mentioned the similarities in the plumage patterning between great northern and black-throated divers, and that shared black and white dorsal patterning is also present in the breeding plumage of both the white-billed diver (which, apart from the yellowish colour of the bill – in North America it is known as the yellow-billed loon – is very similar in appearance to the great northern diver) and the Pacific diver (which is very similar in appearance to the black-throated diver); the red-throated diver is the only *Gavia* species that lacks the black and white markings over its back.

Reproductive behaviour also appears to be broadly aligned between the species in the genus, with, as one paper put it – referring to the differences between black-throated, great northern and white-billed divers – 'only minor differences' showing in 'posture, displays and nesting behaviour, which else remain basically the same'. The same paper concluded that perhaps the greatest difference between these three species of diver 'lies in the vocalisations', in the different strains of weirdness in their songs.

Late in the afternoon, I witnessed the incubation changeover between the diver pair. For several hours I'd only seen one diver and I couldn't locate the other bird out on the loch. Finally, at 5.45 p.m., I noticed the absent diver swimming in towards the nest from the far end of the loch. The bird on the nest stood up and, for a moment, was posed awkwardly, its neck and chest in the water but its rear still on the islet, as though it couldn't quite get its legs where it wanted them. Then the diver slipped into the water and began to swim out towards its mate. I watched as both birds approached each other, and just at the point where they met, they performed a beautiful manoeuvre, turning around one another, each diver executing half a figure of eight, so that they ended up side by side, facing towards the nest. There was a wonderful symmetry to the movement and in the way they greeted each other like this. I had read about black-throated divers performing 'circle dances', where two or more birds swim towards each other, necks raised high; then, when there is just a body-length between them, the divers start circling around a common centre, often for just half a revolution, but occasionally up to four times around the circle. The way the birds rotate in this gyre is not perfectly synchronised, and there are stops and starts, and drifts away from the centre, so the effect is a bit like a wonky merry-go-round. Anything between two and five birds have been observed participating in this dance, and on one memorable occasion a flock of 32 black-throated divers was seen performing numerous circle dances at the same time.

I'm not sure what I witnessed was a circle dance as such, and these 'dance-offs' tend, anyway, to be associated with threat behaviour, as a ritualised way of settling disputes when territory is encroached (encroachments can also provoke more physical responses such as 'rushing' – running over the water as though taking off; 'splash dives' – kicking up water up to 3 ft high as the bird dives;

'fencing posture' – where the diver rises straight up, treading water, head and neck pulled far back, so the bird forms the shape of a question mark; and occasionally even fights between birds).

Circle dance or not, it was a joy to witness this balletic manoeuvre between the pair, and I watched as they swam together back towards the nest. Niall Rankin describes watching a pair of divers swimming together like this, though the pair he observed were also fishing. He makes the interesting observation of this pair that the birds invariably dived simultaneously, always surfacing only a few metres apart 'within a second or two of each other', as though 'the length of the dive were prearranged'. The pair I watched swimming back to their nest didn't dive, however, and once they reached the nest the diver that had been absent for most of the afternoon took its turn to haul itself up onto the islet, where it appeared to delicately nudge the eggs under its breast with its bill, before settling down on the nest.

After supper at the tent, I headed back to the loch for the evening. The rain had stopped and the air was very clear. I focused my scope on the divers' nest, and the colours of the bird sitting there appeared even sharper. A female hen harrier flew over the loch and suddenly spiralled down at lightning speed, as a meadow pipit, I think, shot out of the way on the other bank. The harrier then began to quarter the hillside, and I watched it tacking back and forth, low over the heather, before it disappeared around a curve of the hill. I could see one of the divers far out on the loch. The bird dipped its head and neck below the surface, so that all that was visible were the twin hillocks of its back and tail. Then it dived, without the slightest splash, as though its head and neck had tugged, and the rest of it had followed.

Three weeks later, at the beginning of June, I returned to the loch, this time with my two sons. I was keen to show the boys the divers. I was also anxious to learn whether the nest had survived its perilous location. There was warm sunshine in the glen and the birch trees were in leaf. We walked quietly to the north-east corner of the loch and I set the scope up among the trees while the boys munched on their sandwiches. I was glad to see the colourful siskins still here, several birds flitting through one of the pine trees like alternating Christmas lights.

And here, too, were the divers, almost just as I had left them on that cold morning three weeks ago. One bird was swimming in the middle of the loch, low in the water, its mate sitting on the nest. I lowered the scope to the boys' height, and they took it in turns to look at the birds. They each spent a long time peering through the scope, neither of them saying much. I asked the boys what they thought of the divers. 'Absolutely beautiful! It had a beautiful beak, almost like a horn, it was so long!' His brother added: 'Strange looking, a long neck; it appeared very protective of its nest.'

We left the loch and walked out further onto the moor to camp for the night. The next morning we followed a path that overlooked a large, shallow loch studded with small islands and rocks. The previous day, when we passed the loch, my diver antennae had twitched at how suitable the loch seemed, but there had been no sign of any birds. In the morning, however, better eyes than mine were trained on the water; one of the boys, ahead of me on the path, pointed and said he could see a large bird flying low over the loch. I was too far behind them to see anything, but as I drew level with the boys, we heard a howling sound that seemed to swirl around us, as though the noise had been caught in the wind. It was almost human-sounding, plaintive, as if someone were hailing to us from the other side of the loch – *Hey-youuuu* – their voice distorted by the wind.

I think that what we heard was a diver's 'moaning' contact call, not the 'yodelling' call; it was too brief for the latter, and what we heard was more like a humming, wavering sound. I took off my pack and sat down to scan the loch properly. 'What did you think it sounded like?' I asked the boys. 'Unusual,' one of them replied, 'quite scary!' I had got my binoculars focused on the loch and was checking each diver-sized rock sticking out of the water. Then one of the rocks moved, and there was the soft grey head, the striped neck, of a black-throated diver.

VII

Little Horn in the Rushes

Lapwing

Seton Gordon wrote that the lapwing:

> Is an extraordinarily pugnacious bird, and during the nesting season pursues with great vigour and dash any intruder near his nesting site. The golden eagle presents no terrors to him, nor does the sparrow-hawk, and he will not hesitate to pursue them with great hatred.

On one occasion Gordon in fact witnessed a lapwing 'pursuing a heedless golden eagle', and on another he saw a lapwing swoop down with such fury on a cormorant flying up an estuary that the cormorant 'half fell' into the water, and only escaped the lapwing by swimming away. 'There is no bird,' he concluded, 'that a lapwing will not venture to attack.' And one morning in early May in the Outer Hebrides, I saw that he was right.

I'd only just arrived on the machair and was walking slowly along a sandy track towards the dunes. Already I was being escorted by two lapwings looping around me, making their loud, wheezy, anxious calls. Then suddenly the pair were whirling away and beating fast towards the dunes, and I became aware of a stream of lapwings, around 20 birds, unfolding from the grassland, all of them heading in the same direction. It was as though someone had taken a giant leaf blower to the ground, and all the birds were being billowed up and out across the plain. Except the birds were being pulled, not blown. A sea eagle was flying low along the line of the dunes; massive brown wings with their frayed, fingered edges; huge, slow wingbeats, like someone shaking a doormat. And every lapwing, every oystercatcher and redshank in the vicinity was tearing across to heckle, shriek and yell at the hapless eagle, to tell it, as impolitely as they could, to 'sod off!'

I noticed that the first birds to reach the eagle, and the last to leave it alone, were the lapwings. The oystercatchers and redshanks did most of the yelling, but the lapwings were the ones that flew closest to the eagle, spinning, ducking around the enormous, lumbering bird, as though the lapwings were tangling it up in a giant knot. I'd witnessed a similar encounter, on a previous visit to the islands, involving a male hen harrier who was engulfed by lapwings as it flew along the wrack line of a beach. But I had never encountered a sea eagle over the machair before, and it was fascinating to observe the lapwings treating the much larger eagle with the same degree of vigour and fearlessness as they had the hen harrier, just as they do – as Gordon pointed out – with any bird that encroaches on their breeding grounds.

After the commotion caused by the eagle, I watched as several lapwings began to drift back across the meadow. As soon as I started to walk again along the track, my movement triggered lapwings to rise from the grass and escort me. I'd thought the black-throated diver the boys and I heard had sounded plaintive, mournful, but there is something about the lapwing's alarm call that is perhaps even more affecting than the diver's call; those two thin, parched notes the lapwing makes have been described as 'acutely distressful-sounding' and 'heartbreakingly shrill'. There is something pleading and, at the same time, questioning about the sound; '*Why* have you come here?' the lapwing seems to ask, more in desperation than anger.

There is an onomatopoeic Welsh name for the lapwing, *gwai fi*, that translates as 'woe is me', which seems to chime well with the sense of despair inherent in the bird's call. There are several archaic adjectives, too, that derive from the character of the lapwing's call:

'peesweepy', for example, means 'poor, shrill, whining, silly' (peesweep being a local name for the lapwing), and to be 'peasweep-like' is to be 'sharp-featured, feeble in appearance, with a thin voice'. There is also a wonderful word associated with Cornwall, 'horniwinky', meaning desolate (horniwink being another local name for the lapwing); so, an old, ruined house, for instance, could be described as a 'horniwinky' place.

An obsolete Berkshire dialect word, 'pee-whit', was the name for a musical instrument fashioned by children by splitting a small stick and inserting an ivy leaf into the slit. I assume the leaf acted like a reed inside the stick, and the noise, when you blew on it, must have sounded like a peewit – a lapwing. This 'pee-whit' instrument is said to have produced 'a curious sound', and I think I can imagine what it must have sounded like; to me, those two squeezed, desolate notes the lapwing makes remind me of someone trying to coax a reedy note from a blade of grass cupped between their hands.

The size of the breeding colony on the machair made the lapwings, cumulatively, an effective predator deterrent. This applies across the lapwing's range, with a strong negative correlation between colony size and predation risk; the larger the colony, the less affected the lapwings are by predation. To give an example of this effectiveness, in one lapwing colony that has been studied in Aberdeenshire, though the birds were unable to prevent some nests being lost to crows over the course of the breeding season, the lapwings were seen repelling all

101 attacks by crows during 109 hours of observation. It must be an extremely uncomfortable thing being a crow in a lapwing colony, with the lapwings mobbing the crows (usually the crows work in pairs) intensely, repeatedly diving at them, until the lapwings have driven them out of their territory. In another study, in Poland, the lapwings' defence against predation by marsh harriers reduced nest losses by around 75 per cent.

Such a fierce and effective anti-predator drive helps not only the lapwing colony, but also other birds nesting in the vicinity. So in the same way that skylarks can benefit from the protective proximity of raven nests, birds such as snipe and redshank, nesting on the machair (often very close to lapwings), also benefit from that defensive shield lapwings offer.

The sea eagles – there were two of them, both juvenile birds – were a presence on the machair over the following days. They appeared to be hunting (or at least annoying) the greylag geese, in particular. I didn't witness them catch one of the geese, but on several occasions I heard a great commotion over the marsh and turned to see the eagles flying at speed, one of them dropping at a greylag, causing the whole flock of geese to rise into the air with a great heaving din. These stoops on the geese seemed, perhaps because the eagles were juveniles, a bit half-hearted, in that the geese never flew very far away from the eagles once they had been dislodged, and the eagles never appeared to pursue the geese; instead, just settling on the ground from where they had ejected the greylags. Then the lapwings and gulls would pile in. On one occasion both eagles were perched beside each other on a low mound, so that the pair were conspicuous from some distance. I stood watching them through my scope from the other side of the marsh, the eagles flinching and ducking as a dozen lapwings swirled around them, like sparks from a fire.

The pugnacity in the lapwing that Gordon highlights is not confined to targeting other species of birds, but really extends to anything the lapwing perceives as a threat, whether it be cattle grazing too close to a lapwing's nest (cattle tend to be more receptive to lapwing deterrent displays than sheep), or dogs and people. Dogs seem to come in for particularly vigorous assaults by lapwings, with one witness recording that they had seen 'big dogs run yelping before his [the lapwing's] fearless power-dives'; a local French name for the lapwing is *pèle chien*: 'skin the dog'.

The fact that people can also come in for the same mobbing treatment as crows and dogs hasn't always endeared the lapwing to everyone. The Scottish ornithologist Robert Gray, writing in the 1870s, mentions that, in some parts of the south of Scotland, the lapwing was 'looked upon with great dislike' due to the bird's association with betrayal; their shrill, persistent cries had revealed the location of persecuted Covenanters who had been forced to hide in the hills from the government militias in the seventeenth century, and a derogatory Dumfriesshire name for the lapwing is 'de'il's plover' (devil's plover), a name the bird earned during this period of religious and political unrest. Gray suggests that mistrust of the lapwing was still prevalent two centuries later in the upland communities of Dumfriesshire and Galloway, citing an anonymous poem from the time, 'To the Peesweep', published in 'the "poet's corner" of a country newspaper', whose bitterness towards the lapwing – 'thou idle, ill-conditioned bird' – reaches a climax in the poem's final two stanzas:

> He minds what Scotland greets for yet,
> When helpless Hill Folk, hard beset,
> Could naewhere but in muirlands get
> A night's safe quarters.
> Ye brocht the troopers on them het,
> And made them martyrs.
>
> O sorra on your wicked din,
> And shame on a' your kith and kin!
> And though there's naething 'neath the skin
> That's fit for pot,
> Wad ony body ca't a sin
> To wuss ye shot?

It's hard to align this sort of vitriol with the grace and beauty of the lapwing, with a bird that Donald Watson, writing a hundred years after Gray about the same part of Scotland, notes farmworkers would save the nests of, by 'lifting and putting back eggs when harrowing or rolling a field'.

That bitterness towards the lapwing in Scotland takes another curious, vindictive form that Robert Gray also cites, referring to an Act passed by the Scottish parliament at the time of the Wars of Independence in the late thirteenth and early fourteenth centuries. This Act, which nods towards the view, expressed in the poem 'To the Peesweep', that lapwings in Scotland were not 'fit for pot' because the birds had insufficient flesh on them, also reflects the view, current at the time, that in England (where it was thought lapwings migrated in the autumn, and where the birds fattened up) they were eaten 'in great numbers'. So, in an unusual appropriation of birds as a weapon of war, the Scottish parliament decreed that 'all the peeseweeps' nests' be demolished and their eggs broken, so that the birds 'might not go south and become a delicious repast to our unnatural enemies the English'.

I sat down in the lee of a fence with just enough shelter from the wind for my scope not to wobble. There was a pair of wigeon on a marshy area in front of me; the male's colours were stunning: a smooth grey back, creamy yellow forehead, pinkish chest, face and neck like the colour of dark, wizened tangerine peel. Most of the lapwings I could see in front of me were males, with their longer, wispy crests and solid black necks. The birds had a shimmering, marine-like iridescence: emerald green along their back (hence the lapwing's other name, 'green plover'); a dark purple stripe along the wing; then a paler, softer green around their tail, with a golden splash beneath that I only saw when a bird raised its tail feathers slightly. Some observers describe the colour of the lapwing's undertail coverts as 'russet brown', others as 'orange', but to me, perhaps due to the quality of light over the machair, the feathers beneath the bird's tail had this golden yellow hue to them, and the jade along their backs was lit like stained glass. There is a children's riddle that goes:

> 'What is up when it's down and down when it's up?'
> Answer: 'A lapwing's crest.'

The lapwing's crest is held high when the bird is on the ground and flattened when the lapwing is in flight. Gaelic has an evocative name for the bird, *adharcan-luachrach*, which means 'little horn in the rushes'; English has the dialect name, 'hornpie'; and another Welsh name for the bird is *corn y wich*: 'squeal horn'. The crest does resemble a small horn, especially when the wind tips it so that it stands at a right angle to the top of the bird's head. I loved watching the way the wind expressed the lapwing's crest differently; sometimes it would flow down the back of the bird's neck like tentacles streaming out from a jellyfish, and sometimes the wind would blow it the other way, over the bird's face, as though casting a fishing line. The usual position for the crest, however, was in the shape of a crescent moon, rising above the lapwing's head.

The female lapwings were less conspicuous, and I suspected most of them were sitting on eggs. But every so often I would spot one of the females, with her slightly shorter, stiffer-looking crest, and the speckled white patches interrupting the black on her neck and face, as though she was wearing the buttons on her collar undone. Despite the openness of the machair, it was surprising how difficult it was to spot the females when they were crouched on their nest scrapes. Like the black-throated diver, the lapwing's colouring also lends the bird crypticity, and the female lapwing's green back – a more earthy, less iridescent green than the male's – must also help to blend the female with the grass when she is incubating. Conversely, similar to the way a lack of vegetation on lake shores diminishes the diver's crypticity, so the modern tendency to produce uniform, bright green grassland also diminishes the lapwing's camouflage. Monoculture has the effect of highlighting lapwings, when, for their safety and for the security of their nests, the birds need to disappear.

Several observers have remarked on this ability of lapwings to disappear against their background. K. G. Spencer, in his monograph on the bird, remarks how, if a group of lapwings stands still, whether the background is grass, shingle or ploughland, 'you will probably see none of them at all, or at best just a few.' And Robert Gray has a lovely description of the lapwing's camouflage against the backdrop of a beach, where, Gray writes, 'the ground is spread over with numerous pools and wet stones resembling the lights and shadows of the birds' plumage, and making their detection almost impossible to an unpractised eye.'

The downy lapwing chicks, which can run, swim and feed themselves soon after they have hatched, are even more camouflaged than the adult birds. The chicks resemble, with their blacks and duns, the colours of a dried cowpat (something the young birds, as though aware of the resemblance, will often lie on). Even the young lapwing's conspicuous white nape – which helps their parents locate the chicks, and which has been described as resembling 'little white riding lights bobbing against the neutral background of the field' – contracts and virtually disappears when the chicks crouch on the ground.

From my spot below the fence I watched two lapwings displaying together in the air – two males flying almost in synchrony, jinking, rolling, turning together, then rushing down, skimming low over the ground, before shooting up again on broad, supple wings. Sometimes the pair flew so close together it looked, for a brief second, as though they had merged into a single pair of wings, wavering black and white. It was difficult to detect any acrimony in this dance between the two birds; the challenge laid down, if there was one, seemed to be more a case of 'follow me, if you can.' The ornithologist Richard Vaughan called these aerial flights between two male lapwings 'one of the most familiar sights of spring', describing them as 'not a chase, more of a duet'. He added that 'actual brushes, still less real fights, between male lapwings on the breeding grounds are relatively rare.'

It might have been because I was there a little later in the breeding season, but my own experience on the machair chimed with this, in that I never witnessed any kind of skirmish between male lapwings. Yet, as with the example of the sea eagles, the lapwings were relentless in attacking other species. Once, an innocuous flock of dunlin landed in front of me and immediately a male lapwing swooped down on the dunlin, sweeping the flock away. There were also frequent mid-air jostles with oystercatchers; a whirring blur of black and white as the lapwing looped around the oystercatcher, though I could usually untangle the two by the agility, the twisting dance of the lapwing, compared with the oystercatcher's compact, stiffer-looking flight. The lapwings always seemed, in their coiling, whirling flight, as though they were wrapping a ball of string around the oystercatcher.

Another bird – though not present on the machair – that frequently comes in for the lapwing's ire is the pheasant; cock pheasants, especially, though they do not appear to pose any threat to lapwings, are not tolerated by the waders. One researcher witnessed the entire lapwing population in a field of 12 pairs 'queueing up to dive bomb' a pheasant that had wandered into the lapwings' territory.

It's a curious thing, this harmony that appears almost to override rivalry between the male lapwings. There are of course disputes, territories are established and defended, and other observers have commented on 'border clashes' between rival males as being a familiar sight, with contenders 'striking one another with their wings before instantly somersaulting apart'. But my own experience, like Vaughan's, was that clashes between male lapwings were an exception, and the tendency was for the males to perform together, to 'duet', rather than skirmish, almost as though the lapwing's supple, graceful flight predisposes them to dance, not fight.

I watched one of these dances between two male lapwings for over 20 minutes. The synchrony in their flight seemed miraculous, in the way each bird knew which way to jink and turn, when to drop or rise. The way they communicated the pattern of the flight to each other, it was as if both birds were somehow joined together; even their corkscrewing dives were beautifully, carefully synchronised. Between these twists and loops, there were pauses where the pair drifted together, one bird hanging a fraction above the other, its feet almost resting on the other lapwing's back. The birds hung like this for between 5 and 10 seconds, before they launched into their next rollercoaster manoeuvre. Sometimes the pair trailed their dance over another lapwing, perched on the ground, who was invariably hoisted up in their wake, and for a while the three birds twisted among each other before the original pair broke loose and resumed their duet. Occasionally, as they danced, they dropped out of sight below the ridge of one of the dunes, always clearing the top of the dune again within a second or two, as though there were a trampoline hidden behind the dunes that sent the lapwings rebounding into the air.

Whenever the pair came close to me during this display, I could hear a humming sound that reminded me of the noise a wind turbine makes when its blades are whirring at speed. Lapwings produce this thrumming note by vibrating the three outermost primaries on each downstroke of their wings, creating a fanning noise, hence the bird's scientific name *Vanellus vanellus*, from the Latin word meaning 'little fan' (referring to the type of hand-held fan used to winnow grain). It's a similar sound to the drumming noise snipe produce when they vibrate their tail feathers. Perhaps because they came closer to me, however, the lapwings' thrumming – a rapid, throbbing *whoop-whoop-whoop-whoop* – sounded louder than the snipe I had heard back at the divers' loch. And sometimes, the first I was aware of a lapwing approaching me was hearing that humming noise, like the sound of a rope being swung very fast, round and round through the air.

The ornithologists Desmond and Maimie Nethersole-Thompson called this sound that male lapwings make 'wing music', a beautiful term that recognises the wing-humming as being as much a part of the lapwing's song as the song itself. What is so distinctive – and mesmerising – about the lapwing's song is that it is made up of these component parts: there is the vocal song, the wing music, and also the song flight. Skylarks combine their flight display with their song; snipe have their own whirring music; ravens their tumbling, rolling dances; but lapwings combine the whole lot – wing music, song, and flight display – in an extraordinary ensemble.

* * *

Besides merging their song with their flight display, lapwings have several other things in common with the skylark. Above all, they share a need for wide, open spaces, preferably free of tall structures like trees and buildings (which provide lookout posts for avian predators), somewhere that gives them the space to perform their song flights. Lapwings also require the height of the vegetation to be kept short enough so that it neither impedes their ability to walk and forage for food, nor blocks their view of threats and predators over the surrounding area (long grass has been used as a lapwing deterrent on airfields, as a way to reduce aircraft bird strikes).

In order to feed, lapwings must be able to access invertebrates living on or just below the surface of the soil. Extensive plant growth, as well as drought (when the ground becomes too hard), can therefore cause problems for the birds during the breeding season, just as frost and snow can impede feeding in the winter. For these reasons, wet grassland habitats used for grazing and hay crops are extremely important for the species, with meadows and rough pastures favoured for nesting, and shorter grass for feeding. Where such wet grassland habitats are maintained, such as the machair in the Outer Hebrides and, notably, in the Netherlands (which holds the largest breeding population of lapwings in Europe), it provides an ideal habitat.

However, outside such areas, the lapwing – like the skylark – is a species that has struggled to adapt to modern agricultural practices. The pressure these agricultural changes have exerted on the lapwing have led to the species, in 2009, joining the skylark on the UK's Birds of Conservation Concern Red List. And the losses have been as stark as they have been for the skylark, with the UK lapwing population having declined by at least 40 per cent between 1970 and 1998. In Northern Ireland, the lapwing population has declined a catastrophic 89 per cent since 1987. Significant factors behind the decline of the lapwing population in Britain include the switch from spring- to winter-sown crops and the curtailment of the breeding season that this causes, as well as a general loss of mixed farmland and the effect of grassland drainage schemes. Perhaps the overriding issue for the lapwing – one that has seriously impeded the species' productivity – has been the bird's inability, through lack of suitable breeding habitat brought about by these agricultural changes, to raise a replacement clutch should the first clutch fail. Agricultural intensification, therefore, has led to this farmland bird now struggling to breed on much of our farmland.

One July, a few years before this trip, I spent a couple of days on the machair, and the difference between how the lapwings arrange themselves at the tail end of the breeding season and in May, near the start of it, is fascinating. By early July, the lapwings had begun to congregate in large, loose flocks, rather than the segregated breeding territories of spring. In fact, such is their gregarious nature and instinct to flock, lapwings that have failed to breed that year will often start to form flocks as early as May.

On one occasion during that summer visit I watched a flock of around a hundred lapwings shaken into flight by an oystercatcher's alarm call. The lapwings rose so lightly they looked like leaves being lifted by the wind. The flock rose to about 30 ft and then hung in the air above a loch, creating a shadow over the water. Then, after a few restless minutes, they began to descend, lowering themselves so hesitantly – flickering, feinting – as though they could no longer trust the ground to touch.

When a large flock of lapwings drifts down to land like this, some of the birds fall softly, like snow; others seem almost to drop out of the sky. Initially, when they land, the flock appears quite bunched, but then the birds will often adjust, arranging themselves roughly 5 ft apart, spacing out even more (about 10 ft between birds) as they begin feeding. The effect of this redistribution is a bit like someone pouring a bag of black and white draughts pieces onto a board, then quickly shuffling the pieces onto their squares. There is something in the way lapwings arrange then disassemble the structure of their flocks that I love. Both in flight, and on the ground, they can alternate between a loose, ragged arrangement and something tighter and more structured. On the ground, the flock seems to exhale as it spreads out across a field; in the air, lapwings can go from these loose, drifting flocks to a tight, synchronised formation, flying fast over the dunes.

Sometimes, other birds will fuse with these lapwing flocks. In the air, golden plovers often flock with lapwings in winter, with the lapwings threading through the plovers' tight, fast formations as though trying to find their way through a maze. On the ground, when a flock of lapwings is foraging, black-headed gulls may station themselves at regular intervals through the lapwing flock. Seton Gordon described the gulls as 'a thorn in the lapwing's flesh', as the black-headed gulls, in this instance, are behaving as kleptoparasites, hoping to intercept the lapwings' food before the lapwings can swallow it (hence an old name for the black-headed gull, 'peewit gull'). This piracy on the part of the gulls is largely a winter phenomenon in Britain, and their presence within a lapwing flock usually indicates what the lapwings are feeding on. With small items of prey, particularly those invertebrates picked from the surface, the gulls don't have time to reach the lapwing before the food has been swallowed. It's only with larger earthworms – which lapwings take time to extract from the ground – that the gulls have the opportunity to swoop in and snatch the worm from the lapwing; if the lapwings are not feeding on these larger, more awkward worms, the gulls tend to move away.

The black-headed gulls are usually spaced among the lapwing flock in such a way that each gull holds its own territory within the flock, monitoring between 10 and 20 lapwings. From a distance, with the larger, white gulls spaced among them, it can seem as though the lapwing flock is moving around the stumps of melted snowmen.

The lapwings, in turn, will shuffle away from the gulls, sometimes flying up, drift-hopping a few feet forward, trying to keep their distance from the sharp-eyed gulls. The presence of the gulls inside the lapwing flock therefore opens the flock up, the gulls creating ripples and eddies that flow through the lapwings as they feed.

The following day it rained heavily all morning. The previous evening had been dry and clear, and I had gone on a long walk along the west side of the island. The beaches felt like a stopover site for birds heading further north, and I saw sanderlings scurrying over the wet sand; also a large grey plover, tall-looking, with its black neck and chest, waiting for a passage to the Arctic to open up. I also saw a large brown rat working its way over the machair, a reminder – alongside hedgehogs, which had been introduced to South Uist in 1974 and had spread north to Benbecula by the 1990s – of the predation pressures the nesting birds faced here. The non-native hedgehogs, in particular, through their predation of eggs, have been implicated as an important cause in the population decline of birds breeding on the machair. Between 1983 and 2014 there was a fall of 18 per cent in the total number of breeding waders over the machair of South Uist, Benbecula and North Uist, with the highest concentration of declines (including lapwings, down by 14 per cent) occurring in those areas colonised by hedgehogs.

Despite the rain, I decided to head to a spot a little further along the machair from where I had been the day before. I walked north, with the dunes on my left and a large marshy area, thick with rushes, on my right. Within a few metres I was surrounded by snipe; five birds, making their scratchy calls, chasing each other in a noisy, high-speed group over the marsh. And everywhere, regardless of the wind and rain, snipe were drumming, the sky humming with that shivering sound the birds made as the air rushed through their tail feathers.

It is easy to be pulled into the orbit of other birds on the machair. Though there were also lapwings present around that marsh and, at one point, I heard both a lapwing's wing music and a snipe drumming at the same time, almost as though one were answering the other, like listening to a conversation between winds. Nevertheless, I found myself so captivated by the snipe, and by seeing and hearing so many of these usually fairly inconspicuous birds together, that I gave the rest of that rainy morning over to watching them.

A long fence separated the sandy pasture from the marsh. As I followed the fence north, a flock of starlings, perched along the wire, talked snipe to me, imitating the snipe's *snitch-snitch* calls before reverting to their squeaky starling chatter. I could hear the occasional burst of bubbling lapwing song, too, coming from the starlings; what a place to be a starling, I thought, with all the different calls and songs of the machair the starlings had to draw on, to imitate and improvise. The starlings had arranged themselves along the fence like notes on a stave, as though the flock were singing the score of itself.

About half a mile along the fence there was a large, rusty trailer wheel lying on the grass. The rain had eased a bit, so I perched on the edge of the wheel and looked back across the marsh. There was this deft movement, a sort of arabesque, that the snipe performed as they dropped in height out of their display flights; just a few feet from the ground the bird would lift both its wings above its back as though deploying a parachute. For a fraction of a second the snipe seemed to stall in the air, so it appeared that it was about to drop to the ground, then there was a sudden jink, and the bird was twisting up and away again.

Sometimes there were as many as 10 or 12 snipe displaying overhead, and, despite hearing them so often, I never got used to that peculiar sound their tail feathers made as they vibrated through the air. The sound is sometimes described as 'bleating', as in a goat's bleating, hence the snipe's Gaelic names, *gobhar athar* (air goat) and *meannan athair* (air kid). To me, however, it feels more like a shivering, whirring, fan-like noise than the sound a goat makes. Each sequence of drumming was brief, lasting only 2 or 3 seconds. The snipe would climb, with rapid wingbeats, at a steady angle (not steeply) in a wide coiling trajectory, as though moving up through the inside of a bowl. The ascents would last around 5 to 6 seconds, then the snipe would pause briefly before tipping out of the climb into a rapid descent. It was during this brief descent that the birds made their drumming sound. Like the climb, the descent was not especially steep, and it seemed as though the snipe were just letting themselves back down to the point in the air where they had begun their climb before commencing the whole thing again. I drew sketches in my notebook of the patterns of these displays. My sketches of the ascents looked like a coiled spring unravelling, with zigzagging lightning bolts representing the brief 'drumming' fall back to earth.

One snipe I watched would frequently hop up from the cover of the marsh onto the top of a fence post, its long, straight bill – almost as long as the bird's body – pointed downwards over the fence. The snipe would then start to sing its rusty, squeaky song, sounding like it was sawing at the fence's wire with a hacksaw. As it sang, I noticed the snipe jerking its bill up and down, opening it like a pair of tweezers, though not widely, as only the last third of the bill appeared to open. It reminded me of the woodcock I had seen over the nightjar's heath, the way the woodcock also never opened its bill fully when it called, and how the two birds – both snipe and woodcock – held their long bills at the same 45° angle to the ground.

Every half-hour or so the snipe popped back up onto the fence post and commenced – sometimes standing on just one leg, sometimes on two – its *chuck-er*, *chuck-er*, *chuck-er* 'train-in-the-distance' song, lasting between 5 and 10 minutes, before the bird dropped back into the marsh. Sometimes I could see the wind ruffling the snipe's white under-feathers, and every so often the bird stopped calling and turned its head around to rest its bill along the length of its back, seeming to sheathe it in its feathers. They are the most beautiful-looking birds, snipe, and to see one perched like that in the open, so that I could trace the patterns and colours – the whorl of browns and blacks and creams – in the bird's plumage, was at least one of the reasons it took me so long to get back to the lapwings that morning.

One snipe, drumming right above my head, sounding like it was shaking the air, suddenly dropped down to a small pool about 20 ft from me. I walked very slowly towards it, then went down on hands and knees and crawled forwards till I was just 8 ft away, looking down at the pool from a tuft of reeds. There was the snipe, drilling its bill into the soft, boggy ground, probing the mud for worms and insects. I watched the bird wade into the shallow pool, where it continued to forage. Each time the snipe pushed its bill into the water, its reflection came up to meet it, so that the snipe's long bill, briefly, like a magic trick, shrank into itself, and it looked as though the snipe were folding into another bird.

Besides the snipe, another bird that held me captivated on the machair was the oystercatcher. This is such a colourful species; dark red eyes, bright orange bill, the way it tilts in flight, tipping its wings to reveal chinks of white. When the oystercatchers were out feeding on the wet sand, the brightness of those colours was even sharper. They are such vigilant, vocal birds, too, as though they provide an early-warning alarm for all the other birds on the machair; lapwings, I noticed, could react to an oystercatcher's alarm call with such rapidity, it was as if the two species were joined by circuitry.

The oystercatchers' flocking behaviour, like the lapwings', could also be mesmerising. There was a moment that I looked for inside an oystercatcher flock; I didn't always catch it, but when it occurred it was very beautiful to observe. A flock would be flying quickly over the dunes, for instance, and then suddenly there was this pause, a collective mid-air hesitation; their wings stopped and lifted above their heads, not unlike that parachute-opening movement I had seen in the snipe. The flock of oystercatchers stalled, hanging there, as though holding its breath, then exhaled: a flash of white, and the birds flicked back into flight.

They could be just as mesmerising on the ground, the oystercatchers, as they were in the air. Several times I witnessed a flock of oystercatchers perform a strange, beautiful dance known as a 'piping party'. Within the flock, some birds would be resting, their bills tucked under their wings; others were alert, pacing about. Every so often, a troop of four birds broke off from the rest to perform a tense, shuffling dance; beaks open, pointed downwards, the dancers started up a crescendo of trilling, turning around each other in tight synchrony. There was often a rippling, domino effect, as one bird turned and the remaining three then followed in sequence. Those oystercatchers not taking part in the ceremony stood nearby, seemingly indifferent to the dance. But whenever one of the stiff, hunchbacked dancers swayed into a non-dancer, the spectating bird was forced to perform a leapfrog to avoid a collision. Sometimes, too, a pair of dancing birds collided with each other, but usually a hop and brief flight out of the way by one of them – a fan of white tail feathers, outstretched wings – allowed the dance to continue. One collision I witnessed, however, erupted into several minutes of scuffling between the birds, a roiling ball of black and white and orange, as the oystercatchers jabbed and folded over each other in the tussle.

Fights like that appeared to be rare, and the purpose of the 'piping' display seemed more about trying to diffuse tension within the flock, whether that tension had arisen from a dispute about feeding, spacing or some other hierarchical issue. The fact that the oystercatchers' sharp, powerful bills were pointed downwards throughout the display, in what seemed like a purposefully awkward pose, suggested that they wished to avoid injury during these disputes. I found these 'piping parties' hypnotic to watch; the noise the oystercatchers made when they were dancing, a fast-paced trilling, was very loud, and the way a party erupted so suddenly was like a car alarm going off on the machair.

Lapwings, too, perform an unusual display on the ground. When I witnessed this performance, known as 'scraping' or 'nest dancing', by the lapwings on the machair, it was preceded by the lapwing pair mating, though it often occurs the other way round. The male lapwing will use his feet to scrape out several small, rounded depressions across his territory, one of which, after the pair have lined it with grass and moss or whatever vegetation is to hand, the female will eventually lay her eggs in. The male uses these scrapes as sites for his display, often reusing scrapes from previous years.

There are two phases to the nest dance: an initial 'rocking' phase, where the lapwing straddles the scrape, bowing and bobbing, lifting his wings and dipping his tail, often culminating in a second more vigorous display. Here the bird sinks into one of the hollows, leaning on his wing wrists, with the tips of the wings pointed vertically upwards, vibrating and flickering his tail very rapidly, while scraping the hollow with his feet and moving from side to side, so that it looks like the bird is moulding the hollow with his breast. As the lapwing lifts his tail during this latter display, the golden splash of colour on the bird's undertail coverts is clearly revealed and seems to act as an important part of the display, in signalling to the female.

Following this dance, the male lapwing will frequently peck at bits of grass and roots around the scrape and throw them over his shoulder (lapwings also do this when they are agitated); sometimes the grass is real, and sometimes the bird mimes the action of pecking and throwing. Each time the lapwing performs this scraping display he crouches in the hollow facing a different direction from the previous dance, so that the bird eventually carves out a scoop that is perfectly circular. There can be up to as many as 20 of these hollows spread across an individual lapwing's territory; the ground is dented with forms that the birds have cupped, danced inside and briefly warmed.

After that rainy morning watching the snipe, I decided to move camp and head further south down the chain of islands. I pitched my tent close to a rushy field where a corncrake called through the night, a cuckoo on the hillside joining it at dawn. There were snipe here too, drumming at dusk, sounding quieter than the snipe I had heard in the morning, as though the birds from earlier in the day had been drumming to compete with the sound of the wind and rain. At around half past ten that night I went outside the tent to see if I could spot the snipe, as I had done in the early morning in the divers' glen. But the birds had performed their usual invisibility trick and were humming somewhere above me in the cool, dark air.

The next morning I was back on the machair, watching the lapwings. I walked through a field of corncrakes, then along a track with redshanks and snipe calling from the reeds on either side. It struck me, listening to all three of these birds calling together, hidden among the rushes, that there isn't another habitat I know of where the ground itself sings like this. Hearing the corncrakes and snipe together was just such an unusual duet: the corncrakes' percussive rasping and the rapid, swinging, 'chuckering' calls of the snipe, as though they were trying to coax some speed and variation into the corncrakes' song, and above them both, the redshanks' high, quivering notes.

The wind had picked up again, so I headed further into the dunes to look for some shelter. I found a spot where there were several lapwings displaying around a sandy pool, where I could sit with my back against a tall dune and put my scope up. Sand martins were nesting in the cliff-like dunes and buzzing all around me, making a soft, pattering, fizzing call as they flew past.

There was always at least one lapwing up above the pool, calling and displaying, though sometimes as many as six or seven birds would be up, with several of them chasing each other in dizzying, twisting rolls. The luminous pine-green colours on their backs were striking against the backdrop of the pool. Some birds appeared to perform abbreviated versions of their song flights, as I watched them zigzagging back and forth, and just as I thought they were about to rise into a full display, they would touch down next to the pool. But every so often a bird would launch into a full song flight and perform its repertoire of electric bubbling, combined with twisting, climbing, somersaulting flight. When this occurred, it was entrancing to watch, and my heart leapt at the display. Seton Gordon has a good description of the lapwing's song flight:

> Backwards and forwards the male lapwing flies with mad, swerving flight, the broad, rounded, creaking wings being driven fast. He then rises a little way almost vertically into the air, seems to turn a back somersault, and throws to the March wind his loud, defiant love song which sounds something like

> 'whey willuch ou weep, willuch ou willuch ehyuweep.'

The song sequence itself is short, lasting around 3.5 seconds. Each phrase of the song – demarcated by the gaps between the phrases in Gordon's transcription – is assigned to a different stage of the flight itself. Though it can appear a crazily spontaneous thing, the lapwing's song flight is a highly choreographed and ritualised performance. It follows a set sequence of moves and the song slots into that sequence at precisely the same moment for each display. Watching the lapwings displaying above the dunes, I was struck how their song flights, despite adhering to this highly structured routine, never felt repetitive. That, for me, is the beauty of the lapwing's song flight; they somehow dissolve any sense of a routine, without dismantling the flight's underlying structure. In other words, each song flight feels fresh, invigorating, and so fluid and playful in its execution, you forget – or it simply never dawns on you – that it's following a pattern.

Arriving on their breeding grounds as early as they do, from mid-February and all through March, lapwings are vulnerable to late winter blizzards. Occasionally, if the birds don't have time to escape the weather, freezing temperatures and snowstorms can prove catastrophic. Seton Gordon cites a particularly severe March in 1930, when the snow in the Highlands 'lay unbroken until the last week of the month, and the frost had entered so deeply into the ground that some upland farmers were unable to turn a furrow between the last Saturday of January and the opening day of April'. The blizzards that March came, unfortunately, after many waders – curlews, lapwings and oystercatchers – had arrived at their upland breeding grounds; a correspondent wrote to Gordon that, following these storms, he collected over two hundred dead birds, most of them lapwings. This correspondent – a fisherman on the Spey – also informed Gordon that in the space of 15 minutes, 18 dead lapwings floated past him on the river; 'for about 3 days after the storm,' the fisherman added, 'there was deadly silence over field and river.'

Prolonged periods of cold, though rare now in the British Isles, resulted in large exoduses of lapwings in the recent past, as the birds sought milder conditions elsewhere. Some of these cold weather migrations must have been spectacular to witness, with 40,000 lapwings recorded flying south over the Sussex coast on 31 December 1978. If one had witnessed such a large concentration of birds, it must have seemed as though every lapwing in the country was leaving; as they all did in the severe winters of 1962/63 and early in 1982, when there were virtually no lapwings left in Britain.

Lapwings migrating south, away from cold weather, in the autumn, will often fuse with populations of lapwings that have migrated from an entirely different region. When these birds return north in the spring, individuals will often get pulled along in the flow of birds heading to a different region from where they were born and would normally return to. This phenomenon, of getting mixed up with their migration routes, is known as 'abmigration', and seems to be a distinctive feature of lapwing movements, and perhaps explains why, with the resulting gene flow, there is little subspecies differentiation across the lapwing's range; northern lapwings (*Vanellus vanellus*) all essentially look the same, from the machair to Mongolia.

If I slowed down one of the song flights I watched among the lapwings in the dunes, this was what I saw. A lapwing would lift itself from the ground in that loose, floating way they have, as though they are always on the verge of drifting away. It is difficult to know what prompts a display, why one bird would suddenly launch itself into a song flight. There is that domino effect, a sense, as with the skylarks' field, of one song triggering another. But it could be anything or nothing that initiates the lapwing's display; early in the season the males are so primed to perform, the sound of a lapwing way over on the other side of the dunes could be sufficient to prompt a bird into its song flight.

Once airborne, the male lapwing I was watching flew low over the ground with slow, extended wingbeats. His flight was so low that on each downstroke the bird's wingtips almost brushed the ground. There was a sense during this low-level flight of the wings subsuming the bird, of the bird becoming his wings, so that all I could really make out were these broad, flapping wings heaving over the grass. This exaggerated flapping – the initial stage of the song flight – is known as the 'butterfly flight', due to its similarity to the movement of a butterfly's wings, though it's also been compared to the slow, graceful flight of a short-eared owl. 'Owl flight' or 'butterfly flight', watching the lapwing fly like this felt like I was watching a warm-up, the bird limbering, wing-stretching, albeit it was the shortest of warm-ups, lasting only 2, perhaps 3, seconds. Then the lapwing was speeding up, and rising, his wingbeat shallower, more normal in appearance.

As the bird rose, he started to swerve from side to side, throwing himself left, then right, in a zigzagging pattern. Each time he tilted to change course, the bird rolled so that his wings were tipped upwards, almost perpendicular to their level flight. Flicking himself from side to side like this, the black and white patterning on the lapwing's plumage alternated strikingly, and that combination of jerking flight and flickering black and white made me feel like I was watching a speeded-up animation, each tilt another frame in the sequence. This swerving back and forth has, appropriately, been termed the 'alternating flight', though 'rapid alternating flight' perhaps gives a better sense of the speed that the bird injects into this stage of the display. When I observed this flight in the lapwings over the dunes it seemed to last around 5 or 6 seconds, and it felt like the longest stage of the display. Flying like this, the lapwing quickly covered a wide area over the dunes in what appeared to be a long, curving line. When he passed close to me on this line, I could hear the bird's 'wing music', that humming sound coming from his vibrating primaries.

I could never predict when the zigzagging flight would end, at what point along its trajectory the bird would decide to switch to the next stage of the display; it was as though I missed the movement that signalled a change was coming. Perhaps this was because the 'alternating flight' had a hypnotic swinging motion to it, so I only registered that it had come to an end when the lapwing was already shooting steeply upwards. But other observers have identified what is called the 'low flight', between the 'alternating flight' and the 'ascent', where the lapwing drops out of the swerving, zigzagging display, and flies for about 15 to 30 ft very low over the ground, head and neck pulled back and upwards, as though the bird were anticipating the climb that follows.

As soon as I saw the lapwing climbing, I heard that first squeezed phrase of his song, Gordon's *whey willuch ou weep*. The bird climbed to around 15 ft, just clearing the top of the dunes, then, levelling off, he flew straight for a second or two back towards the pool, singing the middle section of his song – *willuch ou willuch*. Now he came to what I thought the most beautiful moment in the display: he turned on his back, not unlike the way I'd seen the ravens perform their mid-air rolls, though unlike the ravens, who quickly flipped back into level flight again, as the lapwing rolled he plunged down towards the ground, so that it looked like the bird was performing a backwards dive, swirling around as he dived and, at the same time, beating his wings. The effect of this – of the bird's wings continuing to beat during the descent – was that the lapwing appeared to be actually flying, rather than just diving, at the ground. As he made his descent, the final *ehy-u-weep* of his song spilled from the bird. It was all over in seconds, and the dive itself was not long, perhaps just a few metres (lapwing dives range anywhere from under 3 ft to up to 30 ft, the average being around 15). But to me the dive appeared longer than it was – and this was the case for all the other display flights I witnessed – because the lapwing fitted so much twisting manoeuvrability into such a brief descent.

Sometimes, when a lapwing came out of its dive, it would level out to glide over the ground before touching down on the grass. Other lapwings seemed to get caught in a display loop; instead of landing, they would flick back out of the dive and accelerate away into another series of swerving tacks around the perimeter of the dunes. After the supple agility of the song display, there was a stiffness to those lapwings that had landed. On the ground the birds had a tall, upright posture; they would make jerky darts over the grass, pause, then bob their heads and necks, as though hiccupping. I often felt with the grounded lapwings that they just wanted to be airborne again; so that when a flock of dunlin, sprinkled with ringed plovers, passed over the pool, and some of the lapwings rose to give chase, it seemed as though the lapwings were not really seeing off a threat, rather that they were just glad of an opportunity to test their mesmerising, twisting flight against another bird.

* * *

It was interesting that, despite the wind over the machair, the lapwings' songs during their displays were very clear and carried some distance. The way the song is structured, with its pauses, rhythmic repetitions (*willuch ou – willuch ou*) and harmonic range (*ehy-u-weep*), seems to equip the lapwing with the ability to communicate effectively in an open, windy, bird-busy habitat, such as the machair.

What *is* the lapwing communicating through its song flight? One way to think about this is to look at the different stages of the display, and, in particular, at what the origins of each stage are. In other words, to ask how has the lapwing's song flight been put together, from what has it been assembled? The ornithologist Torben Dabelsteen ascribed the different stages of the lapwing's display to behavioural traits in the bird. For example, he observed that the 'alternating flight' strongly resembles the flight lapwings use when chasing competitors and reacting to predators. Similarly, the dive sequence is very similar to the aggressive dives lapwings perform to deter predators. Essentially, most of the components of the lapwing's song flight have their origins in aggressively motivated behaviour. Even the song itself, with its distinctive components, is based on the way the bird uses those song phrases outside the song, usually when chasing predators and seeing off (sometimes being seen off by) rivals. The song of the lapwing – with its accumulated parts – is therefore primarily aggressive, 'dominated', in Dabelsteen's phrase, 'by attack tendencies'.

Is that what other lapwings hear and see when they observe a lapwing's song flight? Are the aggressive (though perhaps they should be described as 'defensive', given the lapwing's role in defending its territory) tendencies what other lapwings absorb from the display? I certainly witnessed lapwings employing that cork-screw dive, which is a part of the display flight, when they were diving at the sea eagles perched on the ground. And when the lapwings took off to pursue the eagle flying over the dunes, they did so with that swerving, zigzagging flight. So is the purpose of the song flight, therefore, not just to advertise and hold territory, but to signal the male's fitness and capability to chase off rivals and predators? The answer to this appears to be yes, as female lapwings seem to prefer those males that perform the most acrobatic display. This particularly applies to the arena of the 'alternating flight', where those male lapwings that rolled most steeply before each swerve were more likely to be selected by females. It seems that this component of the song flight – the longest section of the display – and one that is based on the bird's chasing, antagonistic behaviour, carries the most important information within the display as a whole.

It can be difficult, I think, to reconcile the fact that what is an exceptionally beautiful, graceful, acrobatic display has its origins in aggressive behaviour, and that the purpose of the song flight is for the lapwing to assert its competence as an aggressor, an individual that will defend its territory vigorously. But it is an indication of the hazards and predation pressures this ground-nesting bird endures that its ability to counter them is given primacy in its song display. This is a bird that will mob crows relentlessly, 'skin' dogs, stand up to harriers, even eagles. We come back to Gordon's 'extraordinarily pugnacious bird'; the lapwing as part shadow-boxer, part sky-dancer.

Have I been too formulaic in analysing the song and flight of the lapwing? I worry that in detailing such things as the structure and origins of the song display I have diminished the sheer joy of watching a lapwing's song flight, which, when you see and hear it, never feels like it is following any sort of rules. In any case, there are occasions, especially early in the breeding cycle, when lapwings seem to abandon any sort of structure to their displays. One observer described this behaviour as 'crazy flying', and observed that it sometimes resulted in 10 or 12 lapwings 'swooping and twisting about at once'. Occasionally, a group of female lapwings flying over a territory will trigger this crazy flying. When such a visit by females occurs, the male lapwings in the vicinity, although initially prompted to embark on and go through the stages of their song flight, soon develop or diverge from their traditional display into what has been described as 'virtuoso performances': 'high speed diving and twisting and climbing and zigzagging with complete abandon'. I suspect that when I visited the machair I was too late in the season to observe such a flight. But how I would love to have seen one. The lapwing abandoning all pretence of ritual and structure, and throwing itself into crazy, beautiful flight.

VIII

As Though She Lived on Song

Nightingale

A still, clear evening in spring. The wood is starting to grow dark. A song thrush is singing from the top of an ash. A blackbird makes its jittery way to bed. A tawny owl, a church bell, cars on the nearby road. Ten, fifteen minutes go by. The darkness is making me edgy and I'm thinking of heading home. Then I hear it, coming from the bushes behind me; a loud, trembling, pulsing sound, piercing the dark, like nothing else I've heard.

* * *

I'd learnt about a wood that still held a small population of nightingales. Towards the end of April and during the first few weeks of May, I travelled there as often as I could. Sometimes I would drive to the wood straight from work and spend several hours wandering around till well after dark, thinking every loud song thrush was a nightingale before finally giving up, despondent, knowing that I had not heard the real thing. The nightingales were elusive, and I didn't really know what I was doing, or whether the birds were even there at all. It felt like I was trying to spot a face in a crowd of birdsong. What added to my confusion was that the wood was full of song thrushes and many of the thrushes would imitate nightingale song phrases as part of their own song repertoire. It was a wonderfully confusing, tantalising place, where every new path I hadn't yet been down offered the prospect of nightingales, and every song thrush kept me guessing. It was such a large wood, too, with so many paths crisscrossing it; I felt I could spend all spring wandering among its trees, searching for nightingales.

After two visits to the wood, when I still had not heard a nightingale, I thought perhaps I should travel to a different part of England – to Kent or Suffolk – where there remained a much better chance of hearing nightingales. But there was something about the wood that I loved. Walking down the steep bank through the bluebells in the dusk, coming across badgers and roe deer along the rides at night, and once, as though I had wandered into the strange logic of a cartoon, a fox leaping across the path in front of me, being pursued by a barking muntjac. There was a sense of the wood, in springtime, of being a contained space, sealed off by birdsong. I would walk in and out of earshot of different birds, past song thrushes, blackbirds, nuthatches and robins. Then a buzzard, like a siren, would sound in the distance. And even though the song thrushes continued to tease me with their nightingale impersonations, I felt sure there must *be* nightingales somewhere in the wood, for the thrushes to have learnt those phrases in the first place.

One of the things that helped me to locate the nightingales was reading an account by a contemporary wildlife photographer of my great-grandfather. When Seton Gordon was photographing ptarmigan on the high tops of the Cairngorms, Norman Ticehurst, in the springs of 1911 and 1912, was photographing nightingales in a wood in the south of England. Ticehurst's photographs (among the first taken of a nightingale), and his notes that accompany them, achieve remarkable intimacy with the nightingales in the birds' tangled, hidden world. For instance, he writes about the nightingales, when perched, having their tails in constant motion, 'with a characteristic upward flick and a slower subsidence to the horizontal', giving the sense of a bird that is permanently on the move. He also observed how the male nightingale would signal his arrival with food to the female on the nest by 'a burst of song', despite the male having his bill 'crammed with green caterpillars'.

But it is Ticehurst's account of the technical difficulties of photographing the nightingales that steered me towards the sort of habitat where I might locate the birds in the wood. He described the nightingales' nest-site he studied as being so overgrown, and having such a paucity of natural light, that, in order to photograph the birds successfully (and he found it very difficult to do so), he needed to use a long exposure, fast plates and the widest admissible lens aperture. So hidden and tangled is the nightingale's domain (and so dark), Ticehurst found it was virtually impossible for him to spot the juvenile birds after the young nightingales had fledged and, over the subsequent days, they started creeping through the vegetation around the nest. He spent an hour or more every day watching the vicinity of the nest for ten days after the young had fledged, but despite often spotting the adult nightingales during these vigils, anxious and whistling – indicating the fledglings were present – he only once in all that time caught a brief glimpse of one of the young birds.

Ticehurst's vivid account of trying to photograph the birds was a useful guide; listen for nightingales in the most impenetrable part of the wood, it seemed to suggest. Similarly, John Clare encapsulates that advice, most beautifully, in a line from his 1832 poem, 'The Nightingale's Nest', where he describes the singing nightingale as being 'lost in a wilderness of listening leaves'.

What set the south-west corner of the wood apart was that, in places, it was so dense with scrub, it was impossible for a person to enter, let alone walk through. There were fewer large trees there, too, so that through May, as the rest of wood grew darker with the trees coming into leaf, there was still a good deal of light in that corner of the wood, allowing the understorey to thrive. The result was a tangled thicket of blackthorn, hazel, honeysuckle and bramble. The remainder of the wood was fairly open, and I could walk easily among the trees. But in the south-west corner it was as though the interstices between the trees had widened, and scrub, like a wave, had poured into the gaps. Perfect for nightingales.

The first time I heard a nightingale was just before noon on the last day of April. I'd returned to the wood to spend the whole of that day and evening there. My thinking was that, rather than these snatched visits I'd been making up till then, I should just go and spend an entire day in the wood and focus on its overgrown corner, where, if nightingales were present, then at some point during the day or night I was sure to hear them.

Nightingales sing both during the day and at night. Again, John Clare reminds us of this in 'The Nightingale's Nest'. In the poem he recalls listening to nightingales 'at morn and eve nay all the live long day', 'as though', in another beautiful line from this poem, 'she lived on song'.

There is a difference in character between the nightingale's nocturnal and daytime song; the daytime song is usually shorter, contains less variety and greater repetition than the nocturnal song. The purpose of the two also appears to be different; the night-time song is more concerned with courtship, with securing a mate, while the diurnal song has more of a territorial significance.

Male nightingales arrive on their breeding territories around a week before the females (those males that arrive earlier are more successful in attracting a female than late arrivals), and the males commence singing at night to attract the female nightingales passing overhead. A study looking at the differences between nocturnal and diurnal singing in nightingales found that daytime singing activity among males was comparatively low until after the females had arrived. Thereafter, once the females had settled on their territories, male nightingales that sung frequently during the day suffered fewer territorial incursions from other males.

The essential pattern, therefore, is that male nightingales sing through the night to attract a mate, then sing through the day to fend off other males. Most males cease singing at night once they have formed a pair with a female, resuming nocturnal singing for a brief period of around three nights when the female lays her eggs. Those nightingales that do continue to sing at night through the remainder of the breeding season are most likely unpaired males. There can often be quite a number of these unattached male nightingales (as many as 50 per cent) present in a given area, which can sometimes make it difficult to identify the number of actual breeding pairs. But those male nightingales that have not yet attracted a mate will continue to use the night as a vehicle for their song.

The stance from which the nightingale's daytime and night-time song is delivered is different too. The daytime song is more fidgety, often given from different locations within the bird's territory, while the nocturnal song tends to be performed from a single perch. When singing, the nightingale adopts an almost upright stance, its head tilted up, white throat feathers puffed out, wings beating rapidly, with the bird's wide-open bill showing a yellow-and-orange gape. The diurnal song seems to be more a case of the nightingale beating the bounds of its territory; the nocturnal song about finding a stage on which the bird can perform uninterrupted. *How* uninterrupted varies, but there is an account of one bird singing for 23.5 hours in a single day! Somewhere between 5 and 30 minutes, however, is more the norm.

There are other types of song the nightingale performs. In winter, for example, nightingales sometimes sing a more subdued version of their song. This subsong starts to acquire more variety and be sung more frequently as spring approaches, and nightingales will sing on passage when they migrate to their breeding territories, as though the birds are rehearsing their songs as they travel north. Males will also perform a quieter courtship song to the female. This usually takes place low down among the bushes or on the ground, and the song is accompanied by a fluttering, waltz-like display by the male – bowing, opening and spreading his tail, shivering his wings – a performance that the naturalist and wildlife photographer Oliver Pike described as 'exceedingly graceful', adding that he had 'never watched a more beautiful display by any bird'.

Some nightingales include mimicry of other bird songs in their repertoire, but this does not appear to be a common trait. While I sometimes detected phrases of the nightingale's song in the song thrush, I could never detect it the other way around; the nightingale's song always seemed to be of itself (though some writers have been able to discern examples of where each bird has borrowed from the other). Where there is an overlap between common nightingales and thrush nightingales (the species of nightingale found in northern and eastern Europe), is when common nightingales will sometimes mimic aspects of the thrush nightingale's slower, less varied song, and thus have a slower and more repetitive song themselves.

I arrived at the wood that morning around 10 a.m. It was cold and overcast, and already, largely on account of the temperature, I thought I would be in for a long day and night of not hearing anything; Oliver Pike had cautioned that it was 'almost useless' to visit a nightingale wood on 'cold evenings when a north wind is blowing', as in such conditions the birds simply hunker down with their bills tucked under their feathers.

I parked the car off a narrow lane, packed a small daysack and set off walking along the sunken track that led into the wood. As I descended the bank, which dropped away towards the south of the wood, I counted off the different birds I could hear singing: blackbird, blackcap, robin, wren, then (yes, even here) a raven in the distance. Beside a puddle on the track, I spotted a male and female blackcap and admired the dance of colours between them, the soft light of the female's chestnut cap beside the male's inky black beret. This stretch of the track was wet and muddy, and some of the puddles were soupy with frogspawn. As I was looking at the blackcap pair, I heard a loud, rapid *keer-keer-keer* call, and looked up to see a hobby flying fast on its long, pointed wings. It landed on the branch of a tall pine and straight away another hobby joined it there, and I watched as the pair scuffled through the tree together. Through my binoculars I could make out the falcons' distinctive dark moustachial stripe and the red blush around their legs.

I was in the south-west corner of the wood now, and as I turned the next bend there was a narrow, overgrown path leading up a bank to my right. Immediately I disturbed a male blackbird, who shot off down the path's tunnel, making a rapid, bubbling alarm call. I followed the blackbird, and as I stepped onto the path there was a short burst of liquid-sounding song, very loud, coming from about halfway down the path. I knew it was a nightingale. Its sheer volume was extraordinary, and the notes had this deep, quivering intensity to them. A burst of clear, rapid whistling notes, then a long pause of maybe 6 seconds, before there was another burst, this time of clattering sounds, like a speeded-up magpie's rattle. Another pause, and I walked a little further along the path, then froze as the nightingale let off a series of pulsing notes, sounding like the stuttering laser blasts of a *Space Invaders* game.

I was so relieved to have found this bird. And I suddenly felt a bit foolish at how confused I'd been, on those previous visits, by the song thrushes. All that confusion dropped away on hearing the nightingale; the sound – the loud, fast-flowing clarity of the bird's notes – was utterly distinctive. The song, however, was quite fragmented, and it felt like this individual was delivering just a few brief phrases of its song. At least, it felt like the nightingale kept interrupting its song, and I had a sense of the bird moving around in the thicket, releasing a burst of pulsating notes, then moving to a different perch to release another burst.

I sat down on a stump in the middle of the path and took out my binoculars to scan the undergrowth in front of me. Each time the nightingale released another rush of song I fixed my binoculars on where I thought the sound was coming from, trying to make sense of the tangle of branches, looking for gaps in the foliage where a bird might be perched. I caught a movement along the branch of a hawthorn bush, and there was a mouse weaving through the leaves. Then there was another sequence of song, this time slightly longer, a rattling *churr-churr-churrrr*, extremely close and loud, feeling like the nightingale was only a few feet in front of me. Still, though, I couldn't locate the singer. A robin was singing on the other side of the path as well, and each time the robin paused in its song, the nightingale responded with a rattling, whistly sequence of notes.

I'd read how nightingales are often prompted to sing even louder when they are accompanied, or challenged, by other birdsong, particularly when this involves loud songsters such as thrushes, blackbirds and blackcaps. The louder the competition, the more the nightingale comes into its own, seemed to be the general rule. So much so that Oliver Pike, who in 1932 made a film about the nightingale for *The Secrets of Nature* series, commented, slightly impatiently, that the famous BBC radio broadcasts of a cellist accompanying a nightingale, which ran between 1924 and 1942, employed both the wrong sort of instrument and music (the cello being too 'slow' and 'soft') to bring out the best in a nightingale's song. 'If the nightingale listens to slow music it will give slow music in return,' was Pike's assessment; he thought that 'loud, lively jazz music' or even thunderstorms were more effective inducements for a nightingale to sing at its best. Poignantly, Pike also witnessed a nightingale that was prompted to sing in a wood in northern France in the spring of 1916 during a heavy artillery bombardment, though its song was cut short when the bird was killed by an explosion, together with five men who were standing nearby.

I found it hard to discern whether the nightingales along the path sang more loudly when other birds were singing close by. But as with the robin singing on the other side of the path, I often had the sense of the nightingales being part of an ensemble of birdsong. Just as I was listening to the robin and nightingale duet together, a chiffchaff began to sing from one of the trees overlooking the path, as though keeping rhythm with its repeated notes. Then a wren joined them, trilling beneath the nightingale, and often, like an echo, filling the nightingale's long silences.

There were several variations on these ensembles, with different birds duetting, at different times of day, with the nightingales. The bird that seemed to induce a nightingale to sing, more than any other, was the blackbird. And on several occasions when I had been waiting a long time to hear a nightingale, it was a blackbird who appeared to prompt the nightingale, finally, to sing. A blackbird would start singing in that slow, soft way they have, so that it seems like they are thinking through their song's progression. And within a few phrases of the blackbird's song a nightingale would launch into a series of extraordinary loud clicking, strobe-like beeping sounds: *theew*, *theew*, *theew*, followed by a sequence of long, trembling whistles. All the time, the blackbird kept singing its quiet undertone.

The most interesting duets for me to listen to, I found, were the ones between the nightingales and song thrushes. Again, as with the blackbirds, the thrushes seemed not so much to prompt but more to coax the nightingales into song. These duets tended to occur around dusk, between 8 and 8.30 p.m. A song thrush would be singing from high up in one of the ash trees above the path, running through its eclectic repertoire of sounds, repeating each phrase to itself, then reinterpreting the notes, squeezing them into a different phrase.

And every so often there would be a sequence of whistling notes that sounded like they had been borrowed from a nightingale. Then, as if on cue, a nightingale would start singing below the song thrush, and it always felt to me as though the nightingale had finally been stirred into song by the thrush's prompts and cues.

Were these accompaniments from other birds, however, more like duels than duets? Oliver Pike uses the term 'challenge' when describing the way a nightingale responds through its song to other sounds, as in the bird 'replying' to the 'challenge' of the noise of a thunderstorm. Certainly, it is the case that male nightingales – as with skylarks – perform 'song duels' with other males to settle territorial disputes. The territorial boundary during these quarrels seems to act as a kind of no man's land that the rival nightingales approach by adopting a 'strangled' version of their song or uttering a series of alarm calls instead, the boundary itself seeming to have a distorting effect on the bird's song. Sometimes rival males will chase each other up into the trees and back to ground again during these duels, singing all the time.

Nightingales appear to use their song to settle territorial disputes, but they also use it to both avoid, and initiate, these disputes in the first place. Those nightingales that sing more often and for longer periods suffer fewer incursions from other male nightingales; so the more a nightingale sings, the more their song serves as a deterrent to other males. However, those birds with higher song rates also tend to intrude on other territories more frequently; in other words, the more they sing, the more they are bolstered into making forays into the territories of other nightingales.

I find this relationship between a nightingale's song and the way that song can direct both the movement of the listeners to the song (other nightingales) and the singer itself, fascinating. Of all the birds I've written about in this book the nightingale is the one, culturally, that we most associate with its song, to the extent that the bird and its song are almost inseparable. However, rather than lose something of the reality of the nightingale by approaching it solely through the prism of its song, we in fact touch on a truth about the bird – that the nightingale *is*, to a large extent, its song. The nightingale's song controls the spatial behaviour of the birds; territorial boundaries are composed of walls of song; birds encroach into other territories under the primacy and protection of their own songs; nightingales settle disputes with their songs; and birds that lose these disputes retreat with song-wounds.

The one time I did see a nightingale in the wood, I was sitting on the stump in the middle of the overgrown path and had been listening to a nightingale in front of me. I caught a movement through my binoculars, much deeper inside the bushes than I had been expecting, and there was a large, shiny black eye. The colour of the eye was enhanced by a narrow white ring that encircled the black like the shore around a lake. I could see a rusty, reddish-brown tail, browner wings and greyish patches around the head. The tail feathers gave off a faint glow. A second or two like this, then a flickering movement and the nightingale was gone, back into the wilderness of leaves.

It was a brief glimpse of the hidden world of the nightingale, the world beyond their song. Nightingales are like shy robins, preferring to stay hidden, foraging among the leaf litter on the ground and through the undergrowth, tilting their head to the side, much like a robin does, as they listen out for the minuscule scratchings of their invertebrate prey. Beetles, weevils, earthworms, ants and spiders are all typical prey species, with some berries and seeds also eaten by nightingales later in the summer.

Watching Pike's 1932 film *The Nightingale*, seeing the birds foraging through the undergrowth, you get a sense of the way a nightingale moves, of those characteristic head-tilting, tail-flicking gestures; a sense too of quite a long-legged bird, and so of a taller, slimmer bird than a robin. When the nightingale is perched on a branch, flicking its tail up and down, the movement sometimes fans the nearby leaves, so that the bird's tail appears to be coaxing the leaves to dance.

The same day I caught that glimpse of a nightingale deep in the undergrowth, I had another unexpected encounter on the path. I had seen nobody else in the wood all day, but in the middle of the afternoon four men came round the corner in their green and blue waterproof jackets. They stopped at the top of the path and looked hesitantly down towards where I stood. I nodded back to them, and one of the men began to walk slowly down the path towards me, his jacket making a swishing sound as its sleeves brushed against his side.

'Anything up?' he said when he reached me. I nodded towards the thicket in front of us and told him that there was a nightingale in there, singing on and off. 'Mostly short bursts of song', I said apologetically.

He then turned towards his friends and waved to them, and, one by one, they filed onto the path and walked down to join us. As they passed me, each of the men nodded hello. Then, as though we had already decided the arrangement, all five of us lined up 6 ft apart along the narrow path facing the wall of undergrowth.

The next hour on that path was a lovely experience. We didn't say anything to one another. All of us just stood there in silence, waiting, listening to the nightingale when it sang. Sometimes 5 minutes would go by in silence, then there would be a sudden burst of song from the thicket. The gaps between the song phrases got longer, so that it seemed as though the bird were running down its song in there. And after an hour or so it ceased singing, and the men turned and walked off down the path together.

On another occasion, when I visited the wood at night, I met a man coming towards me down the path. He told me he had taken a detour on his way home from work; 'I don't have long to spare', he said, 'just wanted to see if I could hear them.'

Do any other songbirds do that to people? What is it about the nightingale's song that makes someone take a detour on their way home from work, that pulled those four men into the wood to stand in silence for an hour beside me? Perhaps more than with any other bird, there is something about the nightingale's song that draws us to it. Is that because the song is so celebrated in our culture, in poetry in particular? Is it because the song is so renowned, or is it just that the song itself is remarkable, strange and beautiful, made more so because it is largely – and almost uniquely among songbirds – nocturnal? Or is it perhaps because the song has become precious through its rarity?

I suspect it may be a combination of all these things. But the bird's increasing rarity as a breeding species in England enhances the experience – and the poignancy – of listening to nightingales here. I was acutely aware, for example, that in the wood where I listened to the birds, there were very few nightingales present. The most birds I was able to count in a single night were three, perhaps four, singing males. And one year I only heard one nightingale singing, early in the season, and, despite visiting on several occasions through May, I never heard another bird singing that spring. There was almost the sense, that year, that I was listening to the wood's last remaining nightingale.

The south-east of England, the nightingale's heartland in this country, holds much denser populations of the bird than the wood I visited, which was more like an outlier on the very north-western edge of the bird's range, both in England (nightingales don't breed in Wales or Scotland) and therefore also in Europe. It may even have been the case that the lone nightingale I heard in the wood that dismal spring was indeed the loneliest nightingale in Europe. He was certainly a long way adrift from the bulk of the English population (roughly 5,500 singing males), which are found in Kent, Sussex, Essex and Suffolk. But that number marks a decrease of more than 90 per cent in the last 40 years. And in 2015 – alongside the skylark and lapwing – the nightingale was added to the UK's Birds of Conservation Concern Red List. The rate of decline in the species (only the turtle dove, wood warbler and willow tit have declined to a greater extent over the same period), alongside its geographical contraction towards the south-east, has led to warnings that the nightingale could, in the very near future, become extinct as a breeding species in Britain.

One of the puzzles around the nightingale's range contraction in Britain is that it goes against the modelling for this species, which suggests, due to the impacts of climate change, a northwards expansion. In other words, as the climate warms, nightingales, which are associated with areas that enjoy a more continental climate, should be able to spread north from the south-east of England. But this predicted expansion has not occurred, and many of the factors that have led to the nightingale's decline in Britain are shared by species like the nightjar, skylark and lapwing, habitat loss being a key driver of the nightingale's decline. Scrubland and coppiced woodland, the nightingale's preferred habitats in Britain, are a rarity now. Scrubland – the overgrown, thorny, brambly places nightingales love to nest in – has largely been scrubbed out in Britain to make way for development, agriculture, or, in some places, it has been diminished through overgrazing by deer. Coppiced woodland, apart from when it is deliberately managed for wildlife, is largely a thing of the past, as it no longer carries the commercial incentive it once did, though there has recently been a revival of interest in managing woodland this way.

There may be other factors, outside Britain, that have led to the nightingale's decline, including habitat loss in the bird's wintering sites in Africa, as well as drought conditions in some of the nightingale's migration stop-over sites. But it remains the case that in Britain, while we celebrate – perhaps more than any other bird – the nightingale's song, we have also, through our negligence, through what the writer, Benedict Macdonald has termed Britain's 'ecological tidiness disorder', greatly reduced – almost silenced – that song.

In an echo of Seton Gordon's view, which I referred to at the start of this book, that 'it is impossible to set down the greenshank's song in words', Oliver Pike, similarly, wrote that 'it is not easy to put the nightingale's song into words'; 'If half a dozen people attempted it', Pike thought, 'I doubt if two would use the same syllables.' And Bethan Roberts in her recent book, *Nightingale*, writes of the song that she didn't 'have the words to describe the sound, but I know how it feels'. I think that sentiment gets to the heart of the experience of listening to nightingales; it is a deeply sensory experience. The writer Richard Mabey, too, has described how listening to a nightingale's song can leave him 'puzzling' as to how the song 'can have such an extraordinary effect on one's senses and emotions.' And Sam Lee, in another recent work on the nightingale, writes that, for him, 'the song was visual.' You *see* the nightingale's song, and you *feel* it.

My own experience of listening to nightingales was that I never got used to the song; it never settled into the soundscape as other birdsong does. Sometimes I would feel it almost physically as though the notes were reverberating through me. Both Richard Mabey and the poet Edward Thomas have also remarked on this 'penetrating' quality of the sound; Thomas describing it as 'like steel for coldness and penetration', Mabey as 'astonishingly pure and penetrating'. I was always amazed by the volume of the song, which can be heard more than a mile away; a nightingale singing some way off could sound like it was much closer than it actually was, and when a bird *was* singing close to me it seemed on occasion like the ground itself was trembling. I was also spellbound by the variety of sounds the nightingales made. The long silences that punctuated the songs made it feel as though the birds were using the pauses to run through their extensive repertoire, as though deciding which sequence to play next. Individual nightingales can hold song repertoires containing more than 250 different phrases, and the birds can deliver more than

400 of these phrases per hour, sometimes beginning a series of phrases with a new introduction, sometimes shuffling the phrases around so that they follow a different sequence.

While (especially during the daytime) I might hear only snatched sequences of phrases that didn't seem to be part of a full song, I also – particularly at night – heard long sequences of full song from the nightingales. These renditions often started with a series of trills, rising in volume, the notes echoey and very pure sounding. Edward Thomas described these notes 'as rounded and as full of liquid sweetness as a grape, and they are clustered like a grape'. Thomas also described the notes, memorably, as, 'wild and pure as mountain water in the dawn'.

After the sequence of trills, there would be a pause, then a series of knocks, rattles, Sputnik-beeps, and those pulsing, electric laser blasts, intercut with a beautiful sequence of trembling, whistling notes. I attempted to transcribe some of these sounds in my notebook, but it was always as though the phrases ran away from me as I was writing them down: *chi-eeew – chew-eee – did – did – err – err – rup* ... One feature I noticed in one of the nightingales was that every so often the bird would introduce this plaintive, whistling, almost wheezy sound, as though the singer were trying to catch its breath. It had a captivating fragility, that sound, and those whistling sequences were the most ventriloquial I heard from the nightingale, as they always sounded fainter and further away than the other phrases in the song. When I first heard those notes, they sounded as though they were being made by a different bird.

One other trick the nightingales would perform was that, rather than throw their voice (as the nightjars did), the birds would throw themselves from one side of the narrow path to the other. For instance, I would be listening to a nightingale singing from the bushes in front of me, then there would be a pause of maybe 10 seconds before the bird would start up singing from the bushes on the other side of the path. I might have been mistaken, but I was sure it was the same bird, as I only ever heard it singing from one side of the path at a time, as though the path were simply part of this bird's territory. The trick was that the nightingale always seemed to cross the path without me noticing it. Once, I thought I caught a blurred movement out of the corner of my eye, but I couldn't be sure what it was. The next moment the bird was singing behind me, as if it had slipped by under cover of my blink.

Edward Thomas wrote that the 'onset' of the nightingale's song 'is like nothing else'. And that, for me, rings true. It's partly a feeling of surprise I had each time I heard a nightingale begin to sing; surprised by the loudness of the noise, but also a feeling of being taken aback, not quite trusting that what I heard – its volume, its echoey quality – was coming from a bird. Thomas added that, listening to a nightingale, 'we hear voices that were not dreamed of before', and this perhaps helps to explain the emotional response many people have when they encounter the song; we hear notes and phrases, combinations of sounds and silences in the nightingale's song that dismantle and refresh what we think a bird's song is capable of. A nightingale's song seems to work on us differently to that of other birds. The writer H. E. Bates grasped this when he wrote this description of nightingale song in his 1936 book *Through the Woods*:

> It has some kind of electric, suspended quality that has a far deeper beauty than the most passionate of its sweetness. It is a performance made up, very often, more of silence than of utterance. The very silences have a kind of passion in them, a sense of breathlessness and restraint, of restraint about to be magically broken.

At the start of May I arrived at the wood around 8.30 p.m., just as it was beginning to grow dark. I walked down the track and turned right onto the narrow path. A soft, frog-like grunt sounded above me, and I looked up to see a woodcock passing overhead, wings flickering, its long bill tilted downwards. There was a nightingale singing from the bushes about 30 ft away. I walked towards the song and stopped just in front of it. The bird released a series of trilling notes, rich and clear, which ran like a current along the ground and up through my toes. I could hear all the small ticks, shuffles and breathy whistles in its voice. A pause, and then it let out two quieter whistling notes, like an inhalation of breath.

That performance was the longest I heard any nightingale give in the wood, lasting maybe half an hour. By the time the bird finished singing it was completely dark. I made several recordings of the nightingale's song that evening and, listening back to them, I'm struck how true Bates's description of the song being made up 'more of silence than of utterance' is. I have been referring to these silences as 'pauses' in the song, yet I'm not sure that's quite what they are; there is something occurring in the silences, something expressive about them, as Bates detected. But the silences also, I think, give the nightingale's song a sense of hesitancy and fragility. The song is incredibly loud and expressive, yet, at the same time, there is this sense that it never quite seems certain of itself, that it never quite settles. The effect of the silences (which can sometimes last for as long as 20 or 30 seconds) is that they lend the song a tentativeness. There is a paradox of sorts here, that a bird so celebrated for its music has a song that is composed of so much silence. But the way in which that silence expresses and unsettles the nightingale's song creates something uniquely beautiful.

Another contradiction about nightingales is that they are birds that do not, in fact, really belong in the night. They are essentially diurnal – they don't, for instance, forage at night – and they simply happen to use the conditions of night to sing in, as do some other diurnal birds such as corncrakes, sometimes robins and dunnocks too. As one study of nightingales put it, 'singing at night is an exceptional addition to their daily behavioural routines during the breeding season.' Nightingales trespass the night with their song. And just as their song has this hesitancy to it, there is also a tentativeness to the birds themselves at night. For example, singing nightingales will not tend to move around much in the dark, preferring to perform their song from a single perch, as though the birds don't trust the darkness around them.

That nervousness at night is also apparent whenever a predatory tawny owl calls, prompting nightingales to hush their singing. The energy costs of singing at night are substantial for nightingales; the birds need to prepare for a night's singing through additional feeding so that their body mass at dusk, before they commence singing, is sufficient to see them through the night. Those energy reserves will drain away when they sing, and a nightingale will finish its night shift lighter than when it began it at dusk.

There is therefore a tension behind the nightingale's song at night; the bird is taking a risk, stepping into an element it is not adapted to at a substantial energetic cost so it can perform its song. Yet somehow, despite this tension, this hesitancy – perhaps because of it – the nightingale, through its song, has made the night its own.

I often felt tense at night in the wood. It was sometimes hard to shake off the feeling of unease the dark could bring, and there were nights when I was glad to get back to the warmth of the car and turn for home. One night, when it was especially dark, I saw a figure walking slowly along one of the rides. They kept stopping, then moving on a few paces. I wasn't sure what to do. Leaving felt a bit silly, and I always preferred to say hello to the few people I met in the wood, to share what we had heard or not heard of the nightingales.

But I also felt a little uneasy as it was very late and there was nobody else in the wood that night. By now I could see it was a man and that he was still walking very slowly, stopping every few paces. But then he must have noticed me, as he suddenly turned and started to head in my direction. He was walking quickly now, and his pace was making me nervous. But as he drew closer, I relaxed; the man had a huge, warm smile on his face. I didn't need to ask if he had been listening to the nightingales. 'Just extraordinary,' he said, as he passed me. Then he walked off into the dark.

Acknowledgements

Thank you to my agent, Jessica Woollard for her support and for responding so enthusiastically to the idea for this book at a very early stage. To Nicholas Pearson, who also responded so positively when he acquired *Wild Air* for 4th Estate. To Myles Archibald for his perceptive editorial guidance, and to Eve Hutchings at 4th Estate, both of whom it has been a pleasure to work with. To Mark Bolland for his meticulous copy-edit and index. To Norman Arlott for his wonderful illustrations of the birds. To Andrew McNeillie for his support and for publishing work in progress from this book in *Archipelago* magazine. To Sophie Wilcox at the Alexander Library of Ornithology in Oxford, and to the staff at the Vere Harmsworth Library, Oxford. Thank you also to Jim Manthorpe and Lesley Watt for their helpful advice on the shearwater colony on Rum. Lastly, thank you as ever to Nicki, C & J.

Notes

Full publication details of the titles listed in this section are given in the Bibliography.

Introduction

2 **'I would strongly advise ...'**: Seton Gordon, *Hill Birds of Scotland*, p. vii.
2 **consider tuning up his bagpipes**: Ibid., p. 113.
3 **'It was plain that the keeper ...'**: Seton Gordon, *Birds of the Loch and Mountain*, p. 176.
4 **before his deafness took hold**: see also Adam Watson, *Some Days from a Hill Diary*, p. 9: 'He [Seton] said the Braemar, Ballater and Aboyne chaffinches have different songs, but on account of increasing deafness he cannot now hear birdsong.'
6 **'in certain respects ...'**: Seton Gordon, *Thirty Years of Nature Photography*, p. 69.
6 **'It is impossible to set down ...'**: Ibid., p. 69.
6 **'On returning home ...'**: Ibid., p. 69.
7 **birds can sing with 'two voices'**: Roderick A. Suthers, 'Contributions to Birdsong from the Left and Right Sides of the Intact Syrinx'.
7 **Each of these chambers in the syrinx can produce sounds ...**: Ibid.
7 **'eludes all verbal description'**: Daines Barrington, 'Experiments and Observations on the Singing of Birds', p. 284.

8 **'everywhere in Scotland … much scarcer'**: Seton Gordon, *Highland Summer*, p. 13.
8 **like the lapwing**: see also Seton Gordon, *In the Highlands*, p. 44: 'I should like to see passed an Act of Parliament protecting this attractive and useful bird in all districts of Britain throughout the year, and not only during the nesting season.'

I. The Bird that Hides Its Shadow: *Nightjar*

10 **is close to mimicry**: David L. Lack, 'Some Diurnal Observations on the Nightjar'.
11 **some climatic variation across the species**: Charles Vaurie, 'Systematic Notes on Palearctic Birds, No. 40, Caprimulgidae'.
11 **focus on the contours of the patterning**: Lack, 'Some Diurnal Observations'.
11 **habitually roost lengthways**: Ibid.
11 **a thin slit through which the bird keeps watch**: Ibid.
11 **'closing up'**: John Walpole-Bond, *A History of Sussex Birds, Vol. II*, p. 156.
11 **'the narrowest of railings'**: Ibid., p. 161.
11 **more likely to roost during the day on the ground**: Lack, 'Some Diurnal Observations'.
12 **shifting their position so they are always facing the sun**: Peter Tate, *The Nightjar*, p. 17.
12 **eggs have not evolved the level of protective colouration**: Lack, 'Some Diurnal Observations'.
12 **locate them in the dark**: Nigel Cleere, 'Goatsuckers'.
12 **exceptionally close sitters**: Lack, 'Some Diurnal Observations'.
13 **roll away from under them**: Ibid.
13 **incubating their first egg as soon as it is laid**: Ibid.
13 **removal of the eggshells**: Peter Tate, *The Nightjar*, p. 19
13 **A study of nightjars in Dorset**: Giselle Murison, 'The Impact of Human Disturbance on the Breeding Success of Nightjar *Caprimulgus europaeus* on Heathlands in South Dorset, England'.
14 **as long as 9 minutes … up to 19.5 minutes**: Tate, *The Nightjar*, p. 21.

14 **described as 'skirling'**: Walpole-Bond, *A History of Sussex Birds*, p. 151.
14 **comprises 28 to 42 notes ...**: Tate, *The Nightjar*, p. 21.
14 **in particular, the mole-cricket**: J. F. Burton & E. D. H. Johnson, 'Insect, Amphibian or Bird?'
15 **exploits the air passage that connects a bird's two inner ear cavities ...** Charles H. Brown, 'Ventroloquial and Locatable Vocalizations in Birds'.
15 **much easier to locate a call made up of multiple frequencies**: http://www.birdingisfun.com/2011/01/bird-ventriloquism.html
16 **overlap with the timing of their song**: Burton & Johnson, 'Insect, Amphibian or Bird?'
16 **'In fine weather ...'**: Gilbert White, *A Natural History of Selborne*, p. 241.
16 **more 'chirr' than 'churr'**: Burton & Johnson, 'Insect, Amphibian or Bird?'
16 **confuse even seasoned ornithologists**: Ibid.
16 **chorus of wood-crickets ...**: Ibid.
16 **acoustic camouflage**: Ibid.
16 **insect-like songs of some warbler species**: Ibid.
17 **'like the sound of a stream of wine ...'**: J. A. Baker, *The Peregrine*, p. 11.
17 **small-engined motorbike ... sometimes stood in for a churring nightjar**: Michael Clegg, 'Insect, Amphibian or Bird?'
18 **The many names for the nightjar ...**: Tate, *The Nightjar*, p. 23; also, Charles Swainson, *The Folk Lore and Provincial Names of British Birds*, pp. 96–8.
18 **'The buzzing dor-hawk, round and round, is wheeling'**: William Wordsworth, 'The Waggoner'.
18 ***engana pastor***: **'shepherd's deceiver'**: Swainson, *Folk Lore*, p. 98.
18 **from the Latin *capra* ...**: Cleere, 'Goatsuckers'.
19 **derives from a skin infection**: Tate, *The Nightjar*, p. 23.
19 **White was quick to dismiss this belief ...**: https://naturalhistoryofselborne.com/1789/08/09/august-9-1789/
19 **whole baggage of folklore ...**: Swainson, *Folk Lore*, p. 98.
19 **distinctive plip-plop call**: Cleere, 'Goatsuckers' (in side article titled 'A landmark encounter' by Simon Colenutt).

20 **'aural litter' or 'audible trash'**: Bernie Krause, *The Great Animal Orchestra*, p. 157.

20 **two principal phrases to the nightjar's song ...**: Hunter, Jr., Malcolm L., 'Vocalization During Inhalation in a Nightjar'.

21 **like a 'clockwork toy running down'**: Tate, *The Nightjar*, p. 21.

21 **2020 study of nightjars in Nottinghamshire**: Stephen Docker *et al.*, 'Identification of Different Song Types in the European Nightjar *Caprimulgus europaeus*'.

22 **result of the bird's breathing rhythm**: Tate, *The Nightjar*, p. 21

22 **appears to lie with the pattern of the song ...**: Hunter, Jr., Malcolm L., 'Vocalization During Inhalation in a Nightjar'.

23 **key to both sexual selection ...**: Ibid.

23 **by the middle of August, the churr is usually weaker**: David L. Lack, 'Some Breeding-habits of the European Nightjar'.

23 **identify individual males from their song**: M. Rebbeck *et al.*, 'Recognition of Individual European Nightjars *Caprimulgus europaeus* from their Song'.

27 **entering a state of torpidity**: V. A. Peiponen, 'On Hypothermia and Torpidity in the Nightjar (*Caprimulgus europaeus* L.)'; also, Nigel Cleere & Dave Nurney, *Nightjars: A Guide to Nightjars and Related Nightbirds*, p. 25.

27 **common poorwill ... enter a state of hibernation**: Ibid., pp. 24–5.

27 **require some degree of light**: Alexander M. Mills, 'The Influence of Moonlight on the Behaviour of Goatsuckers (Caprimulgidae)'.

27 **bulk of their prey species ...**: Tate, *The Nightjar*, pp. 21–2.

28 **several notable adaptations ...**: Cleere, 'Goatsuckers'.

28 **Another specialised adaptation ...**: Ibid.

28 **recent study in Switzerland concluded**: A. Sierro & A. Erhardt, 'Light Pollution Hampers Recolonization of Revitalised European Nightjar Habitats in the Valais (Swiss Alps)'.

29 **synchronise their reproductive cycle with the lunar cycle**: Alexander M. Mills, 'The Influence of Moonlight on the Behaviour of Goatsuckers (Caprimulgidae)'.

29 **lunarphilic in their behaviour**: Ibid.

30 ***papa ventos*** **... 'father of the wind' ...** ***engoulevent*****: 'wind crow'**: Charles Swainson, *The Folk Lore and Provincial Names of British Birds*, p. 98.

35 **produced by the bird striking its wings together above its back**: Tate, *The Nightjar*, p. 21.

35 **theory concerning injury-feigning**: Lack, 'Some Breeding-habits'.

36 **marked decline since at least the 1950s ...**: Greg Conway & Ian Henderson, 'The Status and Distribution of the European Nightjar *Caprimulgus europaeus* in Britain in 2004'.

36 **Contraction has been especially accelerated ...**: Ibid.

37 **66 per cent of the population is located**: Ibid.

37 **population was estimated at 4,024 males**: Ibid.

37 **accounted for 88.6 per cent of the national increase**: Ibid.

37 **closely follows climatic trends**: F. C. Gribble, 'Nightjars in Britain and Ireland in 1981'; also Tate, *The Nightjar*, pp. 9–14.

37 **less common now than it was in the 1930s**: Rob Berry & Colin J. Bibby, 'A Breeding Study of Nightjars'.

37 **severely limiting their ability to catch sufficient insect prey**: Gribble, 'Nightjars in Britain and Ireland'.

38 **close correlation between cold nights ...**: Berry & Bibby, 'A Breeding Study of Nightjars'.

38 **declines in insect populations ...**: Tate, *The Nightjar*, p. 9.

38 **more than 40 per cent of all insect species ...**: Francisco Sánchez-Bayo & Kris A. G. Wyckhuys, 'Worldwide Decline of the Entomofauna: A Review of Its Drivers'.

38 **60 per cent of species documented as being in decline**: Ibid.

38 **337 moth species in England ...**: Ibid.

38 **17 per cent per decade**: Ibid.

38 **Habitat loss has been another significant factor**: Gribble, 'Nightjars in Britain and Ireland'.

38 **Fragmentation of these habitats also impacts**: Tate, *The Nightjar*, p. 11.

39 **collision with vehicles**: Ibid., p. 3

39 **in the 2004 national survey, 46.4 per cent**: Conway & Henderson, 'The Status and Distribution of the European Nightjar'.

39 **A study in Belgium**: Ruben Evens *et al.*, 'Study on the Foraging Behaviour of the European Nightjar *Caprimulgus europaeus* Reveals the Need for a Change in Conservation Strategy in Belgium'.
40 **makes a bubbling call to her ...**: Tate, *The Nightjar*, p. 17.

II. Mountain of the Trolls: *Shearwater*

45 **also eat the shearwaters themselves**: R. W. Furness, 'Predation on Ground-nesting Seabirds by Island Populations of Red Deer *Cervus eluphus* and Sheep *Ovis*'.
48 **possessing a high concentration of olfactory cells**: Adam Nicolson, *The Seabird's Cry*, p. 222.
48 **oldest Manx shearwater recorded**: https://www.bto.org/understanding-birds/species-focus/manx-shearwater
49 **breed around the British and Irish coasts in large numbers**: Michael Brooke, *The Manx Shearwater*, p. 52.
49 **70 centimetres and 3 metres deep**: Ibid., p. 5.
49 **Shearwaters are diligent gardeners**: P. Wormell, 'The Manx Shearwaters of Rhum', p. 105.
50 **will often find their burrows still buried under snow**: SNH leaflet 'Manx Shearwater: The Wandering Mariner': http://www.isleofrum.com/pulsepro/data/img/uploads/files/Manx%20Shearwaters%20SNH%20Leaflet.pdf
50 **losing around 10 g in weight per day**: Brooke, *The Manx Shearwater*, p. 105.
50 **male's larger size means they lose**: Ibid., p. 106.
50 **lowering their body temperature by around 2°C**: Ibid., p. 106.
51 **enter a state of mild torpor**: Ibid., p. 106.
51 **withstand lengthy periods of cooling**: Ibid., pp. 108–9; also, G. V. T. Matthews, 'Some Aspects of Incubation in the Manx Shearwater Procellaria Puffins, with Particular Reference to Chilling Resistance in the Embryo'.
51 **turns a slightly darker grey**: Brooke, *The Manx Shearwater*, p. 15.
52 **one and a half times the weight of its parents**: Ibid., p. 5.
52 **a darker, blacker bird above**: Ibid., p. 15.
54 **non-breeding birds that make all the noise**: A. E. Storey, 'Function of Manx Shearwater Calls in Mate Attraction', pp. 74–6.

54 **experiments that tested the shearwater's use of smell**: Katherine Russell Thompson, 'The Ecology of the Manx Shearwater *Puffinus puffinus* on Rhum, West Scotland', p. 178; also, Paul C. James, 'The Vocal and Homing Behaviour of the Manx Shearwater *Puffinus puffinus* with Additional Studies on other Procellariiformes', p. 218; also, Paul C. James, 'How do Manx Shearwaters *Puffinus puffinus* Find their Burrows?'

54 **high percentage of colourless droplets in the receptor cells**: Brooke, *The Manx Shearwater*, pp. 206–7.

54 **a relatively flat cornea**: Graham R. Martin, 'Designer Eyes for Seabirds of the Night'; also, Graham R. Martin & M. de L. Brooke, 'The Eye of a Procellariiform Seabird, the Manx Shearwater, *Puffinus puffinus*: Visual Fields and Optical Structure'.

54 **for example, a pigeon, a similar-sized diurnal bird**: Ibid.

55 **it may be that the open habitat**: Ibid., pp. 75–6.

56 **as has been suggested, 'proprioception'**: Brooke, *The Manx Shearwater*, pp. 215–16.

56 **Ronald Lockley's homing experiments**: R. M. Lockley, *Shearwaters*.

56 **Boston, Massachusetts**: Rosario Mazzeo, 'Homing of the Manx Shearwater'.

56 **navigate the oceans using their sense of smell**: Nicolson, *The Seabird's Cry*, pp. 229–31.

59 **rafts may assemble**: C. A. McSorley *et al.*, 'Manx Shearwater *Puffinus puffinus* Evening Rafting Behaviour around Colonies on Skomer, Rum and Bardsey'.

60 **rafts are located**: C. Richards, *et al.*, 'Manx Shearwater (*Puffinus puffinus*) Rafting Behaviour Revealed by GPS Tracking and Behavioural Observations'.

60 **possible that this is a mass gathering**: Ibid.

61 **create herb-rich mossy gardens**: for overview of flora and fauna of the shearwater 'greens', see Wormell, 'The Manx Shearwaters of Rhum', pp. 105–6.

62 **not negatively impacted**: Thompson, 'The Ecology of the Manx Shearwater', p. 140.

62 **Burrow flooding**: Ibid., p. 54.

66 **'Invisible birds made weird music ...'**: Seton Gordon, *In the Highlands*, p. 76.

66 **'At times through the dusk the swift ...'**: Seton Gordon, *Wild Birds in Britain*, p. 84.
66 **'crossed the vision like a meteor'**: Gordon, *In the Highlands*, p. 76.
67 **able to recognise females calling**: Storey, 'Function of Manx Shearwater Calls', pp. 74–6.
68 **find and pair with each other in the dark**: Brooke, *The Manx Shearwater*, p. 202.
69 **also seen the call transcribed as**: Keith C. Hamer, '*Puffinus puffinus* Manx Shearwater'.
69 **Gordon's phonetic sonogram**: Seton Gordon, *In Search of Northern Birds*, p. 138.
69 **'like wandering spirits'**: Ibid., p. 64.
69 **trolls were precisely what the Norse settlers**: Thompson, 'The Ecology of the Manx Shearwater', p. 14.
70 **within is a safer option**: Storey, 'Function of Manx Shearwater Calls', p. 75.
70 **like a megaphone**: Ibid., p. 75.
71 **architecture of the burrow**: Ibid., p. 75.
71 **Sonograms of individual male shearwater calls**: Brooke, *The Manx Shearwater*, p. 192.
71 **anecdote concerning Cory's shearwaters**: Dietrich Ristow & Michael Wink, 'Cory's Shearwater, A Clever Energy Conserver Among our Birds', p. 34.
71 **indicator or sentinel species**: Maíra Duarte Cardoso *et al.*, 'The Manx Shearwater (*Puffinus puffinus*) as a Candidate Sentinel of Atlantic Ocean Health'.
72 **5.25 trillion particles**: M. Eriksen *et al.*, 'Plastic Pollution in the World's Oceans: More than 5 Trillion Plastic Pieces Weighing over 250,000 Tons Afloat at Sea'.
72 **A study in Brazil in 2009**: Fernanda I. Colabuono *et al.*, 'Plastic Ingestion by Procellariiformes in Southern Brazil'.
72 **emits a similar chemical profile**: Matthew S. Savoca *et al.*, 'Marine Plastic Debris Emits a Keystone Infochemical for Olfactory Foraging Seabirds'.
73 **recent model predicted**: Chris Wilcox *et al.*, 'Threat of Plastic Pollution to Seabirds is Global, Pervasive, and Increasing'.

III. The Blacksmith of the Stream: *Dipper*

80 **origin of the dipper's old Russian name**: Sergei Volkov, *Birds Forever* blogpost, 1 August 2015 (translated by Ruth Addison).

80 **generic name, *Cinclus*, derives from**: Stephanie Tyler & Stephen Ormerod, *The Dippers*, p. 2; also, James A. Jobling, *The Helm Dictionary of Scientific Bird Names*, p. 108; subsequently, Stephen Ormerod has suggested, 'The word predates the ancient Greek "Kinklos" and has Sanskrit origins: Cañcalā (चञ्चला) implies quivering, trembling, moving to-and-fro.': https://twitter.com/SteveOrmerod/status/1484140762707157001

81 **Gordon frequently observed**: Seton Gordon, *Hill Birds of Scotland*, pp. 262–3.

81 **air bubbles trapped in their feathers**: Tyler & Ormerod, *The Dippers*, p. 20.

82 **would be to risk appearing conspicuous**: Stephanie J. Tyler & Stephen J. Ormerod, *The Dipper*, p. 6.

82 **purpose of the bird's conspicuous white bib**: Tyler & Ormerod, *The Dippers*, p. 20.

83 **recorded blinking up to 50 times per minute**: Ibid., p. 21.

84 **a risk, living in such a loud**: Lucy Magoolagan *et al.*, 'The Structure and Context of Male and Female Song in White-throated Dippers'.

85 **longest dipper dives on record**: Tyler & Ormerod, *The Dippers*, p. 25.

86 **Nor is there evidence**: see Twitter question from Stephen Ormerod addressing this issue: https://twitter.com/SteveOrmerod/status/1370374156311744514

86 **with the aid of their short, powerful wings**: William R. Goodge, 'Locomotion and other Behaviour of the Dipper'.

89 **a thick downy layer between the feather tracts**: John Davenport *et al.*, 'Comparison of Plumages of White-throated Dipper *Cinclus cinclus* and Blackbird *Turdus merula*'.

89 **One study of five dippers counted**: William R. Goodge, 'Structural and Functional Adaptations for Aquatic Life in the Dipper, *Cinclus mexicanus*', p. 23.

89 **six times higher a density**: Cassondra L. Williams *et al.*, 'Hidden Keys to Survival: The Type, Density, Pattern and Functional Role of Emperor Penguin Body Feathers'.

89 **exceptionally dense plumage means**: David E. Murrish, 'Responses to Diving in the Dipper, *Cinclus mexicanus*'.

90 **reports of dippers from zoos**: Goodge, 'Locomotion and other Behaviour of the Dipper'.

91 **more developed iris sphincter**: William R. Goodge, 'Adaptations for Amphibious Vision in the Dipper *Cinclus mexicanus*'.

91 **also control their heart rate**: Murrish, 'Responses to Diving in the Dipper'.

93 **root of many local names for the dipper**: Tyler & Ormerod, *The Dippers*, p. 2; also Charles Swainson, *The Folk Lore and Provincial Names of British Birds*, p. 30.

94 **languages other than English**: Tyler & Ormerod, *The Dippers*, p. 2.

97 **'Somewhat lark-like are the notes'**: H. E. Forrest, *The Fauna of North Wales*, p. 101.

97 **a narrow frequency belt of 4.0 to 6.5 kHz**: Magoolagan *et al.*, 'Structure and Context'.

97 **seeking out quieter parts of the river**: Ibid.

98 **Both the male and the female dipper sing**: Lucy Magoolagan & Stuart P. Sharp, 'Song Function and Territoriality in Male and Female White-throated Dippers *Cinclus cinclus*'; also, Magoolagan *et al.*, 'Structure and Context'.

99 **Analysis of their respective songs suggests**: Ibid.

99 **a distinctive display flight**: C. Moody, 'Display-flight of Dipper'; also, Raymond Hewson, 'Territory, Behaviour and Breeding of the Dipper in Banffshire'.

100 **'were lost to sight as they moved into the glare of the sun'**: Ibid.

100 **fly at great heights over watersheds**: H. Galbraith & S. J. Tyler, 'The Movements and Mortality of the Dipper as Shown by Ringing Recoveries'; also, Stephanie J. Tyler & Stephen J. Ormerod, *The Dipper*, p. 16.

101 **extraordinary gathering of a hundred dippers**: Donald Watson, *Birds of Moor and Mountain*, p. 119.

102 **often under stone bridges, or somewhere sheltered and out of the wind**: Kenneth W. Perry, *The Irish Dipper*, p. 41.

102 **approaching a roost will often start to sing**: Stephanie J. Tyler & Stephen J. Ormerod, *The Dipper*, p. 8.

103 **seemed like the extent of these shallow feeding areas**: This observation is also made by Perry in *The Irish Dipper*, p. 33: 'It therefore seems that the extent of such shallow water controls the size of each territory.'

104 **of 'extraordinary sweetness ...'**: Seton Gordon, *Birds of the Loch and Mountain*, p. 135.

104 **'One should owe a debt of thankfulness ...'**: Gordon, *Hill Birds of Scotland*, p. 260.

105 **The subsong is a warm-up, a rehearsal**: see John Bevis, *Aaaaw to Zzzzzd: The Words of Birds*, p. 12 for an excellent summary of subsong; also, W. H. Thorpe & P. M. Pilcher, 'The Nature and Characteristics of Sub-Song'.

106 **borrowed from the sand martin, chaffinch and greenfinch**: Perry, *The Irish Dipper*, p. 30.

106 **with a spotted flycatcher's nest built on top**: Gordon, *Hill Birds of Scotland*, p. 262.

106 **interior is a bowl of woven grasses**: for a detailed description of a dipper's nest, see Perry, *The Irish Dipper*, p. 76.

107 **helping to feed grey wagtail nestlings**: Stephanie J. Tyler & Stephen J. Ormerod, *The Dipper*, p. 18.

107 **two principal nuclei associated with song**: Lucy Magoolagan, *The Structure, Development and Role of Song in Dippers*, p. 5.

108 **interesting research into the relationship**: Magoolagan, *Structure, Development and Role of Song*, pp. 6–10; also, L. Magoolagan *et al.*, 'The Effect of Early Life Conditions on Song Traits in Male Dippers, *Cinclus cinclus*'.

109 **indicator species for the health of a river**: Stephanie J. Tyler & Stephen J. Ormerod, *The Dipper*, p. 23.

109 **include acidification**: S. J. Ormerod, *et al.*, 'Is the Breeding Distribution of Dippers Influenced by Stream Acidity?'; also, S. J. Ormerod *et al.*, 'The Distribution of Breeding Dippers (*Cinclus cinclus* (L.); Aves) in Relation to Stream Acidity in Upland Wales'.

110 **removal of natural tree cover**: Tyler & Ormerod, *The Dippers*, p. 195.

110 **watering troughs or guttering**: Perry, *The Irish Dipper*, p. 35.

110 **examined the transfer of plastics**: J. M. D'Souza *et al.*, 'Food Web Transfer of Plastics to an Apex Riverine Predator'.
110 **an account, published in *Country Life***: John Lawton Roberts, 'Dippers on the Stream'.

IV. Up in the Lift Go We: *Skylark*

116 **may have its origins in the Anglo-Saxon word**: Paul F. Donald, *The Skylark*, p. 204.
116 **varies markedly between different populations**: Ibid., p. 41.
116 **some must bathe**: Ibid., p. 41.
117 **use their claws to strike at the eyes of sheep**: Ibid., p. 52.
117 **an old Scottish rhyme**: Robert Chambers, *Popular Rhymes of Scotland*, pp. 192–3.
118 **70 per cent of the UK population**: Donald, *The Skylark*, p. 60; also S. Browne *et al.*, 'Densities and Population Estimates of Breeding Skylarks *Alauda arvensis* in Britain in 1997'.
118 **structure of a habitat**: Donald, *The Skylark*, p. 66.
118 **Vegetation at around 60 centimetres high**: Ibid., p. 62.
119 **concentrate their feeding**: Ibid. p. 155.
119 **vicinity of raven nests**: Ibid. p. 65; also, Piotr Tryjanowski, 'Proximity of Raven (*Corvus corax*) Nest Modifies Breeding Bird Community in an Intensively Used Farmland'.
119 **red-breasted geese have been observed**: https://odnature.naturalsciences.be/bebirds/en/research/red-breasted-geese-and-peregine-falcons
119 **shelter next to people**: Eric Simms, *British Larks, Pipits & Wagtails*, p. 54.
119 **study showing that their densities adjacent to roads**: T. P. Milson, *et al.*, 'Coastal Grazing Marshes as a Breeding Habitat for Skylarks *Alauda arvensis*', p. 48.
121 **conducted a beautifully conceived survey**: Eric Simms, *Voices of the Wild*, pp. 154–63.
123 **not the lark's only form of descent**: Donald, *The Skylark*, p. 83.
124 **Victorian naturalists thought**: Ibid., p. 82.
124 **go above 160 ft**: Ibid., p. 82.

125 **average height reached of 400 ft**: Anders Hedenström & Thomas Alerstam, 'Skylark Optimal Flight Speeds for Flying Nowhere and Somewhere'.
125 **rate of 3 ft per second**: Ibid., p. 82.
125 **song can't keep pace**: Michael Csicsáky, 'The Song of the Skylark (*Alauda arvensis*) and Its Relation to Respiration'.
125 **reason male skylarks have longer wings**: Donald, *The Skylark*, p. 81.
125 **provides the most information**: Ibid., p. 82.
126 **higher the lark goes, the longer it spends**: Ibid., p. 83.
126 **majority of song flights last between 2 to 4 minutes**: Ibid., p. 84.
126 **tendency to decrease**: Ibid., p. 84.
126 **performed by unpaired males**: Ibid., p. 87.
126 **stabilises its speed at around 20 ft per second**: Ibid., p. 83.
126 **If the wind speed drops**: Ibid., p. 83.
126 **curtailed or abandoned altogether**: Ibid., p. 85.
127 **According to Pliny the Elder**: James A. Jobling, *The Helm Dictionary of Scientific Bird Names*, p. 37.
127 **over 300 syllables**: E. Briefer *et al.*, 'Are Bird Song Complexity and Song Sharing Shaped by Habitat Structure?'
127 **skylarks and one of their principal avian predators**: Will Cresswell, 'Song as a Pursuit-deterrent Signal'.
128 **Wading birds**: Donald, *The Skylark*, p. 76.
129 **keeping the larks 'honest'**: Ibid., p. 77.
129 **a 'good singer' – often blinded**: Ibid., p. 76.
129 ***mauviettes en surprise aux truffes***: Ibid., p. 221.
132 **as little as a mile**: Ibid., p. 77.
132 **use a distinctive temporal arrangement of syllables**: E. Briefer *et al.*, 'How to Identify Dear Enemies: The Group Signature in the Complex Song of the Skylark *Alauda arvensis*'.
133 **skylark's cognitive skills**: E. Briefer *et al.*, 'Does True Syntax or Simple Auditory Object Support the Role of Skylark Song Dialect?'
134 **hopping dance**: Donald, *The Skylark*, p. 90.
134 **shivers his wing**: Ibid., p. 90.
135 **description of another unusual performance**: C. Suffern, 'Sky-larks Making "Forms"'.
135 **10 to 14 days**: Donald, *The Skylark*, p. 109.

136 **fall into a drought-crack**: Ibid., p. 116.
136 **three-quarters – fail**: Ibid., p. 129.
136 **three broods per season**: Ibid., p. 136.
140 **Both displays also involve song**: Ibid., p. 96.
140 **revert to 'song duels'**: Ibid., p. 96.
141 **'low-belling'**: Ibid., p. 211.
142 **less than half what it was in the early 1980s**: Ibid., p. 67.
142 **a million and a million and a half pairs**: Ibid., p. 67.
142 **declined by 75 per cent between 1972 and 1996**: https://www.rspb.org.uk/birds-and-wildlife/wildlife-guides/bird-a-z/skylark/threats/
142 **British farmland may have lost**: Donald, *The Skylark*, p. 69.
142 **half of all European countries**: Ibid., p. 70.
142 **estimated 3 to 4 million birds are harvested each year**: https://ec.europa.eu/environment/nature/conservation/wildbirds/hunting/docs/skylark.pdf
143 **most important factor**: Donald, *The Skylark*, p. 186; also, https://app.bto.org/birdtrends/species.jsp?year=2019&s=skyla
143 **also seen significant population declines**: Dan E. Chamberlain & Humphrey Q. P. Crick, 'Population Declines and Reproductive Performance of Skylarks *Alauda arvensis* in Different Regions and Habitats of the United Kingdom'.
143 **'lark mirror'**: Donald, *The Skylark*, pp. 213–14.

V. Xylophone in the Trees: *Raven*

152 **returning to the same nesting cliffs**: Derek Ratcliffe, *The Raven*, p. 139.
152 **'so wary has the raven become …'**: Seton Gordon, *The Immortal Isles*, p. 22.
153 **over the ice of the Arctic and over the sands of the desert**: Ratcliffe, *The Raven*, p. 242.
153 **majority of females … sitting on eggs**: Ibid., p. 168.
153 **'Nest at Candlemas …'**: Gordon, *The Immortal Isles*, p. 21; also, Alexander Nicolson (ed.), *A Collection of Gaelic Proverbs and Familiar Phrases*, p. 332.
153 **tenderly arranging this lining**: Ratcliffe, *The Raven*, p. 175.
153 **burying the nestlings deep**: Derek Goodwin, *Crows of the World*, p. 141.

153 **to increase ventilation**: Ibid., p. 141.
153 **wet her underparts**: Ibid., p. 141.
153 **torn out the wool lining**: Ratcliffe, *The Raven*, p. 171.
153 **opportunist scavengers**: Ibid., p. 242.
154 **large black slugs**: Ibid., p. 90.
154 **'perhaps the cold storage of winter ...'**: Bernd Heinrich, *Mind of the Raven*, p. 52.
154 **coincide with the lambing season**: Sylvia Bruce Wilmore, *Crows, Jays, Ravens and Their Relatives*, p. 153.
155 **study conducted in the Welsh uplands**: I. Newton *et al.*, 'Ravens and Buzzards in Relation to Sheep-Farming and Forestry in Wales'.
155 **Donald Watson suggested**: Donald Watson, *Birds of Moor and Mountain*, p. 138.
163 **Studies of raven territories in the Cheviots**: M. Marquis, *et al.*, 'The Decline of the Raven *Corvus corax*, in Relation to Afforestation in Southern Scotland and Northern England'.
163 **become permanently deserted**: Ratcliffe, *The Raven*, pp. 226–8.
164 **Heinrich recounts a vivid experience**: Bernd Heinrich, *Mind of the Raven*, p. 201.
165 **'more wooden than ...'**: Ibid., p. 229
165 **'distinctly different calls'**: Ibid., p. 196.
166 **'heard sounds or nuances ...'**: Ibid., p. 246.
166 **study in Switzerland**: Peter Enggist-Dueblin & Ueli Pfister, *Cultural Transmission of Vocalizations in Ravens.*
166 **tended to be 'bilingual'**: Bernd Heinrich, *Mind of the Raven*, p. 197.
166 **own personal variation**: Goodwin, *Crows of the World*, p. 142.
166 **will call to its lost mate**: Ibid., p. 142.
171 **sliding down roofs**: Heinrich, *Mind of the Raven*, p. 248.
171 **banks of snow**: Charles C. Bradley, 'Play Behaviour in Northern Ravens'.
171 **bathing in the spray**: Edmund C. Jaeger, 'Aerial Bathing of Ravens'.
171 **upside down on branches**: Richard D. Elliot, 'Hanging Behaviour in Common Ravens'.
171 **and on power lines**: Heinrich, *Mind of the Raven*, p. 248.
171 **for at least a hundred metres**: Sydney Evershed, 'Ravens Flying Upside Down'.

171 **typical playful behaviour includes**: Wilmore, *Crows, Jays, Ravens*, p. 148.
171 **gathering objects such as**: Ratcliffe, *The Raven*, p. 116.
171 **onto nesting kittiwakes**: W. A. Montevecchi, 'Corvids Using Objects to Displace Gulls from Nests'.
171 **'the size of a golf ball'**: Stewart W. Janes, 'The Apparent Use of Rock by a Raven in Nest Defense'.
172 **pine cones thrown**: Heinrich, *Mind of the Raven*, p. 304.
172 **Gordon once observed**: Seton Gordon, *Wild Birds in Britain*, pp. 52–3.
173 **signal to the pack**: Heinrich, *Mind of the Raven*, p. 237.
173 **uncomfortable ... where wolves are *not* present?**: Ibid., pp. 231–2.
173 **Many Inuit communities believed**: Ibid., pp. 246–7.
173 **choicest titbits**: Ibid., p. 252.
173 **game wardens in the US**: Ibid., p. 242.
174 **a 2020 study**: Simone Pika *et al.*, 'Ravens Parallel Great Apes in Physical and Social Cognitive Skills'.
174 **'Do ravens show consolation?'**: O. N. Fraser & T. Bugnyar, 'Do Ravens Show Consolation? Responses to Distressed Others'.
176 **Heinrich's ravens in Maine recognised him**: Heinrich, *Mind of the Raven*, pp. 174–5.
176 **Another study, conducted in 2016**: Thomas Bugnyar *et al.*, Ravens Attribute Visual Access to Unseen Competitors.
177 **numerous anecdotal reports**: Heinrich, *Mind of the Raven*, p. 305.
177 **came from a trapper**: Ralph Whitlock, *Guardian Weekly (Leisure)*, 25 June 1995, p. 24; also, Heinrich, *Mind of the Raven*, pp. 305–6.
177 **Heinrich also addressed the question**: Ibid., pp. 332–42.
177 **largest brain cephalisation** : Ibid., p. 326.
177 **intelligence relates to the complexity**: Ibid., p. 356.
178 **'are able to manipulate ...'**: Ibid., p. 356.

VI. Rather like the Howl of a Dog: *Black-throated Diver*

184 **'perhaps the weirdest'**: Donald Watson, *Birds of Moor and Mountain*, p. 3.
184 **'swelling from a guttural twanging'**: Ibid., p. 5.

184 **'as if a lost spirit'**: H. A. Gilbert & Arthur Brook, *The Secrets of the Eagle and of Other Rare Birds*, p. 76.
184 **'strikingly like the unavailing cries'**: Alexander Carmichael, *Carmina Gadelica, Vol. II*, p. 314.
184 **'dismal and melancholy'**: Niall Rankin, *Haunts of British Divers*, p. 55.
184 **'weird, strident, metallic calls'**: Mike Tomkies, *On Wing and Wild Water*, p. 72.
184 **'like those of a large lost cat'**: Ibid., p. 72.
184 **'no more unearthly bird sound'**: Mike Tomkies, *A Last Wild Place*, p. 109.
184 **'strange goose-like sounds'**: Ibid., p. 114.
184 **'a loud yelp'**: Seton Gordon, *The Immortal Isles*, p. 69.
184 **'a strange and powerful clamour'**: Seton Gordon, *Highland Summer*, p. 83.
184 **'very like the howling of a wolf'**: Sverre Sjölander, 'Reproductive Behaviour of the Black-Throated Diver *Gavia arctica*', p. 53.
184 **'weird and discordant cries'**: Norman Gilroy, *Field-Notes on the Nesting of Divers*.
184 **'a remarkable and far-carrying goose-like clamour'**: H. F. Witherby *et al.*, *The Handbook of British Birds, Vol. IV*, p. 120.
184 **'strange hollow call'**: Charles St John, *The Wild Sports and Natural History of the Highlands*, p. 242.
184 **'mingled laughter'**: Charles St John, *Natural History and Sport in Moray*, p. 291.
184 **appears to be a territorial call**: Sjölander, 'Reproductive Behaviour'.
184 **in response to calls from divers**: Stanley Cramp, *Handbook of the Birds of Europe*, p. 53.
185 **'dominating all other sounds ...'**: Ibid., p. 42.
185 **over 6 miles away**: Sjölander, 'Reproductive Behaviour'.
185 **like a human humming**: Ibid.
185 **function is probably as a contact call**: Cramp, *Handbook of the Birds of Europe*, p. 54.
185 **alternating duet**: Sjölander, 'Reproductive Behaviour.
185 **has been disturbed**: Cramp, *Handbook of the Birds of Europe*, p. 54.
185 **variations on these calls**: Sjölander, 'Reproductive Behaviour'.

185 **low-intensity form of yodelling**: Ibid.
185 **adopted in territorial encounters**: Cramp, *Handbook of the Birds of Europe*, p. 54.
186 **'did not arise from …'**: St John, *Natural History and Sport*, p. 290.
186 **'solitary hiker …'**: Gordon, *Highland Summer*, p. 156.
186 **'has a very human quality'**: Edward A. Armstrong, *The Folklore of Birds*, p. 63.
186 **'quasi-human wails'**: Ibid., p. 64.
187 **Gordon wrote about at length**: Gordon, *The Immortal Isles*, pp. 65–78.
189 **closely attending to their young**: Graham Bundy, 'Breeding and Feeding Observations on the Black-throated Diver', p. 34.
189 **for over three months**: Sjölander, 'Reproductive Behaviour'.
189 **the day the ice thaws**: Ibid.
189 **usually sometime in September**: Gordon, *Highland Summer*, p. 83.
190 **'The air was mild and still …'**: Ibid., p. 83.
190 **'smoother than seems possible for feathers'**: Watson, *Birds of Moor and Mountain*, p. 3.
190 **'seems to have been drawn by a fine brush'**: Ibid., p. 3.
192 **'She gives the impression …'**: Gordon, *The Immortal Isles*, p. 77.
193 **an account from 1925**: Gilbert & Brook, *The Secrets of the Eagle*, p. 79.
193 **sibling aggression**: Sjölander, 'Reproductive Behaviour'.
193 **egg-collecting ornithologist Norman Gilroy**: see Donald Watson, *The Hen Harrier*, pp. 73–4 for a description of Gilroy; also, Desmond & Maimie Nethersole-Thompson, *Waders: Their Breeding, Haunts and Watchers*, p. 28.
193 **paper published in 1923**: Gilroy, *Field-Notes*.
194 **'a most devious character'**: Watson, *The Hen Harrier*, p. 74; also, Desmond & Maimie Nethersole-Thompson described Gilroy as 'quite amoral' in *Waders*, p. 28.
195 **struck many observers**: see also Watson, *Birds of Moor and Mountain*, p. 4: 'Compared with the cormorant's muscular plunge, the diver sinks effortlessly below the surface of the water.'

195 **widely thought to be the reasons**: G. P. Mudge *et al.*, 'Changes in the Breeding Status of Black-throated Divers in Scotland'.
195 **'of recent years the ...'**: Gilroy, *Field-Notes.*
196 **'A few pairs of black-throated divers ...'**: Osgood Mackenzie, *A Hundred Years in the Highlands*, p. 131.
196 **'the nest was always wet'**: St John, *Wild Sports and Natural History*, p. 242.
197 **'to speak ... in a low voice'**: Seton Gordon, 'First Days in the Life of a Black-throated Diver'.
197 **Seton Gordon recalled**: Gordon, *Highland Summer*, pp. 82–3.
198 **cites an example**: Seton Gordon, *In the Highlands*, p. 61.
198 **between about 1 and 3 ft**: David Merrie, 'To Build an Island'.
198 **12 ft from the loch and 3 ft above**: Ibid.
199 **'like the propellers of a boat'**: Ibid.
199 **Old Norse *lum*, meaning 'clumsy', or the Old English *lumme*, meaning 'awkward'**: Judith W. McIntyre, *The Common Loon*, p. 2; also, https://en.wikipedia.org/wiki/Loon; also, Ernest A. Choate, *The Dictionary of American Bird Names*, p. 43.
199 ***lómr*, meaning 'moaning'**: Mark Cocker & Richard Mabey, *Birds Britannica*, p. 4. ; also, W. B. Lockwood, *The Oxford Book of British Birds Names*, p. 97.
199 **smaller, lighter red-throats**: see also McIntyre, *The Common Loon*, p. 129: 'Red-throated Loons have the largest wing area relative to body size, and can make the most efficient takeoff for flight.'
199 **stay on their lochan**: Gordon, *Highland Summer*, p. 158.
199 **'swims below the surface ...'**: Ibid., p. 158.
200 **a particularly hazardous one**: Ibid., p. 158.
200 **strong breeze to assist**: Ibid., p. 158.
200 **a runway to take off from**: T. D. H. Merrie, 'Relationship between Spatial Distribution of Breeding Divers and the Availability of Fishing Waters'.
202 **'surprisingly difficult to locate'**: Bundy, 'Breeding and Feeding Observations'.
202 **'the extraordinary white domino ...'**: Watson, *Birds of Moor and Mountain*, p. 3.

203 **'herdsman of the tide-race'**: Gordon, *The Immortal Isles*, p. 42.

203 **Gaelic for the steep-crested waves**: Ibid., p. 42.

203 **marked correlation between the crypticity**: John Hurrell Crook, 'The Adaptive Significance of Avian Social Organizations', p. 186; also, Henning Dunker, 'Habitat Selection and Territory Size of the Black-throated Diver, *Gavia arctica* (L.), in South Norway', p. 24.

204 **breed on single-territory lochs**: L. J. Brown, 'Investigation into the Causes of Black-throated Diver *Gavia arctica* Breeding Failure on Loch Maree, 2006–2009'.

204 **research conducted in Norway**: H. Dunker & K. Elgmork, 'Nesting of the Black-throated Diver, *Gavia arctica* (L.) in Small Bodies of Water'.

204 **Nordic countries hold 99 per cent**: Erick Hemmingsson & Mats O. G. Eriksson, 'Ringing of Red-throated Diver *Gavia stellata* Black-throated Diver *Gavia arctica* in Sweden'.

204 **100 m or 200 m across**: Merrie, 'Relationship'.

204 **'very exposed shores …'**: Dunker & Elgmork, 'Nesting of the Black-throated Diver'.

205 **Charles St. John's account**: St John, *Natural History and Sport*, p. 290.

206 **less than 1 per cent of the global population**: L. J. Brown, 'Investigation into the Causes'.

206 **'a bulkier grey head'**: Watson, *Birds of Moor and Mountain*, p. 4.

208 **'a miniature pearl necklace'**: Rankin, *Haunts of British Divers*, p. 53.

209 **impounded for hydro-electric schemes**: Dunker & Elgmork, 'Nesting of the Black-throated Diver'.

209 **breeding success is almost negligible**: Merrie, 'To Build an Island'.

209 **no more than 15 or so feet deep**: Bundy, 'Breeding and Feeding Observations'.

209 **exclusively in that shallow zone**: Ibid.

209 **survey conducted in the late 1970s**: Ibid.

210 **so rare in the British Isles**: Rankin, *Haunts of British Divers*, p. 50.

211 **following Gaelic song**: Carmichael, *Carmina Gadelica, Vol. II*, p. 314.

211 **in his book on British divers**: Rankin, *Haunts of British Divers*, p. 50.
212 **around 30 per cent of failures**: M. Hancock, 'Artificial Floating Islands for Nesting Black-throated Divers *Gavia arctica* in Scotland'.
212 **exacerbated by human interference**: G. P. Mudge & T. R. Talbot, 'The Breeding Biology and Causes of Nest Failure of Scottish Black-throated Divers *Gavia arctica*'.
212 **for the purposes of fishing**: Ibid.
212 **'increased the chick productivity ...'**: Hancock, 'Artificial Floating Islands'.
212 **Otters and pine martens were identified**: Brown, 'Investigation into the Causes'.
212 **13 per cent of nest failures to human egg collectors**: Mudge & Talbot, 'The Breeding Biology'.
212 **has remained stable**: Brown, 'Investigation into the Causes'.
214 **speeds of up to 8 mph**: Merrie, 'To Build an Island'.
214 **Trout, char and minnows**: Roy Dennis, *Divers*, p. 39.
214 **dragonflies and beetles**: Ibid., p. 39.
214 **small cod and gobies**: Ibid., p. 39.
214 **48 dives in a 30-minute period**: Bundy, 'Breeding and Feeding Observations'.
214 **often over 40 seconds**: Ibid.
214 **submerged for around 2 minutes ... last less than a minute**: Dennis, *Divers*, p. 39.
214 **between a quarter and a third of a mile underwater**: L. Lehtonen, 'Zur Biologie des Prachttauchers, *Gavia a. arctica* (L.)'.
215 **'very homogeneous group'**: McIntyre, *The Common Loon*, p. 129.
215 **'only minor differences ...'**: Sjölander, 'Reproductive Behaviour'.
215 **'lies in the vocalisations'**: Ibid.
216 **performing 'circle dances'**: Ibid.
216 **a flock of 32 black-throated divers**: Ibid.
216 **associated with threat behaviour**: Ibid.
216 **more physical responses such as ...**: Ibid.
217 **'the length of the dive were prearranged'**: Rankin, *Haunts of British Divers*, p. 54.

VII. Little Horn in the Rushes: *Lapwing*

221 **'is an extraordinarily pugnacious bird ...'**: Seton Gordon, *The Charm of the Hills*, p. 181.
222 **'pursuing a heedless golden eagle'**: Seton Gordon, *Wild Birds in Britain*, p. 34.
222 **swoop down with such fury**: Gordon, *The Charm of the Hills*, p. 181.
222 **'There is no bird ...'**: Gordon, *Wild Birds in Britain*, p. 34.
223 **'acutely distressful-sounding'**: Donald Watson, *Birds of Moor and Mountain*, p. 78.
223 **'heartbreakingly shrill'**: Lars Svensson *et al.*, *Collins Bird Guide*, p. 136.
223 ***gwai fi***: K. G. Spencer, *The Lapwing in Britain*, p. 122.
223 **several archaic adjectives ...**: Ibid., p. 123.
224 **a 'horniwinky' place**: Ibid., p. 125.
224 **'pee-whit', was the name for a musical instrument**: Ibid., p. 124.
224 **'a curious sound'**: Barzillai Lowsley, *A Glossary of Berkshire Words and Phrases*, p. 136.
224 **correlation between colony size and predation risk**: Michael Shrubb, *The Lapwing*, p.62.
225 **all 101 attacks by crows**: Ibid., p. 162; also, Richard D. Elliot, 'The Effects of Predation Risk and Group Size on the Anti-Predator Responses of Nesting Lapwings *Vanellus vanellus*'.
225 **mobbing the crows**: Ibid., p. 162: 'Nesting lapwings mob crows closely and severely, diving at them from the front and behind and harassing them right out of the territory.'
225 **another study, in Poland**: Ibid., p. 163.
225 **(often very close to lapwings)**: Shrubb, *The Lapwing*, p. 131.
225 **benefit from that defensive shield**: Ibid., p. 131.
226 **cattle tend to be more receptive**: Ibid., p. 160.
226 **'big dogs run yelping ...'**: Spencer, *The Lapwing in Britain*, p. 67.
226 ***pèle chien*, 'skin the dog'**: Ibid., p. 67.
226 **'looked upon with great dislike'**: Robert Gray, *Birds of the West of Scotland*, p. 263.
226 **'de'il's plover'**: Watson, *Birds of Moor and Mountain*, p. 76.

227 **'the "poet's corner" of a country newspaper'**: Gray, *Birds of the West of Scotland*, p. 264.
227 **'lifting and putting back eggs ...'**: Watson, *Birds of Moor and Mountain*, p. 76.
228 **Robert Gray also cites**: Gray, *Birds of the West of Scotland*, p. 266 (Gray mentions several other references to this Act of Parliament, though, despite his research, he is unable to find evidence the Act was actually passed).
228 **'in great numbers'**: Ibid., p. 266.
228 **'all the peeseweeps' nests ...'**: Ibid., p. 266.
229 **'russet brown'**: Desmond & Maimie Nethersole-Thompson, *Waders: Their Breeding, Haunts and Watchers*, p. 85.
229 **'orange'**: Shrubb, *The Lapwing*, p. 128.
229 **a children's riddle that goes ...**: Spencer, *The Lapwing in Britain*, p. 132.
229 **'little horn in the rushes'**: Ibid., p. 121.
229 **'hornpie'**: Ibid., p. 119.
229 **'squeal horn'**: Ibid., p. 121.
230 **must also help to blend**: Shrubb, *The Lapwing*, p. 17.
230 **uniform, bright green grassland also diminishes**: Ibid., p. 161.
230 **'you will probably see none of them at all ...'**: Spencer, *The Lapwing in Britain*, p. 2.
230 **'the ground is spread ...'**: Gray, *Birds of the West of Scotland*, p. 265.
231 **run, swim and feed themselves soon after they have hatched**: Gordon, *Wild Birds in Britain*, p. 34; also, Nethersole-Thompson, *Waders*, pp. 97–8; ref. to swimming within 24 hours of hatching: Shrubb, *The Lapwing*, p. 167.
231 **dried cowpat ... will often lie on**: Watson, *Birds of Moor and Mountain*, p. 76.
231 **'little white riding lights ...'**: E. A. R. Ennion, *The Lapwing*, p. 27.
231 **contracts and virtually disappears**: Watson, *Birds of Moor and Mountain*, p. 76.
231 **'one of the most familiar sights ...'**: Richard Vaughan, 'Amorous Lapwings'.
231 **'not a chase, more of a duet'**: Ibid.
231 **'actual brushes ...'**: Ibid.
232 **'queueing up to dive bomb'**: Shrubb, *The Lapwing*, p. 132.
232 **'border clashes'**: Spencer, *The Lapwing in Britain*, p. 34.

233 **'striking one another ...'**: Nethersole-Thompson, *Waders*, p. 86.
234 **outermost primaries**: Shrubb, *The Lapwing*, p. 126.
234 **'little fan'**: Peter Weaver, *The Lapwing*, p. 2.
234 **to winnow grain**: Spencer, *The Lapwing in Britain*, p. 113.
234 **'wing music'**: Nethersole-Thompson, *Waders*, p. 100.
235 **need for wide, open spaces**: Weaver, *The Lapwing*, p. 4.
235 **height of the vegetation**: Ibid., p. 4.
235 **deterrent on airfields**: T. P. Milson *et al.*, 'Diurnal Use of an Airfield and Adjacent Agricultural Habitats by Lapwings *Vanellus vanellus*'.
235 **on or just below the surface of the soil**: Weaver, *The Lapwing*, p. 6.
235 **wet grassland habitats ...**: Shrubb, *The Lapwing*, p. 26.
235 **favoured for nesting ...**: Weaver, *The Lapwing*, p. 4.
235 **Netherlands (which holds the largest ...)**: Shrubb, *The Lapwing*, p. 22.
236 **at least 40 per cent**: https://www.rspb.org.uk/our-work/conservation/conservation-and-sustainability/farming/advice/helping-species/lapwing/
236 **89 per cent since 1987**: https://app.bto.org/birdtrends/species.jsp?year=2020&s=lapwi
236 **seriously impeded the species' productivity**: Shrubb, *The Lapwing*, pp. 195–6.
236 **Agricultural intensification, therefore**: Ibid., pp. 195–6.
237 **often as early as May**: Weaver, *The Lapwing*, p. 10.
237 **drop out of the sky**: Ibid., p. 10.
237 **5 ft apart**: Ibid., p. 10.
237 **10 ft between birds**: Ibid., p. 9.
238 **a winter phenomenon in Britain**: Shrubb, *The Lapwing*, p. 108.
238 **indicates what the lapwings are feeding on**: Ibid., p. 107.
238 **gulls tend to move away**: Ibid., p. 107.
238 **station themselves at regular intervals**: Weaver, *The Lapwing*, p. 12.
238 **'a thorn in the lapwing's flesh'**: Gordon, *Wild Birds in Britain*, p. 35.
238 **'peewit gull'**: Spencer, *The Lapwing in Britain*, p. 124.
238 **between 10 and 20 lapwings**: Weaver, *The Lapwing*, p. 12.
239 **shuffle away from the gulls**: Ibid., p. 12.

239 **implicated as an important cause**: John Calladine *et al.*, 'Continuing Influences of Introduced Hedgehogs *Erinaceus europaeus* as a Predator of Wader (Charadrii) Eggs Four Decades after their Release on the Outer Hebrides, Scotland'.

239 **a fall of 18 per cent**: Ibid.

239 **lapwings, down by 14 per cent**: John Calladine *et al.*, 'Changes in Breeding Wader Populations of the Uist Machair between 1983 and 2014'.

241 **snipe's Gaelic names …**: J. A. Harvie-Brown & T. E. Buckley, *A Vertebrate Fauna of the Outer Hebrides*, p. 131.

245 **trying to diffuse tension**: Nethersole-Thompson, *Waders*, p. 69.

246 **lined it with grass and moss**: Shrubb, *The Lapwing*, pp. 135–6.

246 **often reusing scrapes**: Nethersole-Thompson, *Waders*, p. 86.

246 **'rocking'**: Ibid., p. 86.

246 **leaning on his wing wrists**: Ibid., p. 87.

246 **wings pointed vertically …**: Vaughan, 'Amorous Lapwings'.

246 **moulding the hollow with his breast**: Shrubb, *The Lapwing*, p. 128.

246 **in signalling to the female**: R. W. H. Scroggs & H. H. Williams, 'Annual Breeding Bird Survey 1980 Lapwing'.

246 **peck at bits of grass and roots**: Vaughan, 'Amorous Lapwings'.

246 **also do this when they are agitated**: Nethersole-Thompson, *Waders*, p. 90.

246 **sometimes the grass is real**: Scroggs & Williams, 'Annual Breeding Bird Survey'.

246 **perfectly circular**: Vaughan, 'Amorous Lapwings'.

246 **as many as 20 of these hollows**: Shrubb, *The Lapwing*, p. 128.

248 **'Backwards and forwards …'**: Gordon, *Wild Birds in Britain*, p. 34.

249 **3.5 seconds**: Torben Dabelsteen, 'An Analysis of the Song-Flight of the Lapwing (*Vanellus vanellus* L.) with Respect to Causation, Evolution and Adaptations to Signal Function'.

249 **'lay unbroken until …'**: Seton Gordon, *In the Highlands*, p. 15.

250 **A correspondent wrote to Gordon**: Ibid., p. 15.
250 **40,000 lapwings**: Shrubb, *The Lapwing*, p. 186.
250 **virtually no lapwings left in Britain**: Ibid., p. 186; also, H. M. Dobinson & A. J. Richards, 'The Effects of the Severe Winter of 1962/63 on Birds in Britain': 'Scarcely any Lapwings were present in Britain during late January and February, although large numbers gathered in Ireland and suffered heavy mortality there, possibly from exhaustion rather than lack of food.'
251 **distinctive feature of lapwing movements**: Shrubb, *The Lapwing*, p. 188.
251 **resulting gene flow**: Ibid. p. 188.
251 **little subspecies differentiation**: Ibid., p. 188.
251 **so primed to perform**: Dabelsteen, 'An Analysis of the Song-Flight of the Lapwing': 'the behaviour can be released by only slight changes of the external situation.'
252 **flight of a short-eared owl**: Shrubb, *The Lapwing*, p. 125.
252 **termed the 'alternating flight'**: Dabelsteen, 'An Analysis of the Song-Flight of the Lapwing'.
253 **other observers have identified**: Ibid.
254 **from under 3 ft to up to 30 ft**: Ibid.
255 **way the song is structured**: Ibid., p. 174.
255 **open, windy ... habitat**: Ibid., p. 174.
255 **Dabelsteen ascribed the different stages**: Ibid.
255 **primarily aggressive**: Spencer, *The Lapwing in Britain*, p. 24.
255 **'dominated by attack tendencies'**: Dabelsteen, 'An Analysis of the Song-Flight of the Lapwing'.
256 **prefer those males that perform the most acrobatic display**: G. B. Grønstøl, 'Aerobatic Components in the Song-flight Display of Male Lapwings *Vanellus vanellus* as Cues in Female Choice'.
257 **'crazy flying'**: Spencer, *The Lapwing in Britain*, p. 73.
257 **'swooping and twisting ...'**: Ibid., p. 73.
257 **will trigger this crazy flying**: Shrubb, *The Lapwing*, p. 127.
257 **'virtuoso performances'**: Ibid., p. 127.

VIII. As Though She Lived on Song: *Nightingale*

261 **tails in constant motion**: N. F. Ticehurst, 'Some Notes on the Breeding-Habits of Nightingales'.
261 **'a burst of song' …**: Ibid.
262 **long exposure, fast plates …**: Ibid.
263 **usually shorter, contains less variety …**: Peter Clement & Chris Rose, *Robins and Chats*, p. 262.
264 **more successful in attracting a female**: V. Amrhein *et al.*, 'Temporal Patterns of Territory Settlement and Detectability in Mated and Unmated Nightingales *Luscinia megarhynchos*'.
264 **comparatively low**: V. Amrhein *et al.*, 'Nocturnal and Diurnal Singing Activity in the Nightingale: Correlations with Mating Status and Breeding Cycle'.
264 **suffered fewer**: Ibid.
264 **cease singing at night …**: Ibid.
264 **for a brief period of around three nights**: Ibid.
264 **most likely unpaired males**: Ibid.
264 **quite a number of these unattached male nightingales**: Amrhein *et al.*, 'Nocturnal and Diurnal Singing'.
265 **given from different locations …**: Clement & Rose, *Robins and Chats*, p. 262.
265 **adopts an almost upright stance …**: Ibid., p. 262.
265 **23.5 hours**: Richard Mabey, *Whistling in the Dark*, p. 23.
265 **between 5 and 30 minutes**: Ibid., p. 24.
265 **a more subdued version**: Clement & Rose, *Robins and Chats*, p. 262.
265 **will sing on passage**: Ibid., p. 262.
265 **perform a quieter courtship song**: Stanley Cramp (ed.), *Handbook of the Birds of Europe, the Middle East and North Africa*, p. 632.
265 **low down among the bushes**: Oliver G. Pike, *The Nightingale: Its Story and Song*, p. 23.
265 **'exceedingly graceful' …**: Ibid., pp. 23–4.
266 **does not appear to be a common trait**: Clement & Rose, *Robins and Chats*, p. 262.
266 **writers have been able to discern examples**: Sam Lee, *The Nightingale*, p. 154.
266 **mimic aspects of the thrush nightingale's song**: Clement & Rose, *Robins and Chats*, p. 262.

266 **a slower and more repetitive song**: Bethan Roberts, *Nightingale*, p. 38.
266 **'almost useless' to visit …**: Pike, *The Nightingale*, p. 43.
268 **prompted to sing even louder**: Ibid., p. 13.
269 **in 1932 made a film about the nightingale**: https://secrets-of-nature.co.uk/2021/04/07/the-nightingale-1932/
269 **too 'slow' and 'soft'**: Pike, *The Nightingale*, p. 12.
269 **'If the nightingale listens to slow music …'**: Ibid., p. 12.
269 **'loud, lively jazz music'**: Ibid., p. 12.
269 **during a heavy artillery bombardment**: Ibid., pp. 19–20.
271 **uses the term 'challenge'**: Ibid., pp. 18 & 20.
271 **perform 'song duels'**: Cramp (ed.), *Handbook of the Birds of Europe, the Middle East and North Africa*, p. 632.
271 **'strangled' version of their song**: Ibid., p. 632.
271 **will chase each other … all the time**: Ibid., p. 632.
271 **suffer fewer incursions**: M. Naguib *et al.*, 'The Nightingale in Britain: Status, Ecology and Conservation Needs'.
271 **intrude on other territories more frequently**: Ibid.
272 **the one, culturally, that we most associate with its song**: see Roberts, *Nightingale*, for an excellent account of nightingales in art and culture.
272 **spatial behaviour of the birds**: Naguib *et al.*, 'The Nightingale in Britain'.
273 **tilting their head to the side, much like a robin**: Clement & Rose, *Robins and Chats*, p. 263.
276 **roughly 5,500 singing males**: https://app.bto.org/birdfacts/results/bob11040.htm
276 **more than 90 per cent in the last 40 years**: C. Holt *et al.*, 'The Nightingale in Britain: Status, Ecology and Conservation Needs'.
276 **only the turtle dove …**: Ibid.
276 **become extinct as a breeding species in Britain**: Ibid.; also, Roberts, *Nightingale*, p. 147.
276 **the modelling for this species …**: Holt *et al.*, 'The Nightingale in Britain'.
276 **areas that enjoy a more continental climate**: Ibid.
277 **other factors, outside Britain**: Ibid.
277 **'ecological tidiness disorder'**: Benedict Macdonald, *Rebirding*, pp. 189–91.
277 **'it is not easy to put …'**: Pike, *The Nightingale*, p. 40.

277 **didn't 'have the words ...'**: Roberts, *Nightingale*, p. 18.
278 **'can have such an extraordinary effect ...'**: Mabey, *Whistling in the Dark*, p. 7.
278 **'the song was visual'**: Lee, *The Nightingale*, p. 5.
278 **'like steel for coldness and penetration'**: Edward Thomas, *The South Country*, p. 33.
278 **'astonishingly pure and penetrating'**: Mabey, *Whistling in the Dark*, p. 3.
278 **can be heard more than a mile away**: Lee, *The Nightingale*, p. 158.
278 **more than 250 different phrases ...**: Clement & Rose, *Robins and Chats*, p. 262.
279 **follow a different sequence ...**: Ibid., p. 262.
279 **'as rounded and as full ...'**: Thomas, *The South Country*, p. 33.
280 **'is like nothing else'**: Ibid., p. 33.
280 **'we hear voices that were not dreamed of before'**: Ibid., p. 34.
281 **'It has some kind of electric, suspended quality ...'**: H. E. Bates, *Through the Woods*, p. 61.
282 **as long as 20 or 30 seconds**: Pike, *The Nightingale*, p. 42.
282 **essentially diurnal**: Robert J. Thomas, *The Costs of Singing in Nightingales*.
282 **'singing at night is an exceptional addition ...'**: Ibid.
283 **will not tend to move around much in the dark**: Ibid.
283 **whenever a predatory tawny owl calls**: Ibid.
283 **energy costs of singing at night are substantial**: Ibid.
283 **will finish its night shift lighter than when it began it at dusk**: Ibid.

Bibliography

Introduction

Barrington, Daines, 'Experiments and Observations on the Singing of Birds – Letter XXXI', *Philosophical Transactions of the Royal Society of London*, 63, 249–91, 1773
Gordon, Seton, *Birds of the Loch and Mountain*, Cassell, 1907
Gordon, Seton, *Hill Birds of Scotland*, Edward Arnold, 1915
Gordon, Seton, *In the Highlands*, Cassell, 1931
Gordon, Seton, *Thirty Years of Nature Photography*, Cassell, 1936
Gordon, Seton, *Highland Summer*, Cassell, 1971
Suthers, Roderick A., 'Contributions to Birdsong from the Left and Right Sides of the Intact Syrinx', *Nature*, 347, 473–7, 1990
Watson, Adam, *Some Days from a Hill Diary: Scotland, Iceland, Norway, 1943–50*, Paragon, 2012

I. The Bird that Hides Its Shadow: *Nightjar*

Abs, Michael, 'Field Tests on the Essential Components of the European Nightjar's Song', *Proceedings XIII International Ornithological Congress*, 202–5, 1963
Berry, Rob and Bibby, Colin J., 'A Breeding Study of Nightjars', *British Birds*, 74, 4, 161–9, 1981
Brown, Charles H., 'Ventroloquial and Locatable Vocalizations in Birds', *Zeitschrift für Tierpsychologie/Journal of Comparative Ethology*, 59, 4, 338–50, 1982
Burton, J. F. and Johnson, E. D. H., 'Insect, Amphibian or Bird?', *British Birds*, 77, 3, 1984

Cleere, Nigel, 'Goatsuckers', *Birdwatch*, 32–7, June 2002

Cleere, Nigel, 'Reaction by European Nightjar to Displaying Wood Pigeon', *British Birds*, 95, 531–2, 2002

Cleere, Nigel and Nurney, Dave, *Nightjars: A Guide to Nightjars and Related Nightbirds*, Pica Press, 1998

Clegg, Michael, 'Insect, Amphibian or Bird?', *British Birds*, 78, 4, 198, 1985

Conway, Greg and Henderson, Ian, 'The Status and Distribution of the European Nightjar *Caprimulgus europaeus* in Britain in 2004', *BTO*, 398, 2005

Docker, Stephen, Lowe, Andrew and Abrahams, Carlos, 'Identification of Different Song Types in the European Nightjar *Caprimulgus europaeus*', *Bird Study*, 67, 1, 119–27, 2020

Evens, Ruben, Beenaerts, Natalie, Witters, Nele, Artois, Tom, 'Study on the Foraging Behaviour of the European Nightjar *Caprimulgus europaeus* Reveals the Need for a Change in Conservation Strategy in Belgium', *Journal of Avian Biology*, 48, 9, 1238–45, 2017

Gribble, F. C., 'Nightjars in Britain and Ireland in 1981', *Bird Study*, 30, 3, 1983

Hunter, Jr., Malcolm L., 'Vocalization During Inhalation in a Nightjar', *Condor*, 82, 101–3, 1980

Lack, David L., 'Some Diurnal Observations on the Nightjar', *London Naturalist*, 1929

Lack, David L., 'Double Brooding of the Nightjar', *British Birds*, 23, 9, 242–4, 1930

Lack, David L., 'Some Breeding-habits of the European Nightjar', *Ibis*, 266–84, 1932

Lack, David L., 'Notes on Nesting Nightjars', *British Birds*, 50, 7, 273–7, 1957

Mills, Alexander M., 'The Influence of Moonlight on the Behaviour of Goatsuckers (Caprimulgidae)', *The Auk*, 103, 2, 370–8, 1986

Murison, Giselle, 'The Impact of Human Disturbance on the Breeding Success of Nightjar *Caprimulgus europaeus* on Heathlands in South Dorset, England', *English Nature Research Reports*, 483, 2002

Peiponen, V. A., 'On Hypothermia and Torpidity in the Nightjar (*Caprimulgus europaeus* L.)', *Annales AcademiæScientiarum Fennicæ*, Series A, IV. Biologica, 87, 1965

Peiponen, V. A., 'The Diurnal Heterothermy of the Nightjar (*Caprimulgus europaeus* L.)', *Annales AcademiæScientiarum Fennicæ*, Series A, IV. Biologica, 101, 1966

Peiponen, V. A., 'Body Temperature Fluctuations in the Nightjar (*Caprimulgus e. europaeus* L.) in Light Conditions of Southern Finland', *Annales Zoologici Fennici*, 7, 239–50, 1970

Perrins, Christopher M., 'The Purpose of the High-Intensity Alarm Call in Small Passerines', *Ibis*, 110, 200–1, 1968

Perrins, Christopher M., Crick, H. Q. P., 'Influence of Lunar Cycle on Laying Dates of European Nightjars (*Caprimulgus europaeus*)', *The Auk*, 113, 3, 705–8, 1996

Rebbeck, M., Corrick, R., Eaglestone, B., Stainton, C., 'Recognition of Individual European Nightjars *Caprimulgus europaeus* from their Song', *Ibis*, 143, 468–75, 2001

Sánchez-Bayo, Francisco and Wyckhuys, Kris A. G., 'Worldwide Decline of the Entomofauna: A Review of Its Drivers', *Biological Conservation*, 232, 8–27, 2019

Sierro, A. and Erhardt, A., 'Light Pollution Hampers Recolonization of Revitalised European Nightjar Habitats in the Valais (Swiss Alps)', *Journal of Ornithology*, 160, 3, 749–61, 2019

Swainson, Charles, *The Folk Lore and Provincial Names of British Birds*, Elliot Stock, 1886

Tate, Peter, *The Nightjar*, Shire Natural History, 1989

Vaurie, Charles, 'Systematic Notes on Palearctic Birds, No. 40, Caprimulgidae', *American Museum of Natural History*, 1997, 1960

Walpole-Bond, John, *A History of Sussex Birds, Vol. II*, H. F. & G. Witherby, 1938

Weller, Milton W., 'Observations on the Incubation Behaviour of a Common Nighthawk', *The Auk*, 75, 1958

White, Gilbert, *A Natural History of Selborne*, Dent, 1974, first published 1789

II. Mountain of the Trolls: *Shearwater*

Brooke, M. de L., 'The Breeding Biology of the Manx Shearwater', DPhil thesis, Oxford University, 1977

Brooke, M. de L., 'Sexual Differences in the Voice and Individual Vocal Recognition in the Manx Shearwater *Puffinus puffinus*', *Animal Behaviour*, 26, 622–9, 1978

Brooke, Michael, *The Manx Shearwater*, T. & A. D. Poyser, 1990

Cardoso, Maíra Duarte, de Moura, Jailson Fulgencio, Tavares, Davi C., *et al.*, 'The Manx Shearwater (*Puffinus puffinus*) as a Candidate Sentinel of Atlantic Ocean Health', *Aquatic Biosystems*, 10, 6, 2014

Colabuono, Fernanda I., Barquete, Viviane, Domingues, Beatriz S., Montone, Rosalinda C., 'Plastic Ingestion by Procellariiformes in Southern Brazil', *Marine Pollution Bulletin*, 58, 93–96, 2009

Eriksen, M., Lebreton, L. C. M., Carson, H. S., Thiel, M., Moore, C. J., *et al.*, 'Plastic Pollution in the World's Oceans: More than 5 Trillion Plastic Pieces Weighing over 250,000 Tons Afloat at Sea', *PloS ONE*, 9(12), e111913, 2014

Furness, R. W., 'Predation on Ground-nesting Seabirds by Island Populations of Red Deer *Cervus eluphus* and Sheep *Ovis*', *Journal of Zoology*, 216, 565–73, 1988

Gordon, Seton, *In the Highlands*, Cassell, 1931

Gordon, Seton, *Wild Birds in Britain*, Batsford, 1938

Gordon, Seton, *In Search of Northern Birds*, Eyre & Spottiswoode, 1941

Hamer, Keith C., '*Puffinus puffinus* Manx Shearwater', *BWP Update*, 5, 2, 203–13, 2003

James, Paul C., 'The Vocal and Homing Behaviour of the Manx Shearwater *Puffinus puffinus* with Additional Studies on other Procellariiformes', DPhil thesis, Oxford University, 1984

James, Paul C., 'How do Manx Shearwaters *Puffinus puffinus* Find their Burrows?', *Ethology*, 71, 287–94, 1986

Lockley, R. M., *Shearwaters*, J. M. Dent, 1942

Martin, Graham R., 'Designer Eyes for Seabirds of the Night', *New Scientist*, 3, November 1990

Martin, Graham R. and Brooke, M. de L., 'The Eye of a Procellariiform Seabird, the Manx Shearwater, *Puffinus puffinus*: Visual Fields and Optical Structure', *Brain, Behaviour and Evolution*, 37, 65–78, 1991

Matthews, G. V. T., 'Some Aspects of Incubation in the Manx Shearwater Procellaria Puffins, with Particular Reference to Chilling Resistance in the Embryo', *Ibis*, 96, 432–49, 1954

Mazzeo, Rosario, 'Homing of the Manx Shearwater', *The Auk*, 70, 2, 200–1, 1953

McSorley, C. A., Wilson, L. J., Dunn, T. E., *et al.*, 'Manx Shearwater *Puffinus puffinus* Evening Rafting Behaviour around Colonies on Skomer, Rum and Bardsey: Its Spatial Extent and Implications for Recommending Seaward Boundary Extensions to Existing Colony Special Protection Areas in the UK', *JNCC Report*, 406, 2008

Morgan-Grenville, Roger, *Shearwater: A Bird, an Ocean and a Long Way Home*, Icon, 2021

Nicolson, Adam, *The Seabird's Cry: The Lives and Loves of Puffins, Gannets and Other Ocean Voyagers*, William Collins, 2017

Richards, C., Padget, O., Guilford, T., Bates. A. E., 'Manx Shearwater (*Puffinus puffinus*) Rafting Behaviour Revealed by GPS Tracking and Behavioural Observations', *PeerJ*, 7, e7863, 2019

Ristow, Dietrich and Wink, Michael, 'Cory's Shearwater, A Clever Energy Conserver Among our Birds', Nature *Bulletin of the Hellenic Society for the Protection of Nature*, 46/47, July, December 1989

Rutt, Stephen, *The Seafarers: A Journey Among Birds*, Elliott & Thompson, 2019

Savoca, Matthew S., Wohlfeil, Martha E., Ebeler, Susan E., Nevitt, Gabrielle A., 'Marine Plastic Debris Emits a Keystone Infochemical for Olfactory Foraging Seabirds', *Science Advances*, November 2016

SNH leaflet 'Manx Shearwater: The Wandering Mariner': http://www.isleofrum.com/pulsepro/data/img/uploads/files/Manx%20Shearwaters%20SNH20Leaflet.pdf

Storey, A. E., 'Function of Manx Shearwater Calls in Mate Attraction', *Behaviour*, 89, 1/2, 73–89, 1984

Storey, A. E. and Grimmer, B. L., 'Effect of Illumination on the Nocturnal Activities of Manx Shearwaters: Colony Avoidance or Inconspicuous Behaviour?', *Bird Behaviour*, 6, 2, 1986

Thompson, Katherine Russell, 'The Ecology of the Manx Shearwater *Puffinus puffinus* on Rhum, West Scotland', PhD thesis, Glasgow University, 1987

Warham, John, 'Photographing the Manx Shearwater', *Country Life*, 20 October 1950

Wilcox, Chris, Van Sebille, Erik, and Hardesty, Britta Denise, 'Threat of Plastic Pollution to Seabirds is Global, Pervasive, and Increasing', *PNAS*, 112, 38, 11899–904, 2015

Wormell, P., 'The Manx Shearwaters of Rhum', *Scottish Birds*, 9, 2, 1976

III. The Blacksmith of the Stream: *Dipper*

Adler, James, 'Behaviour of Dippers at the Nest During a Flood', *British Birds*, 56, 73–6, 1963

Davenport, John, O'Halloran, John, Hannah, Fiona, McLaughlin, Orla and Smiddy, Pat, 'Comparison of Plumages of White-throated Dipper *Cinclus cinclus* and Blackbird *Turdus merula*', *Waterbirds: The International Journal of Waterbird Biology*, 32, 1, 169–78, 2009

D'Souza, J. M., Windsor, F. M., Santillo, D., Ormerod, S. J., 'Food Web Transfer of Plastics to an Apex Riverine Predator', *Global Change Biology*, 26, 3846–57, 2020

Forrest, H. E., *The Fauna of North Wales*, Witherby & Co., 1907

Galbraith, H. and Tyler, S. J., 'The Movements and Mortality of the Dipper as Shown by Ringing Recoveries', *Ringing & Migration*, 4, 1, 9–14, 1982

Goodge, William R., 'Structural and Functional Adaptations for Aquatic Life in the Dipper, *Cinclus mexicanus*', PhD thesis, University of Washington, 1957

Goodge, William R., 'Locomotion and other Behaviour of the Dipper', *Condor*, 61, 4–17, 1959

Goodge, William R., 'Adaptations for Amphibious Vision in the Dipper *Cinclus mexicanus*', *Journal of Morphology*, 107, 1, 79–91, 1960

Gordon, Seton, *Birds of the Loch and Mountain*, Cassell, 1907

Gordon, Seton, *Hill Birds of Scotland*, Edward Arnold, 1915

Hewson, Raymond, 'Territory, Behaviour and Breeding of the Dipper in Banffshire', *British Birds*, 60, 244–52, 1967

Jobling, James A., *The Helm Dictionary of Scientific Bird Names, From Aalge to Zusii*, Christopher Helm, 2010

Jones, J. W. and King, G. M., 'The Underwater Activities of the Dipper', *British Birds*, 45, 400–1, 1952

Magoolagan, Lucy, 'The Structure, Development and Role of Song in Dippers', PhD thesis, Lancaster University, 2017

Magoolagan, L., Mawby, P. J., Whitehead, F. A. and Sharp, S. P., 'The Effect of Early Life Conditions on Song Traits in Male Dippers, *Cinclus cinclus*', *PLoS ONE*, 13(11), e0205101, 2018

Magoolagan, Lucy and Sharp, Stuart P., 'Song Function and Territoriality in Male and Female White-throated Dippers *Cinclus cinclus*', *Bird Study*, 65, 3, 396–403, 2018

Magoolagan, Lucy, Mawby, Peter J., Whitehead, Flora A. and Sharp, Stuart P., 'The Structure and Context of Male and Female Song in White-throated Dippers', *Journal of Ornithology*, 160, 195–205, 2019

Moody, C., 'Display-flight of Dipper', *British Birds*, 48, 184, 1955

Murrish, David E., 'Responses to Diving in the Dipper, *Cinclus mexicanus*', *Comparative Biochemistry and Physiology*, 34, 4, 853–8, 1970

Murrish, David E., 'Responses to Temperature in the Dipper, *Cinclus mexicanus*', *Comparative Biochemistry and Physiology*, 34, 4, 859–69, 1970

Ormerod, S. J., Tyler, Stephanie J. and Lewis, J. M. S., 'Is the Breeding Distribution of Dippers Influenced by Stream Acidity?', *Bird Study*, 32, 1, 32–9, 1985

Ormerod, S. J., Allenson, N., Hudson, D., Tyler, Stephanie J., 'The Distribution of Breeding Dippers (*Cinclus cinclus* (L.); Aves) in Relation to Stream Acidity in Upland Wales', *Freshwater Biology*, 16, 501–7, 1986

Perry, Kenneth W., *The Irish Dipper*, privately published, 1986

Rankin, M. Neal and Rankin, Denis H., 'The Breeding Behaviour of the Irish Dipper', *The Irish Naturalists' Journal*, 7, 10, 273–82, 1940

Roberts, John Lawton, 'Dippers on the Stream', *Country Life*, 25 January 1979

Swainson, Charles, *The Folk Lore and Provincial Names of British Birds*, Elliot Stock, 1886

Thorpe, W. H. and Pilcher, P. M., 'The Nature and Characteristics of Sub-Song', *British Birds*, 51, 509–13, 1958

Tyler, Stephanie J. and Ormerod, Stephen J., *The Dipper*, Shire Natural History, 1988

Tyler, Stephanie and Ormerod, Stephen, *The Dippers*, T. & A. D. Poyser, 1994

Watson, Donald, *Birds of Moor and Mountain*, Scottish Academic Press, 1972

Williams, Cassondra L., Hagelin, Julie C. and Kooyman, Gerald L., 'Hidden Keys to Survival: The Type, Density, Pattern and Functional Role of Emperor Penguin Body Feathers', *Proceedings of the Royal Society B*, 282, 1817, 2015

IV. Up in the Lift Go We: *Skylark*

Briefer, E., Aubin, T., Lehongre, K. and Rybak, F., 'How to Identify Dear Enemies: The Group Signature in the Complex Song of the Skylark *Alauda arvensis*', *Journal of Experimental Biology*, 211, 317–26, 2008

Briefer, E., Osiejuk, T. S., Rybak, F. and Aubin, T., 'Are Bird Song Complexity and Song Sharing Shaped by Habitat Structure? An Information Theory and Statistical Approach', *Journal of Theoretical Biology*, 262, 151–64, 2010

Briefer, E. F., Rybak, F., and Aubin, T., 'Does True Syntax or Simple Auditory Object Support the Role of Skylark Song Dialect?', *Animal Behaviour*, 86, 6, 1131–7, 2013

Browne, S., Vickery, J. and Chamberlain, D., 'Densities and Population Estimates of Breeding Skylarks *Alauda arvensis* in Britain in 1997', *Bird Study*, 47, 1, 52–65, 2000

Chamberlain, Dan E. and Crick, Humphrey Q. P., 'Population Declines and Reproductive Performance of Skylarks *Alauda arvensis* in Different Regions and Habitats of the United Kingdom', *Ibis*, 141, 1, 38–51, 1999

Chambers, Robert, *Popular Rhymes of Scotland*, W. & R. Chambers, 1870

Clark, R. B., 'Seasonal Fluctuations in the Song of the Sky-lark', *British Birds*, 40, 1, 34–43, 1947

Cresswell, Will, 'Song as a Pursuit-deterrent Signal, and Its Occurrence Relative to other Anti-predation Behaviours of Skylark (*Alauda arvensis*) on Attack by Merlins (*Falco columbarius*)', *Behavioural Ecology and Sociobiology*, 34, 217–23, 1994

Crumley, Jim, *Skylark: Encounters in the Wild*, Saraband, 2016

Csicsáky, Michael, 'The Song of the Skylark (*Alauda arvensis*) and Its Relation to Respiration', *Journal für Ornithologie*, 119, 249–64, 1978

Delius, Juan D., 'A Population Study of Skylarks *Alauda arvensis*', *Ibis*, 107, 466–92, 1965

Donald, Paul F., *The Skylark*, T. & A. D. Poyser, 2004

Hedenström, Anders, 'Song Flight Performance in the Skylark *Alauda arvensis*', *Journal of Avian Biology*, 26, 4, 337–42, 1995

Hedenström, Anders and Alerstam, Thomas, 'Skylark Optimal Flight Speeds for Flying Nowhere and Somewhere', *Behavioral Ecology*, 7, 2, 121–6, 1996

Jobling, James A., *The Helm Dictionary of Scientific Bird Names, From Aalge to Zusii*, Christopher Helm, 2010

Milson, T. P., Langton, S. D., Parkin, W. K., Allen, D. S., Bishop, J. D. and Hart, J. D., 'Coastal Grazing Marshes as a Breeding Habitat for Skylarks *Alauda arvensis*'. In Donald, P. F. and Vickery, J. A. (eds), *The Ecology and Conservation of Skylarks* Alauda arvensis, RSPB, 41–51, 2001

Simms, Eric, *Voices of the Wild*, Putnam, 1957

Simms, Eric, *British Larks, Pipits & Wagtails*, HarperCollins, 1992

Suffern, C., 'Sky-larks Making "Forms"', *British Birds*, 44, 9, 387–8, 1951

Tryjanowski, Piotr, 'Proximity of Raven (*Corvus corax*) Nest Modifies Breeding Bird Community in an Intensively Used Farmland', *Annales Zoologici Fennici*, 38, 2, 131–8, 2001

V. Xylophone in the Trees: *Raven*

Ackerman, Jennifer, *The Genius of Birds*, Corsair, 2017

Bradley, Charles C., 'Play Behaviour in Northern Ravens', *The Passenger Pigeon*, 40, 4, 493–5, 1978

Bugnyar, Thomas, Reber, Stephen A. and Buckner, Cameron, 'Ravens Attribute Visual Access to Unseen Competitors', *Nature Communications*, 7, 10506, 2016

Conner, Richard N., 'Vocalizations of Common Ravens in Virginia', *Condor*, 87, 3, 379–88, 1985

Cramp, Stanley and Perrins, C. M. (eds), *Handbook of the Birds of Europe, the Middle East and North Africa: The Birds of the Western Palearctic, Vol. VIII Crows to Finches*, Oxford University Press, 1994

Elliot, Richard D., 'Hanging Behaviour in Common Ravens', *The Auk*, 94, 4, 777–8, 1977

Enggist-Dueblin, Peter and Pfister, Ueli, 'Cultural Transmission of Vocalizations in Ravens, *Corvus corax*', *Animal Behaviour*, 64, 831–41, 2002

Evershed, Sydney, 'Ravens Flying Upside Down', *Nature*, 126, 3190, 956–7, 1930

Fraser, O. N. and Bugnyar, T., 'Do Ravens Show Consolation? Responses to Distressed Others', *PLoS ONE*, 5(5), e10605, 2010

Fraser, O. N. and Bugnyar, T., 'Ravens Reconcile after Aggressive Conflicts with Valuable Partners', *PLoS ONE* 6(3), e18118, 2011

Goodwin, Derek, *Crows of the World*, British Museum [Natural History], 1976
Gordon, Seton, *The Immortal Isles*, Williams & Norgate, 1926
Gordon, Seton, *Thirty Years of Nature Photography*, Cassell, 1936
Gordon, Seton, *Wild Birds in Britain*, Batsford, 1938
Gordon, Seton, *In Search of Northern Birds*, Eyre & Spottiswoode, 1941
Heinrich, Bernd, *Mind of the Raven: Investigations and Adventures with Wolf-Birds*, Cliff Street Books, 2000
Heinrich, Bernd, *Ravens in Winter*, Simon & Schuster, 2014
Jaeger, Edmund C., 'Aerial Bathing of Ravens', *Condor*, 65, 3, 246, 1963
Janes, Stewart W., 'The Apparent Use of Rock by a Raven in Nest Defense', *Condor*, 78, 3, 409, 1976
Marquis, M., Newton, I. and Ratcliffe, D. A., 'The Decline of the Raven *Corvus corax*, in Relation to Afforestation in Southern Scotland and Northern England', *Journal of Applied Ecology*, 15, 1, 129–44, 1978
Montevecchi, W. A., 'Corvids Using Objects to Displace Gulls from Nests', *Condor*, 80, 3, 349, 1978
Newton, I., Davis, P. E. and Davis, J. E., 'Ravens and Buzzards in Relation to Sheep-Farming and Forestry in Wales', *Journal of Applied Ecology*, 19, 3, 681–706, 1982
Nicolson, Alexander (ed.), *A Collection of Gaelic Proverbs and Familiar Phrases*, Maclachlan & Stewart, 1882
Pika, Simone, Sima, Miriam Jennifer, Blum, Christian R., Herrmann, Esther and Mundry, Roger, 'Ravens Parallel Great Apes in Physical and Social Cognitive Skills', *Scientific Reports*, 10, 20617, 2020
Ratcliffe, Derek, *The Raven*, T. & A. D. Poyser, 1997
Shute, Joe, *A Shadow Above: The Fall and Rise of the Raven*, Bloomsbury, 2018
Watson, Donald, *Birds of Moor and Mountain*, Scottish Academic Press, 1972
Wilmore, Sylvia Bruce, *Crows, Jays, Ravens and Their Relatives*, David & Charles, 1977

VI. Rather like the Howl of a Dog: *Black-throated Diver*

Armstrong, Edward A., *The Folklore of Birds*, Dover, 1970

Brown, L. J., 'Investigation into the Causes of Black-throated Diver *Gavia arctica* Breeding Failure on Loch Maree, 2006–2009', Scottish Natural Heritage Commissioned Report, 379, 20698, 2010

Bundy, Graham, 'Breeding and Feeding Observations on the Black-throated Diver', *Bird Study*, 26, 33–6, 1979

Carmichael, Alexander, *Carmina Gadelica, Vol. II*, T. & A. Constable, 1900

Choate, Ernest A., *The Dictionary of American Bird Names*, Gambit, 1973

Cocker, Mark and Mabey, Richard, *Birds Britannica*, Chatto & Windus, 2005

Cramp, Stanley (ed.), *Handbook of the Birds of Europe, the Middle East and North Africa: The Birds of the Western Palearctic, Vol. I, Ostrich to Ducks*, Oxford University Press, 1977

Crook, John Hurrell, 'The Adaptive Significance of Avian Social Organizations', *Symposia of the Zoological Society of London*, 14, 181–218, 1965

Dawson, M. J., *The Black-Throated Diver*, Oriel Stinger, 1984

Dennis, Roy, *Divers*, Colin Baxter, 1993

Dunker, Henning, 'Habitat Selection and Territory Size of the Black-throated Diver, *Gavia arctica* (L.), in South Norway', *Norwegian Journal of Zoology*, 22, 15–21, 1974

Dunker, H. and Elgmork, K., 'Nesting of the Black-throated Diver, *Gavia arctica* (L.) in Small Bodies of Water', *Norwegian Journal of Zoology*, 21, 1, 33–7, 1973

Dunning, Joan, *The Loon: Voice of the Wilderness*, Yankee Books, 1986

Gilbert, H. A. and Brook, Arthur, *The Secrets of the Eagle and of Other Rare Birds*, Arrowsmith, 1925

Gilroy, Norman, 'Field-Notes on the Nesting of Divers', *British Birds*, 16, 12, 318–21, 1923

Gordon, Seton, *The Immortal Isles*, Williams & Norgate, 1926

Gordon, Seton, *In the Highlands*, Cassell, 1931

Gordon, Seton, *Highland Summer*, Cassell, 1971

Gordon, Seton, 'First Days in the Life of a Black-throated Diver', *Scottish Birds*, 8, 5/6, 319, 1975

Hancock, M., 'Artificial Floating Islands for Nesting Black-throated Divers *Gavia arctica* in Scotland: Construction, Use and Effect on Breeding Success', *Bird Study*, 47, 2, 165–75, 2000

Hemmingsson, Erick and Eriksson, Mats O. G., 'Ringing of Red-throated Diver *Gavia stellata* Black-throated Diver *Gavia arctica* in Sweden', *Wetlands International Diver/Loon Specialist Group Newsletter*, 4, 8–13, 2002

Hulka, S. and Stirling, J., 'A Study of Breeding Black-throated Divers *Gavia arctica* Based on Observation from Vantage Points', *Bird Study*, 47, 1, 117–21, 2000

Lehtonen, L. 'Zur Biologie des Prachttauchers, *Gavia a. arctica* (L.)', *Annales Zoologici Fennici*, 7, 25–60, 1970

Lockwood, W. B., *The Oxford Book of British Bird Names*, OUP, 1984

Mackenzie, Osgood, *A Hundred Years in the Highlands*, National Trust for Scotland, 1988

McIntyre, Judith W., *The Common Loon: Spirit of Northern Lakes*, University of Minnesota Press, 1988

Merrie, David, 'To Build an Island', *The Scots Magazine*, 113, 12–19, 1980

Merrie, T. D. H., 'Relationship between Spatial Distribution of Breeding Divers and the Availability of Fishing Waters', *Bird Study*, 25, 2, 119–22, 1978

Mudge, G. P., Dennis, R. H., Talbot, T. R. and Broad, R. A., 'Changes in the Breeding Status of Black-throated Divers in Scotland', *Scottish Birds*, 16, 2, 77–84, 1991

Mudge, G. P. and Talbot, T. R., 'The Breeding Biology and Causes of Nest Failure of Scottish Black-throated Divers *Gavia arctica*', *Ibis*, 135, 2, 113–20, 1993

Rankin, Niall, *Haunts of British Divers*, Collins, 1947

St John, Charles, *Natural History and Sport in Moray*, Edmonston & Douglas, 1863

St John, Charles, *The Wild Sports and Natural History of the Highlands*, John Murray, 1948, first published 1846

Sjölander, Sverre, 'Reproductive Behaviour of the Black-Throated Diver *Gavia arctica*', *Ornis Scandinavica*, 9, 1, 51–65, 1978

Tomkies, Mike, *A Last Wild Place*, Jonathan Cape, 1984

Tomkies, Mike, *On Wing and Wild Water*, Jonathan Cape, 1987

Watson, Donald, *Birds of Moor and Mountain*, Scottish Academic Press, 1972

Witherby, H. F, Jourdain, F. C. R., Ticehurst, Norman F. and Tucker, Bernard W. (eds), *The Handbook of British Birds, Vol. IV*, Witherby, 1940

VII. Little Horn in the Rushes: *Lapwing*

Calladine, John, Pakeman, Robin J., Humphreys, Elizabeth, Huband, Sally and Fuller, Robert J., 'Changes in Breeding Wader Assemblages, Vegetation and Land Use within Machair Environments over Three Decades', *Bird Study*, 61, 3, 287–300, 2014

Calladine, J., Humphreys, E. M. and Boyle, J., 'Changes in Breeding Wader Populations of the Uist Machair between 1983 and 2014', *Scottish Birds*, 34, 3, 207–15, 2015

Calladine, John, Humphreys, Elizabeth M., Gilbert, Lucy, *et al.*, 'Continuing Influences of Introduced Hedgehogs *Erinaceus europaeus* as a Predator of Wader (Charadrii) Eggs Four Decades after their Release on the Outer Hebrides, Scotland', *Biological Invasions*, 19, 1981–87, 2017

Dabelsteen, Torben, 'An Analysis of the Song-Flight of the Lapwing (*Vanellus vanellus* L.) with Respect to Causation, Evolution and Adaptations to Signal Function', *Behaviour*, 66, 1/2, 136–78, 1978

Dobinson, H. M. and Richards, A. J., 'The Effects of the Severe Winter of 1962/63 on Birds in Britain', *British Birds*, 57, 10, 373–434, 1964

Elliot, Richard D., 'The Effects of Predation Risk and Group Size on the Anti-Predator Responses of Nesting Lapwings *Vanellus vanellus*', *Behaviour*, 92, 1/2, 168–87, 1985

Ennion, E. A. R., *The Lapwing*, Methuen, 1949

Fuller, R. J. and Jackson, D. B., 'Changes in Populations of Breeding Waders on the Machair of North Uist, Scotland, 1983–1998', *Wader Study Group Bulletin*, 90, 47–55, 1999

Gordon, Seton, *The Charm of the Hills*, Cassell, 1912

Gordon, Seton, *The Land of the Hills and the Glens*, Cassell, 1920

Gordon, Seton, *In the Highlands*, Cassell, 1931

Gordon, Seton, *Wild Birds in Britain*, Batsford, 1938

Gray, Robert, *Birds of the West of Scotland*, Thomas Murray, 1872

Grønstøl, G. B., 'Aerobatic Components in the Song-flight Display of Male Lapwings *Vanellus vanellus* as Cues in Female Choice', *Ardea*, 84, 45–55, 1996

Harvie-Brown, J. A. and Buckley, T. E., *A Vertebrate Fauna of the Outer Hebrides*, David Douglas, 1888
Lowsley, Barzillai, *A Glossary of Berkshire Words and Phrases*, The English Dialect Society, 1888
Milson, T. P., Holditch, R. S. and Rochard, J. B. A., 'Diurnal Use of an Airfield and Adjacent Agricultural Habitats by Lapwings *Vanellus vanellus*', *Journal of Applied Ecology*, 22, 313–26, 1985
Nethersole-Thompson, Desmond and Maimie, *Waders: Their Breeding, Haunts and Watchers*, T. & A. D. Poyser, 1986
Scroggs, R. W. H. and Williams, H. H., 'Annual Breeding Bird Survey 1980 Lapwing', *Banbury Ornithological Society*, July 1980
Shrubb, Michael, *The Lapwing*, T. & A. D. Poyser, 2007
Spencer, K. G., *The Lapwing in Britain*, A. Brown, 1953
Svensson, Lars, Grant, Peter J., Mullarney, Killian and Zetterström, Dan, *Collins Bird Guide*, HarperCollins, 1999
Tucker, G. M., Davies, S. M. and Fuller, R. J., 'The Ecology and Conservation of Lapwings *Vanellus vanellus*', *UK Nature Conservation*, 9, 1994
Vaughan, Richard, 'Amorous Lapwings', *Country Life*, 1 December 1977
Vaughan, Richard, *Plovers*, Terence Dalton, 1980
Watson, Donald, *Birds of Moor and Mountain*, Scottish Academic Press, 1972
Weaver, Peter, *The Lapwing*, Shire Natural History, 1987

VIII. As Though She Lived on Song: *Nightingale*

Amrhein, Valentin, Korner, Pius and Naguib, Marc, 'Nocturnal and Diurnal Singing Activity in the Nightingale: Correlations with Mating Status and Breeding Cycle', *Animal Behaviour*, 64, 6, 939–44, 2002
Amrhein, Valentin, Kunc, Hansjoerg P. and Naguib, Marc, 'Seasonal Patterns of Singing Activity Vary with Time of Day in the Nightingale (*Luscinia megarhynchos*)', *The Auk*, 121, 1, 110–17, 2004
Amrhein, Valentin, Kunc, Hansjoerg P., Schmidt, Rouven and Naguib, Marc, 'Temporal Patterns of Territory Settlement and Detectability in Mated and Unmated Nightingales *Luscinia megarhynchos*', *Ibis*, 149, 2, 237–44, 2007

BIBLIOGRAPHY

Bates, H. E., *Through the Woods: The English Woodland, April to April*, Little Toller, 2011, first published 1936

Clement, Peter and Rose, Chris, *Robins and Chats*, Christopher Helm, 2015

Cramp, Stanley (ed.), *Handbook of the Birds of Europe, the Middle East and North Africa: The Birds of the Western Palearctic, Vol. V, Tyrant Flycatchers to Thrushes*, Oxford University Press, 1988

Henderson, Andrew and Bayes, Kevin, *Conservation Advice: Nightingales and Coppice Woodland*, RSPB, 1989

Holt, Chas A., Hewson, Chris M. and Fuller, Robert J., '*The Nightingale in Britain: Status, Ecology and Conservation Needs*', *British Birds*, 105, 172–87, 2012

Lee, Sam, *The Nightingale: Notes on a Songbird*, Century, 2021

Mabey, Richard, *Whistling in the Dark: In Pursuit of the Nightingale*, Sinclair-Stevenson, 1993

Mabey, Richard, *The Barley Bird: Notes on the Suffolk Nightingale*, Full Circle Editions, 2010

Macdonald, Benedict, *Rebirding: Rewilding Britain and Its Birds*, Pelagic, 2019

Naguib, M., Altenkamp, R. and Griessmann, B., 'Nightingales in Space: Song and Extra-territorial Forays of Radio Tagged Song Birds', *Journal für Ornithologie*, 142, 3, 306–12, 2001

Pike, Oliver G., *The Nightingale: Its Story and Song, and Other Familiar Song-Birds of Britain*, Arrowsmith, 1932

Roberts, Bethan, *Nightingale*, Reaktion, 2021

Rothenberg, David, *Nightingales in Berlin: Searching for the Perfect Sound*, University of Chicago Press, 2019

Thomas, Edward, *The South Country*, Hutchinson, 1984, first published 1909

Thomas, Robert J., 'The Costs of Singing in Nightingales', *Animal Behaviour*, 63, 5, 959–66, 2002

Ticehurst, N. F., 'Some Notes on the Breeding-Habits of Nightingales', *British Birds*, 6, 6, 170–6, 1912

General Reading

Armstrong, Edward A., *A Study of Bird Song*, Dover, 1973

Bevis, John, *Aaaaw to Zzzzzd: The Words of Birds*, MIT Press, 2010

Catchpole, Clive K., *Vocal Communication in Birds*, Edward Arnold, 1979

Catchpole, C. K. and Slater, P. J. B., *Bird Song: Biological Themes and Variations*, Cambridge University Press, 1995

Delamain, Jacques, *Why Birds Sing*, Victor Gollancz, 1932

Greenewalt, Crawford H., *Bird Song: Acoustics and Physiology*, Smithsonian Institution Press, 1968

Hartshorne, Charles, *Born to Sing: An Interpretation and World Survey of Bird Song*, Indiana University Press, 1973

Krause, Bernie, *The Great Animal Orchestra*, Profile, 2012

Lovatt, Steven, *Birdsong in a Time of Silence*, Particular, 2021

Marler, Peter and Slabbekoorn, Hans (eds), *Nature's Music: The Science of Birdsong*, Elsevier, 2004

Rothenberg, David, *Why Birds Sing: One Man's Quest to Solve an Everyday Mystery*, Penguin, 2006

Smyth, Richard, *A Sweet, Wild Note: What We Hear when the Birds Sing*, Elliot & Thompson, 2017

Turnbull, A. L., *Bird Music: An Introduction to the Study of the Vocal Expressions of British Birds with Appreciations of Their Songs*, Faber & Faber, 1943

Witchell, Charles A., *The Evolution of Bird-Song*, A. & C. Black, 1896

Index